Routledge Revivals

Was Stalin Really Necessary?

First published in 1964, *Was Stalin Really Necessary?* is a thought-provoking work which deals with many aspects of the Soviet political economy, planning problems and statistics. Professor Nove starts with an attempt to evaluate the rationality of Stalinism and discusses the possible political consequences of the search for greater economic efficiency, which is followed by a controversial discussion of Kremlinology. The author goes on to analyse the situation of the peasants as reflected in literary journals, then looks at industrial and agricultural problems. There are elaborate statistical surveys of occupational patterns and the purchasing power of wages, followed by an examination of the irrational statistical reflection of irrational economic decisions. Professor Nove's essay on social welfare was, unlike some of his other work, used in the Soviet press as evidence against over-enthusiastic cold-warriors, among whom the author was not always popular. Finally, the author seeks to generalise about the evolution of world communism. This reissue will be very welcome to all those with an interest in Soviet politics, economics and history.

Was Stalin Really Necessary?

Some Problems of Soviet Political Economy

Alec Nove

Routledge
Taylor & Francis Group

First published in 1964
by George Allen & Unwin Ltd

This edition first published in 2011 by Routledge
2 Park Square, Milton Park, Abingdon, Oxon, OX14 4RN

Simultaneously published in the USA and Canada
by Routledge
711 Third Avenue, New York, NY 10017

Routledge is an imprint of the Taylor & Francis Group, an informa business

Publisher's Note
The publisher has gone to great lengths to ensure the quality of this reprint but points out that some imperfections in the original copies may be apparent.

Disclaimer
The publisher has made every effort to trace copyright holders and welcomes correspondence from those they have been unable to contact.

A Library of Congress record exists under LC Control Number: 64019788

ISBN 13: 978-0-415-69207-6 (set)
ISBN 13: 978-0-415-68240-4 (hbk)
ISBN 13: 978-0-203-80282-3 (ebk)
ISBN 13: 978-0-415-68496-5 (pbk)

WAS STALIN REALLY NECESSARY?

by the same author

THE SOVIET ECONOMY

'A shrewd and well informed book . . . essential information about the Soviet economy for economists and students of economics.' *Times Literary Supplement*

'The most balanced attempt yet in the English language to describe Soviet economy as it is . . . sane and perceptive analysis.' *The Economist*

Was Stalin Really Necessary?

SOME PROBLEMS OF
SOVIET POLITICAL ECONOMY

BY

ALEC NOVE

James Bonar Professor of Economics
Director of Institute of Soviet and East European Studies
at the University of Glasgow

London

GEORGE ALLEN & UNWIN LTD

RUSKIN HOUSE MUSEUM STREET

FIRST PUBLISHED IN 1964

PRINTED IN GREAT BRITAIN
in 11 point Times type
BY SIMSON SHAND LTD
LONDON, HERTFORD AND HARLOW

To

Irene, David, Perry and Charles

who make it all worth while

INTRODUCTION

Most of the papers comprising the present volume have appeared in various journals, conference reports or compendia, in the course of the last ten years. They have, I trust, sufficient homogeneity in subject-matter to justify their coexistence within the same binding, being all concerned with Soviet communism. In a rapidly-changing setting, it is important to observe the dates on which the previously-published papers first saw the light of day. I have tried to bring the facts and arguments up to date, when necessary, by adding a few paragraphs to some of the papers, and in some instances also adding footnotes or modifying a now obsolete statement, and there will be no difficulty in identifying such after-thoughts. I am most grateful to the editors of journals and synopses for permission to reprint, and acknowledgments are made in each instance.

I am very conscious of the existence of a number of loose ends in argument, which partly reflects the fact that this collection includes essays written at different times and for different purposes, and partly genuine and continuing perplexities. The critical reader will doubtless query the meaning or meanings which should be attached to the word 'rationality', and such a reader would be right. Many of the articles are concerned with a search for rationality in many of its various senses. For we are here very close to the heart of the problem of Soviet (or any other) 'political economy'. Rationality can be considered from many different points of view. Thus, one may define a set of objectives and consider to be rational the achievement of these objectives with the least expenditure of resources. However, even within this rather narrow conception of the problem, complications arise. Thus supposing the *economically* most rational means of achieving certain economic objectives would give rise to grave political embarrassment, or to rebellion, or could not be effectively carried through by the existing administrative or planning machine; are the resulting compromises, representing distinctly sub-optimal paths from the economic point of view, 'irrational'? Are British Governments acting irrationally in not abolishing agricultural subsidies, or the American President in not eliminating agricultural support prices? To assert such propositions means giving to purely economic considerations a primacy they hardly deserve, as well as showing oneself innocent of political realities. Needless to say, political and social considerations (though different ones) exist in the Soviet Union also. There are political and social rationalities with patterns of their own, alongside economic ones.

But this is far from being the end of the matter. There are micro and macro rationalities, *levels* of rationality, which may conflict with one another. Thus a form of organization which coped adequately with problems of a war economy in Great Britain, and was in principle certainly rational, necessarily involved bureaucratic inefficiencies and inflexibilities which would not have arisen in a free enterprise economy. Each isolated manifestation of such errors or omissions is an example of irrational allocation or behaviour. But the system of economic controls did its job and it was impossible to run a war by giving free play to market forces. The micro-irrationalities must then be seen as part of the *cost* of running the economy in a certain basically rational way; it is generally conceded that the cost was worth paying. This must greatly affect our judgment of the war economy as such. One is reminded here of the political economy of development, on which so much good sense has been written by Albert O. Hirschman. The effective 'strategy' is one which enables one to overcome political, economic and social obstacles, using highly imperfect instruments for the purpose (and by 'instruments' one can mean both economic measuring-rods and institutions). In practice, a further complication must be introduced. Ends and means are not distinct, but shade into one another and interact. Hardly ever, in the Soviet Union or elsewhere, can economic policy be related to a clear and unambiguous objective, which can then be reached by some optimum route which provides a criterion of 'rationality'.

Why not abandon the term, then? Because to do so is to evade the duty of identifying error. The duty exists, even though it is a hard and complex task. Misuse of resources can and does occur on a vast scale, which no 'higher rationality' can excuse. Systems or methods can outlive their usefulness. The cost of a given organizational or institutional arrangement might become intolerably high, because of the evolution of the economy and of society, and/or because the special conditions which had given rise to these arrangements no longer exist. There is then a conflict, growing 'contradictions', and the would-be reformers argue that rationality demands change while 'conservatives' resist it, often with success. One sees this in England, where the educational system designed for training rulers of empire is challenged by the requirements of modern European reality. One sees it on a larger scale in political and economic problems currently faced in the Soviet Union.

It is important to distinguish rationality and rationale. Thus there was a rationale in Stalin's massacre of military officers in 1937–38, or for Khrushchev's agricultural campaigns in more recent years, in the sense that there was a logical explanation for these events. Yet these actions must be seen as manifestations of irrationality, viewed from the standpoint of military and agricultural efficiency respectively.

Mention of 'logic', 'rationality', 'rationale', is apt to lead to accusations of determinism, historicism and other -isms with a pejorative flavour. Suffice it to say that events can have a logic without being inevitable, and that, as we well know, men may even be conscious of the rationality of a given course of action without necessarily acting. Scottish sporting landlords may know that they stand in the way of a more economic use of deer 'forests', but they may still prefer economic irrationality and go on stalking deer undisturbed. Soviet leaders must be aware that private plots are a valuable addition to peasant income and to food supplies, but adopt a negative attitude to them all the same. In passing, it is perhaps worth mentioning that some philosopher-critics of alleged 'determinism' seem never to have heard of the law of large numbers. The validity of generalizations about social-economic 'regularities' (*Zakonomernosti*, *Gesetzmässigkeiten*, odd that there is no real English equivalent) cannot be upset merely by proof that an individual is often free to choose. Thus the birth rate in the United Kingdom in 1964 can be forecast with fair accuracy, but the birth of any one child is a matter where unpredictable and 'free' individual behaviour (plus accident) is indeed the determinant. The increase in secondary education in this country since the war is a 'determined' necessity, but the educational career of young Robinson or McTavish depends on luck, personal ambition and other unpredictable factors. But I had better resist the temptation to enter into an argument which goes beyond the scope of the present book.

The principal emphasis in these pages is on matters economic. This reflects the professional preoccupations of the author and not his estimate of the relative importance of economic factors in the development of Soviet society. The reader can deduce the author's views on this controversial topic from the first two papers in the collection. It is my hope that in some of the pages that follow some readers may find ideas, facts or figures which will help in the understanding of Soviet reality. No doubt errors of fact and interpretation can also readily be found, but this will be due to the numerous human failings of the author and not to any attempt to prove the validity of any particular political line. It is always worth trying to seek explanations for events, without either denouncing or justifying.

We are moving into a period in which many of the sterile controversies of the past no longer obstruct the task of scholarship. Thus virtually every scholar in the field now accepts that Stalin's rule was a bloody tyranny, although of course we can and do differ about its causes and the political morals which should be drawn from its existence. There is also a wide concensus about both the extent and the limitations of Soviet economic achievement, although there is room for legitimate disagreement about the relative 'weight' of elements of strength and weakness. Of course, there is plenty of scope for debate, but increasingly it can be conducted in scholarly language and can be made to rest upon an accepted basis of fact. Even statistical argument across ideological dividing lines can occasionally be polite, both sides using data and not abuse as the basis of their case. We have even had a most convincing demonstration, in a Soviet periodical, of the error of an American calculation, the American error consisting in an exaggeration of Soviet relatively to American industrial performance.[1] Admittedly this is, so far, a unique event, but greater confidence, sophistication, successes in a number of endeavours, may be breeding new attitudes and can lead to an increase in the range of subjects on which scholarly exchange of differing views is possible. Which will be all to the good. But where, as in agriculture, there is a wide gap between plan and performance, of which prominent politicians are particularly sensible, serious discussion is still very difficult. In fact, Soviet economic journals too are handicapped in dealing with

[1] See V. Kudrov, *Vestnik Statistiki* No. 7, 1963.

farming questions, which is doubtless why the best material about the village appears in the literary monthlies. Hence the article in this volume on peasants in literature is not primarily an exercise in *belles-lettres*. (Incidentally, a very critical reviewer of my book on the Soviet economy chose to accuse me of 'borrowing' my literary references from secondary American sources, apparently on the assumption that mere economists cannot or do not read Russian literature for themselves. Perhaps Monsieur Barton, the reviewer, will admit that in this respect he was wrong, though he is fully entitled to dislike everything else in the book in question.)

Dubravko Matko, now of the University of Glasgow, did much in the preparation of this collection and in bringing some of the articles up to date. Alastair McAulay, research scholar at Glasgow, read several papers and made some valuable suggestions. J. A. Newth, lecturer at Glasgow, greatly helped with the paper on the comparison of living standards. R. Beermann, also of Glasgow, found several references and publications which were most useful in the paper on the peasants. Some of the papers are based on presentations at Seminars, at the London School of Economics, St Antony's College, Oxford, and elsewhere, and benefited from being subjected to the fire of many deserved criticisms. Among critics perhaps I may mention particularly Leonard Schapiro, who, without converting me to his interpretation of certain events, has over a long period compelled me to rethink many important questions, and also Jacob Miller for his constant refusal to accept superficial explanations for events great and small. To everyone are due my grateful thanks, and all mistakes are due not to them but to me. Finally, the fact that a confused jumble of offprints, photostats and addenda ever got organized is due in no small measure to Mrs M. Chaney.

September 1963

CONTENTS

I. POLITICAL ECONOMY

1. *Was Stalin really necessary?**

Stalin has suffered a dramatic post-mortem demotion, and a monument to his victims is to be erected in Moscow. The present Soviet leadership is thus disassociating itself publicly from many of the highly disagreeable features of Stalin's rule, while claiming for the Party and the Soviet system the credit for making Russia a great economic and military power. Is this a logically consistent standpoint? How far was Stalin, or Stalinism, an integral, unavoidable, 'necessary' part of the achievements of the period? How much of the evil associated with the Stalin system is attributable to the peculiar character of the late dictator, and how much was the consequence of the policies adopted by the large majority of the Bolshevik party, or of the effort of a small and dedicated minority to impose very rapid industrialization on a peasant country?

To ask these questions is of interest from several standpoints. Firstly, in trying to answer them we might be able to see a little more clearly the meaning of such misused terms as 'determinism', causality, or the role of personality in history, and so continue to explore some of the problems which E. H. Carr presented in so stimulating a way in his Trevelyan lectures. Secondly, an examination of the circumstances which brought Stalin to power and led to—or provided an opportunity for—crimes on a massive scale is surely of very practical interest, since it might help in understanding how to avoid a repetition of these circumstances, particularly in those underdeveloped countries which are being tempted by their very real difficulties to take the totalitarian road.

To some people, the word 'necessary' smacks of 'historicism',

* From *Encounter*, April 1962.

of a belief in inevitability, or suggests that the author wishes to find some historic justification, a whitewash to be applied to Stalin and his system. This is far from being my intention. 'Necessity' is used here with no moral strings attached. If I say that to travel to Oxford it is necessary to go to Paddington station, this implies no approval, moral or otherwise, of the service provided by the Western Region of British Railways, still less of the project of making the journey to Oxford. It is simply that *if* I wish to do A, it involves doing B.

It is true that there may be alternatives. One might, for instance, do not B but C, or D. Thus I could go to Oxford by car, or by bus. However, it could be that these physically possible methods are not in fact open to me; I may not own a car, and shortage of time precludes taking the bus. Thus a judgment on the 'necessity' or otherwise of an action in pursuit of a given purpose requires some consideration of what could have been done instead.

The range of choice is not, in practice, limited only by what is *physically* possible. There are also actions which are excluded by religious or ideological principle. For example, it is not in fact open to a rabbi to eat a ham sandwich or an orthodox Hindu to eat cow-meat. Thus if an 'alternative' happens to involve such acts, it is not *for them* an alternative at all. This is because, were they to act otherwise, they would cease to be what they in fact are. A rabbi does not eat pork; were he to do so, he would not be a rabbi. The fact that he is a rabbi would also affect his outlook, his 'freedom' to choose between alternative modes of conduct, where religious law is less strict: for instance, there is nothing in the Talmud or in Deuteronomy about smoking on the Sabbath, but rabbis would tend to be the kind of people who, faced with this 'new' problem, would give the answer 'no'.

Thus, to come nearer our subject, there may have been a number of solutions to the problems posed by Russia of the 'twenties which the Communists could not have chosen because they were Communists, and in considering the practical alternatives before them we have to bear this in mind. In doing so, we are by no means driven to any generalizations about the 'inevitability' of the Russian revolution or of the Bolshevik seizure of power, and *a fortiori* we need not assume that non-

Bolsheviks could not have found some other ways of coping with the problems of the period. (Indeed, though the problems would still have been acute, they might in important respects have been different.) Before his assassination in 1911, the last intelligent Tsarist Prime Minister, Stolypin, expressed the belief that his land reform measures would create in about twenty years a prosperous peasantry which would provide a stable foundation for society and the throne. No one will know if he would have been right, if he had not been murdered, if the Tsar had been wise, if Rasputin had not existed, if the war had not broken out. . . . But of what use is it to indulge in such speculations? A nineteenth-century Russian blank-verse play provides, if somewhat inaccurately, a relevant comment:

If, if, if grandma had a beard,
She would be grandpa. . . .

In assessing the choices open to the Bolsheviks in, say, 1926, the events before that date must be taken as given. The real question, surely, is to consider the practical alternatives which Stalin and his colleagues had before them.

In doing so, we should certainly not assume that what happened was inevitable. 'Necessity' and 'inevitable' are quite distinct concepts, though some critics seem to confuse them. Two simple and probably uncontroversial propositions will illustrate this: it was necessary for eighteenth-century Poland to make drastic changes in its constitution if she were to survive as an independent state; and for China around 1890 a strong, modernizing government was urgently necessary if many disasters were to be avoided. Yet the 'necessary' steps were not taken and the disasters occurred. Unless we believe that whatever was not avoided was for that reason unavoidable, we would wish to examine the actions which men took, their choices between *available* alternatives, and see whether viable alternatives in fact existed.

At this point, many historians—at times one feels E. H. Carr is among them—tend to brush aside impatiently any talk of what might have been; they are concerned, they would claim, with chronicling and explaining what was. Curiously, this line is often taken both by those who believe in strict historical determinism, i.e. that what happened *had* to happen, and by those who consider history to be merely a chronological series of events, i.e. that by implication *anything* could have happened. Both these apparently opposite extremes agree in not examining the actual possibilities as they were seen by the statesmen of the period. Yet how can one speak meaningfully of the reasons for, or causes of, any political act unless one implicitly or explicitly considers what could have been done instead? In other words, we must be concerned with freedom of choice, or its converse, necessity, whether we like it or not, unless we hold either that freedom of choice is infinite or that it is non-existent.

There are several more things to be said on the subject of 'necessity'. One of these concerns what might be called consequences of consequences, or indirect effects. For example, it is difficult to marry a wife without simultaneously acquiring a mother-in-law. Or, moving nearer to our subject, a sergeant is an unavoidable element in an army, and the needs of discipline involve giving him powers over his men which he is likely to abuse. Bullying NCOs are likely to be found if an army exists, and so, given the necessity for an army, they become an inevitable consequence of its existence, just as the mother-in-law is an unavoidable appendage of a 'necessary' wife. Thus, getting still nearer to the point, a situation which requires many bureaucrats, or which gives exceptional power to many policemen, may bring into action certain forces, certain behavioural tendencies, which are typical of bureaucrats or policemen and which, though not needed or desired as such, cannot in the circumstances be avoided.

The saying that 'you cannot make omelettes without breaking eggs' (or its Russian equivalent: 'if you chop trees, the chips fly') has been used so often as an excuse for excesses and crimes, that we sometimes forget that you really *cannot* make omelettes without breaking eggs. . . .

Now on to Stalin, or rather to Stalinism, since the idea of 'necessity' does not of course mean that the leader had to be a Georgian with a long moustache, but rather a tough dictator ruling a totalitarian state of the Stalinist type. What were the practical alternatives before the Bolsheviks in the late 'twenties, which contributed to the creation of the Stalinist régime, or, if one prefers a different formulation, gave the opportunity to ambitious men to achieve so high a degree of absolutism?

The key problem before the Bolsheviks concerned the linked questions of industrialization and political power. They felt they had to industrialize for several reasons, some of which they shared with non-Bolshevik predecessors. Thus the Tsarist Minister, Count Witte, as well as Stalin, believed that to achieve national strength and maintain independence, Russia needed a modern industry, especially heavy industry. The national-defence argument, relabelled 'defence of the revolution', was greatly strengthened by the belief that the Russian revolution was in constant danger from a hostile capitalist environment, militarily and technically far stronger than the USSR. Then there was the belief that the building of socialism or communism involved industrialization, and, more immediately, that a 'proletarian dictatorship' was insecure so long as it ruled in an overwhelmingly petty-bourgeois, peasant, environment. There had to be a large increase in the number and importance of the proletariat, while the rise of a rich 'kulak' class in the villages was regarded as a dangerous (or potentially dangerous) resurgence of capitalism. It was clear, by 1927, that it was useless to wait for 'world revolution' to solve these problems. These propositions were common to the protagonists of the various platforms of the middle 'twenties. Thus even the 'moderate' Bukharin wrote: 'If there were a fall in the relative weight of the working class in its political and its social and class power, . . . this would subvert the basis of the proletarian dictatorship, the basis of our government.'[1] He too spoke in principle of the 'struggle against the kulak, against the capitalist road', and warned of the 'kulak danger'.[2] He too, even in the context of an attack on Zinoviev and the 'left' opposition, argued the need for 'changing the production relations of our country'.[3]

Until about 1927, a rapid rise in industrial production resulted from the reactivation of pre-revolutionary productive capacity, which fell into disuse and disrepair in the civil war period.

[1] 'The Results of the United Plenum of the Central and Control Commissions of the Party' (1927).

[2] Speech on 'The Results of the 14th Party Congress' (January 5, 1926).

[3] Speech to the XXIII special conference of the Leningrad provincial party organization (1926).

However, it now became urgent to find material and financial means to expand the industrial base. This at once brought the peasant problem to the fore. The revolution had distributed land to twenty-five million families, most of whom were able or willing to provide only small marketable surpluses. Supplies of food to the towns and for export fell, peasant consumption rose. Yet the off-farm surplus must grow rapidly to sustain industrialization, especially where large-scale loans from abroad could scarcely be expected. As the 'left' opposition vigorously pointed out, the peasant, the bulk of the population, had somehow to be made to contribute produce and money, to provide the bulk of 'primitive Socialist accumulation'.

The arguments around these problems were inextricably entangled in the political factional struggles of the 'twenties.[1] The moderate wing, led by Bukharin, believed that it was possible to advance slowly towards industrialization 'at the pace of a tortoise',[2] a pace severely limited by what the peasant was willing to do voluntarily. This was sometimes described as 'riding towards socialism on a peasant nag'. The logic of this policy demanded priority for developing consumers' goods industries, to make more cloth to encourage the peasants to sell more food. At first, Stalin sided with the moderates.

The case against the Bukharin line was of several different kinds. Firstly, free trade with the peasants could only provide adequate surpluses if the better-off peasants (i.e. those known as *kulaks*) were allowed to expand, since they were the most efficient producers and provided a large part of the marketable produce. Yet all the Bolshevik leaders (including, despite momentary aberrations, Bukharin himself) found this ideologically and politically unacceptable. A strong group of independent, rich peasants was Stolypin's dream as a basis for Tsardom. It was the Bolsheviks' nightmare, as totally inconsistent in the long run with their rule or with a socialist transformation of 'petty-bourgeois' Russia. But this made the Bukharin approach of doubtful internal consistency. This was understood at the time by intelligent non-party men. Thus the

[1] See A. Erlich: *The Soviet Industrialisation Debate* (Harvard, 1960) for a most valuable account of the interaction between the debates and the economic realities of the period. The account given here is necessarily oversimplified.

[2] Bukharin's words, speech of January 5, 1926.

famous economist Kondratiev, later to perish in the purges, declared in 1927: 'If you want a higher rate of accumulation . . . then the stronger elements of the village must be allowed to exploit (the weaker)', in other words that the 'kulaks' must expand their holdings and employ landless labourers.[1] The 'peasant nag' could not pull the cart; or it, and the peasant, would pull in the wrong direction.

A second reason concerned the pace of the tortoise. The Bolsheviks were in a hurry. They saw themselves threatened by 'imperialist interventionists'. Even though some war scarces were manufactured for factional reasons, the Party as a whole believed that war against them would come before very long. This argued not merely for speed, but also for priority to *heavy* and not light industry, since it provided a basis for an arms industry. Still another reason was a less tangible but still very real one: the necessity of maintaining political *élan*, of not appearing to accept for an indefinite period a policy of gradualism based on the peasant, which would have demoralized the Party and so gravely weakened the régime. It was widely felt, in and out of Russia, that by 1927 the régime had reached a *cul-de-sac*. I have in front of me a contemporary Menshevik pamphlet published abroad, by P. A. Garvi,[2] which describes its dilemma quite clearly, and indeed the political and economic problem was extremely pressing: to justify its existence, to justify the Party dictatorship in the name of the proletariat, a rapid move forward was urgent; but such a move forward would hardly be consistent with the 'alliance with the peasants' which was the foundation of the policy of the moderates in the 'twenties. Stalin at this point swung over towards the left, and his policy of all-out industrialization and collectivization was a means of breaking out of the *cul-de-sac*, of mobilizing the Party to smash peasant resistance, to make possible the acquisition of farm surpluses without having to pay the price which any free peasants or free peasant associations would have demanded. He may well have felt he had little choice. It is worth quoting from the reminiscences of another Menshevik, who in the late 'twenties was working in the Soviet planning organs: 'The financial

[1] Paper read at a plenum of the Agricultural Economics Research Institute, Moscow, 1927.

[2] *Zakat bolshevisma* (Twilight of Bolshevism) (Riga, 1928).

base of the first five-year plan, *until Stalin found it in levying tribute on the peasants, in primitive accumulation by the methods of Tamerlane*, was extremely precarious. . . . (It seemed likely that) everything would go to the devil. . . . No wonder that no one, literally no one, of the well-informed economists, believed or could believe in the fulfilment (of the plan).'[1]

It does not matter in the present context whether Stalin made this shift through personal conviction of its necessity, or because this seemed to him to be a clever power-manoeuvre. The cleverness in any case largely consisted in knowing that he would thus strengthen his position by becoming the spokesman of the view which was widely popular among Party activists. The 'leftists', destroyed organizationally by Stalin in earlier years, had a considerable following. Stalin's left-turn brought many of them to his support—though this did not save them from being shot in due course on Stalin's orders. It is probably the case that he had at this time genuine majority support within the Party for his policy, though many had reservations about certain excesses, of which more will be said. But if this be so, the policy as such cannot be attributed to Stalin personally, and therefore the consequences which flowed from its adoption must be a matter of more than personal responsibility.

Let us examine some of these consequences. Collectivization could not be voluntary. Rapid industrialization, especially with priority for heavy industry, meant a reduction in living standards, despite contrary promises in the first five-year plans. This meant a sharp increase in the degree of coercion, in the powers of the police, in the unpopularity of the régime. The aims of the bulk of the people were bound to be in conflict with the aims of the Party. It should be added that this conflict is probably bound to arise in some form wherever *the state* is responsible for financing rapid industrialization; the sacrifices are then imposed by political authority, and the masses of 'small' people do not and cannot provide voluntarily the necessary savings, since in the nature of things their present abstinence cannot be linked with a future return which they as individuals can identify. However, this possibly unavoidable unpopularity was greatly increased in

[1] N. Valentinov, in *Sotsialisticheskii Vestnik* (New York), April, 1961. (Emphasis mine.)

the USSR by the sheer pace of the advance and by the attack on peasant property, and, as we shall see, both these factors reacted adversely on production of consumers' goods and so led to still further hardships and even greater unpopularity. The strains and priorities involved in a rapid move forward required a high degree of economic centralization, to prevent resources from being diverted to satisfy needs which were urgent but of a non-priority character. In this situation, the Party was the one body capable of carrying out enormous changes and resisting social and economic pressures in a hostile environment; this was bound to affect its structure. For a number of years it had already been in process of transformation from a political into a power machine. The problems involved in the 'revolution from above' intensified the process of turning it into an obedient instrument for changing, suppressing, controlling.

This, in turn, required hierarchical subordination, and suppression of discussion; therefore there had to be an unquestioned commander-in-chief. Below him, toughness in executing unpopular orders became the highest qualification for Party office. The emergence of Stalin, and of Stalin-type bullying officials of the sergeant-major species, was accompanied by the decline in the importance of the cosmopolitan journalist-intellectual type of party leader who had played so prominent a role earlier.

The rise of Stalin to supreme authority was surely connected with the belief among many Party members that he was the kind of man who could cope with this kind of situation. Of course, it could well be that Stalin tended to adopt policies which caused him and his type to be regarded as indispensable, and he promoted men to office in the Party because they were loyal to him. Personal ambition, a desire for power, were important factors in shaping events. But this is so obvious, so clearly visible on the surface, that the underlying problems, policy choices and logical consequences of policies need to be stressed.

Let us recapitulate: the Communists needed dictatorial power if they were to continue to rule; if they were to take effective steps towards industrialization these steps were bound to give rise to problems which would require further tightening of political and economic control. While we cannot say, without much further research, whether a Bukharinite or other moderate policy was impossible, once the decision to move fast was taken this had very radical consequences; the need for a tough, coercive government correspondingly increased. Given the nature of the Party apparatus, the mental and political development of the Russian masses, the logic of police rule, these policies were bound to lead to a conflict with the peasantry and to excesses of various kinds. Thus, given the premises, certain elements of what may be called Stalinism followed, were objective 'necessities'. In this sense, and to this extent, Stalin was, so to speak, operating within the logical consequences of Leninism.

It is an essential part of Lenin's views that the Party was to seize power and use it to change Russian society; this is what distinguished him from the Mensheviks who believed that conditions for socialism should ripen within society. Lenin also suppressed opposition parties and required stern discipline from his own followers. (It is impossible to ban free speech outside the Party without purging the Party of those who express 'wrong' views within it.) Indeed Lenin promoted Stalin because he knew he was tough, would 'prepare peppery dishes', though he had last-minute regrets about it. While it would be going too far to describe Stalin as a true Leninist, if only because Lenin was neither personally brutal nor an oriental despot, Stalin undoubtedly carried through some of the logical consequences of Lenin's policies and ideas. This remains true even though Lenin thought that the peasant problem could be solved by voluntary co-operation, and would probably have recoiled at the conditions of forced collectivization.

Is it necessary to stress that this does not make these actions right, or good? Yes, it is, because so many critics assume that to explain is to justify. So it must be said several times that no moral conclusions follow, that even the most vicious acts by politicians and others generally have causes which must be analysed. We are here only concerned to disentangle the special contribution of Stalin, the extent to which Stalinism was, so to speak, situation-determined. This is relevant, indeed, to one's picture of Stalin's personal responsibility, but in no way absolves him of such responsibility. If in order to do A it proves necessary to do B, we can, after all, refuse to do B, abandon or modify the aim of attaining A, or resign, or, in extreme circumstances—

like Stalin's old comrade Ordzhonikidze—commit suicide.

But Stalin's personal responsibility goes far beyond his being the voice and leader of a party majority in a given historical situation. For one cannot possibly argue that all the immense evils of the Stalin era flowed inescapably from the policy decisions of 1928–29. In assessing Stalin's personal role in bringing these evils about, it is useful to approach the facts from two angles. There was, first, the category of evils which sprang from policy choices which Stalin made and which he need not have made; in other words we are here concerned with consequences (perhaps necessary) of unnecessary decisions. The other category consists of evil actions which can reasonably be attributed to Stalin and which are his direct responsibility.

Of course, these categories shade into one another, as do murder and manslaughter. In the first case, the evils were in a sense situation-determined, but Stalin had a large hand in determining the situation. In the second, his guilt is as clear as a politician's guilt can be.

The most obvious examples of the first category are: the brutality of collectivization and the madly excessive pace of industrial development. In each case, we are dealing with '*excessive excesses*', since we have already noted that collectivization without coercion was impossible, and rapid industrialization was bound to cause stresses and strains.

Take collectivization first. Some over-zealous officials were presumably bound to overdo things, especially since the typical Party man was a townsman with no understanding or sympathy for peasants and their problems. But these officials received orders to impose rapid collectivization, to deport *kulaks*, to seize all livestock, and Stalin was surely the source of these orders. The deportation of the *kulaks* (which in reality meant anyone who voiced opposition to collectivization) removed at one blow the most efficient farmers. There had been no serious preparation of the measures, no clear orders about how a collective farm should be run. Chinese experience, at least before the communes, suggests that milder ways of proceeding are possible. In any event, the attempt to collectivize all private livestock ended in disaster and a retreat. It is worth reproducing the figures from the official handbook of agricultural statistics:

LIVESTOCK POPULATION
(Million of Head)

	1928	*1934*
Horses	32·1	15·4
Cattle	60·1	33·5
Pigs	22·0	11·5
Sheep	97·3	32·9

Yet already by 1934 private livestock holdings were again permitted, and in 1938 over threequarters of all cows, over two-thirds of all pigs, nearly two-thirds of all sheep, were in private hands. This is evidence of a disastrous error.

Its consequences were profound. Peasant hostility and bitterness were greatly intensified. For many years there were in fact no net investments in agriculture, since the new tractors merely went to replace some of the slaughtered horses. Acute food shortage made itself felt—though the state's control over produce ensured that most of those who died in the resulting famine were peasants and not townsmen. But once all this happened, the case for coercion was greatly strengthened, the need for police measures became more urgent than ever, the power of the censorship was increased, freedom of speech had still further to be curtailed, as part of the necessities of remaining in power and continuing the industrial revolution in an environment grown more hostile as a result of such policies. So Stalin's policy decisions led to events which contributed greatly to the further growth of totalitarianism and the police state.

The same is true of the attempt to do the impossible on the industrial front in the years of the first five-year plan. Much of the effort was simply wasted, as when food was taken from hungry peasants and exported to pay for machines which rusted in the open or were wrecked by untrained workmen. At the same time, the closing of many private workshops deprived the people of consumers' goods which the state, intent on building steelworks and machine-shops, was quite unable to provide. Again, living standards suffered, the hatred of many citizens for the régime increased, the NKVD had to be expanded and the logic of police rule followed. But Stalin had a big role in the initial decisions to jump too far too fast.[1] (It is interesting to note that Mao, who should have learnt the lessons of history, repeated many of these mistakes in China's 'great leap forward' of 1958–59, which suggests that *there are certain errors which Communists repeatedly commit*, possibly due to the suppression, in 'anti-rightist' campaigns, of the voices of moderation and common sense.)

One of the consequences of these acute hardships was isolation from foreign countries. Economists often speak of the 'demonstration effect', i.e. of the effect of the knowledge of higher living standards abroad on the citizens of poor and underdeveloped countries. This knowledge may act as a spur to effort—but it also generates resistance to sacrifice. Stalin and his régime systematically 'shielded' Soviet citizens from knowledge of the outside world, by censorship, by cutting off personal contacts, by misinformation. The need to do so, in their eyes, was greatly increased by the extent of the drop in living standards in the early 'thirties.

But we must now come to Stalin's more direct contribution to the brutality and terrorism of the Stalin era.

There was, firstly, his needless cruelty which showed itself already in the methods used to impose collectivization. The great purges were surely not 'objectively necessary'. To explain them one has to take into account Stalin's thirst for supreme power, his intense pathological suspiciousness, i.e. matters pertaining to Stalin's personal position and character. These led him to massacre the majority of the 'Stalinist' central committee elected in 1934, who had supported or at the very least tolerated Stalin's policies up to that date. The facts suggest that they believed that relaxation was possible and desirable; many of them seem to have died for the crime of saying so. Nor was there any 'police logic' for the scale and drastic nature of the purges. Indeed, the police chiefs figured prominently among the victims. True, there was a kind of 'snowballing' of arrests, which might have got out of control in 1938, but this was due largely to the effect of the terror on the police, who had to show zeal or go under. Nor can any 'necessity' explain the post-war repressions,

[1] N. Jasny, in his *Soviet Industrialisation, 1938–52* (Chicago, 1961), has much to say about the chaotic planning of the early 'thirties.

the death of Voznesensky, the so-called 'Leningrad affair', the shooting of the Jewish intellectuals, the 'doctors' plot'. Stalin played so prominently a personal role in establishing a reign of terror in the Party and the country that he must bear direct responsibility even where executions were the result of false information supplied to him by his subordinates for reasons of their own.

The atmosphere of terror had, of course, far-reaching consequences in every sphere of Soviet life. It became particularly grotesque and purposeless in the last years of Stalin, when the social and economic developments, plus victory in war, provided the Soviet régime with a much firmer base among the people, so that a considerable part of the discontent was the result, rather than the cause, of repressive measures. Many obviously overdue reforms had to await his death. As did Tsar Nicholas I, a century earlier, Stalin was able to delay 'necessary' changes.

Many other examples can be given of the personal role of Stalin. On the economic front, the miserable state of the peasants in 1953 was due largely to Stalin's obstinate refusal to face the facts and listen to serious advice. He contributed greatly to wasteful and grandiose schemes to 'transform nature', and to a wasteful and grandiose style of architecture. In the military field, history will, I think, support Khrushchev's accusation that Stalin's inability to see the signs of a German attack, his unwillingness to allow preparations, his massacre of the best Soviet officers, all made a personal contribution to the Russian disasters of 1941. Stalin personally insisted on his own deification, the rewriting of history, the creation of myths. Some myths were based on lies which he himself publicly uttered. For instance, in 1935 he announced: 'We have had no poor for two or three years now'—and this when bread had reached the highest price, in relation to wages, that it had ever attained in Soviet history. Or equally ridiculous was his claim, in 1947, that Moscow 'had completely abolished slums'. In this personal way he made impossible all serious discussion either of living standards or the housing problem, just as his wildly false assertions about 'Bukharin and Trotsky, agents of Hitler and the Mikado', made the writing of Soviet history impossible in Russia. One could argue that the myth about 'voluntary collectivization' was an objectively necessary lie, in the sense of transcending Stalin's personality; indeed, this lie figures in the Party programme adopted by the twenty-second Congress last November. But Stalin's lies went very much beyond this, and beyond the distortions and myths which can be ascribed to other politicians in other countries.

Throughout Russia, officials at all levels modelled themselves on Stalin, and each succeeded in imposing more unnecessary misery on more subordinates, stultifying initiative, penalizing intelligence, discouraging originality. The price of all this is still being paid.

The urgent need to prepare for war has often been advanced as an excuse for Stalin's industrial 'tempos' and for the terror. This can hardly be accepted. In the worst years of social coercion and over-ambitious plans, i.e. 1929–33, Hitler was only just climbing to power, and Comintern policy showed that he was not then regarded as the main enemy. It is possible that Stalin was liquidating all potential opponents in the Purges of 1936–38 as a precaution in case war broke out, though this seems doubtful for a variety of reasons. But it is quite false to use the result of the war as ex-post-factum justification of Stalinism. Perhaps, with less harsh policies, the greater degree of loyalty in 1941 would have offset a smaller industrial base? In any event the Purges not only led to the slaughter of the best military officers but also halted the growth of heavy industry.

The attentive reader will have noticed that this analysis has some features in common with Khrushchev's. Before 1934, Stalin had been carrying out policies which commanded the assent of a majority of the Party and which, like collectivization, had been accepted as necessary and irreversible by the bulk of Party members, whatever their reservations about particular mistakes and acts of brutality. However, after that date he took more and more personal, arbitrary measures, massacred much of the Party, behaved like an oriental despot. It is true that he was also arbitrary before 1934, and that he took some wise decisions after that date; but there is a case for placing a qualitative change around then.

But this is by no means the end of the matter. It is not only a question of making some obvious remarks concerning Khrushchev's own role during the terror. Of much more general significance is the fact that the events prior to 1934, including the building-up of Stalin into an all-powerful and infallible dictator (by men many of whom he afterwards massacred), cannot be disassociated with what followed; at the very least they provided Stalin with his opportunity. This is where the historian must avoid the twin and opposite pitfalls of regarding what happened as inevitable, and regarding it as a chapter of 'personalized' accidents. At each stage there are choices to be made, though the range of possible choices is generally much narrower than people suppose. In 1928 any practicable Bolshevik programme would have been harsh and unpopular. It might not have been *so* harsh and unpopular but for choices which need not necessarily have been made. If before 1934, i.e. in the very period of maximum social coercion, Stalin truly represented the will of the Party, and Khrushchev argues that he did, some totalitarian consequences logically follow. One of these, as already suggested, is the semi-militarized party led by a *Fuehrer*, a dictator, because without an unquestioned leader the consequences of the policies adopted could not be faced.

But, even if it is true that the triumph of a dictator may be explained by objective circumstances which certainly existed in the Soviet situation, the acts of a dictator once he has 'arrived' involve a considerable (though of course not infinite) degree of personal choice. Those who gave him the opportunity to act in an arbitrary and cruel way, who adopted policies which involved arbitrariness and coercion on a big scale, cannot ascribe subsequent events to the wickedness of one man or his immediate associates and claim that their hands are clean, even indeed if they were shot themselves on Stalin's orders. The whole-hog Stalin, in other words, was not 'necessary', but the possibility of a Stalin was a necessary consequence of the effort of a minority group to keep power and to carry out a vast social-economic revolution in a very short time. And *some* elements of Stalinism were, in those circumstances, scarcely avoidable.

The serious problem for us is to see how far certain elements of Stalinism, in the sense of purposefully-applied social coercion, imposed by a party in the name of an ideology, are likely or liable to accompany rapid economic development even in non-Communist countries.

For it is surely true that many of the problems tackled by Stalin so brutally are present elsewhere, though events in the USSR were, of course, deeply affected by peculiar features of Russia and of Bolshevism. The West should indeed emphasize the high cost in human and material terms of a Stalin, and show that the rise of such a man to supreme power in the Soviet Union was, to use the familiar Soviet-Marxist jargon phrase, 'not accidental'. Indeed, some Western historians who normally write 'personalist' and empiricist history will begin to see the virtues of an approach they normally deride as 'historicist'; they will analyse Soviet history to establish patterns, regularities, 'necessities', which lead to Stalin. By contrast, an embarrassed Khrushchev will be—is being—forced to give an un-Marxist emphasis to personal and accidental factors.

But, of course, we must not confine our search for 'necessities' in history only to instances which happen to serve a propagandist purpose. This would be a typically Soviet approach to historiography, only in reverse. It is particularly important to think very seriously about the inter-relationship of coercion and industrialization, about the nature of the obstacles and vicious circles which drive men to think in totalitarian terms. Unless we realize how complex are the problems which development brings, how irrelevant are many of our ideas to the practical possibilities open to statesmen in these countries, we may unconsciously drive them towards the road which led to Stalin. They cannot be satisfied with 'the pace of a tortoise'.

NOVE ON STALIN: A COMMENT

Alec Nove's article 'Was Stalin really necessary?' is very stimulating. Although his answer to the basic question posed is not quite clear, one can agree with most of what he says. Still, my own inclination is to say 'Quite, quite unnecessary!' and so I should like to make a few comments on the way Nove handled the three central issues:

(1) What is the meaning of historical necessity?
(2) Was the forcible collectivization necessary?

(3) Was the Great Purge linked with the 1929–31 economic upheaval or was it only a consequence of Stalin's 'excesses'?

1. Nove argues that historical necessity is not historically immanent (why exactly is it historical?) but is to be understood as the existence of objective and subjective factors limiting the range of possible choice. The subjective factors are concerned with the Aristotelian essences of those taking decisions. 'A rabbi does not eat pork; were he to do so, he would not be a rabbi.' Similarly: 'There may have been a number of solutions to the problems posed by Russia of the 'twenties which the Communists could not have chosen because they were Communists.' That may be true, but if historical necessity is so defined then each régime carries within it its own 'inevitability'. The Indian Congress Party, for instance, cannot do certain things without ceasing to be an Indian Congress Party, and Soviet Russia's 'historical necessities' are thus irrelevant to it by definition. Is this the conclusion Mr Nove wanted to draw? He rightly rejects Marxist 'historical inevitability', but then in his reasoning the belief in it is surely a subjective factor without which the Soviet Communists would not be Communists. It thus follows that, however mistaken and however 'voluntaristic' their acts, they are in Nove's scheme in a sense all 'necessary' by definition. This is, of course, part of a genuine paradox; but it largely rests on how the words 'possible' and 'necessary' are defined. Is this begging the whole question? If 'really necessary' is not the same as 'historically necessary', why is it not?

2. The answer to the second question is given in the affirmative: Yes, Nove argues, forcible collectivization was necessary. This is not the answer implied by Gomulka, and Khrushchev himself admitted at the twenty-second Congress the possibility of a different road to socialism in countries 'where peasants are deeply attached to private property'. The Polish Communists have quickly reproduced this passage offering a doctrinal legitimation of their present practice. If this is so, doesn't it cast doubt on the 'necessity' of Stalin's forcible collectivization? Peasants everywhere are attached to their property; so were they in Russia. It is interesting to compare Nove's conclusions on the subject with those given in the official Polish Communist theoretical journal *Nowe Drogi* (No. 12, 1961):

> Apart from objective factors there are also subjective factors. There are no situations in which the Party or the individuals do not have possibility of choice, in which definite problems cannot be solved by different methods, less costly, and avoiding many unnecessary sufferings and negative effects.

Would Nove reject this in favour of the Khrushchevian justification of Stalin's 'necessities' (*minus* his 'excesses')? Is there not enough evidence that the whole monstrous character of Soviet collectivization was connected more with *political* than with economic necessities?

3. According to Nove, forcible collectivization stemmed from objective necessities and only its excesses (which Stalin also condemned) resulted from subjective factors and indirect effects. This apparently is not the case with the great purges of 1936–38. In his view, 'the great purges cannot possibly be derived from any "objective necessity" arising from past policies. They can be derived from Stalin's thirst for supreme power, his intense, pathological suspiciousness'.

This is an astonishing argument. It is enough to look at the record (for example, in the chapter on the subject in Leonard Schapiro's history of *The Communist Party of the Soviet Union*) to see that historical evidence points to a precisely opposite conclusion. The Great Purge was more than intimately linked with the past policies of forcible collectivization. Nobody, of course, would deny Stalin's 'thirst for power', but this was also an operative factor in the previous instances. 'Given the nature of the system', Stalin had at each stage been taking decisions which largely conditioned his subsequent actions (and 'Stalin would not be Stalin, if he had done otherwise').

Collectivization may be regarded either as an end in itself, or as a means to secure industrial growth. In the former case, the problems besetting Soviet agriculture today cast doubt on the economic rationality of collectivization; in the latter case, in the perspective of 1931, Stalin may well have felt that the drastic method of squeezing agriculture in order to build industry quickly may be the only one, but three decades later this does not seem so certain and there is no reason to fall into the trap of *post hoc ergo propter hoc* type of reasoning. In any case the economic perspective is not the only one. What may seem economically necessary may not be 'really necessary' if the human price to be paid is too high. It is only too easy to confuse retrospectively doctrinal necessity with economic necessity and then make it into a 'historical necessity'.

The exclusively economic perspective probably accounts for Nove's conclusion on the great purges. 'Objective necessity' in this context means for him more or less plausible economic reasons; and these, he seems to suggest, may have justified drastic steps in 1931 but not after 1934 when the economic situation improved. But in political perspective there were apparently reasons more compelling than the economic one for Stalin to act as he did.

For an economist there may be a temptation to qualify economic reasons as 'objective necessity', but not political reasons. This reflects a certain economic determinism. It is an oversimplification to regard Stalinism as just a function of the necessities of industrialization in 'backward Russia'. Stalin had risen to power before his 'second revolution' and not as a result of it. There is no historical reason to confer an economic justification on his would-be imitators in the underdeveloped countries, however harsh may be the conditions of the industrial 'take-off' in them.

LEOPOLD LABEDZ

Survey, London.

'WAS STALIN NECESSARY?': A REJOINDER

It is always a pleasure to cross swords with my old friend Leopold Labedz, who never fails to be a stimulating opponent. He takes me to task [*Encounter*, August] for my judgment of the necessity or otherwise of Stalin. I do not deny the validity of some of his comments, but on occasion he seems to misunderstand what I was trying to say. My article [*Encounter*, April] was concerned, first, to discuss the personal role of Stalin, i.e. the extent to which his terror régime was situation-determined; secondly, I was concerned to identify the extent to which the situation itself, including the horrors of forced collectivization, flowed from the existence of a Communist dictatorship which was trying to industrialize a predominantly peasant country quickly. I do not pretend that these are the only questions which should be asked in a survey of the political and economic history of the Soviet Union. Nor indeed are they the kind of questions which permit of a definitive answer. They are, nonetheless, matters which are interesting to discuss.

I do not quite understand the point of Labedz's criticism of my discussion of necessity. He both accepts and rejects the proposition that the choices of politicians are limited by their own ideological attitudes and beliefs. Surely, if one is trying to identify the role of an individual, it is significant to identify the ideological limitations on his choice which would apply not only to him but also to the overwhelming majority of his party comrades. For example, no leader of the British Labour Party is in a position to denationalize an existing nationalized industry, and this is surely an elementary political fact. A Conservative is less limited in this respect, though no doubt he would be precluded by his beliefs from advocating certain solutions which would be acceptable to the Labour Party. All this is obvious, and I do not see why the same kind of logic cannot be applied to the choices available to the Bolsheviks. Labedz complains that 'if historical necessity is so defined, then each régime carries with it its own inevitability'. The word 'inevitability' is his, not mine. It does carry with it its own limitations on the range of practicable choices. He points out that, if my logic were valid, the Indian Congress Party must be seen as having a different field of choices from that which was or would be available to the Communists. A minute's reflection would cause him to see that this is not only the case, but self-evidently the case. Why is this a criticism?

Labedz also asserts that I expressed the view that 'forcible collectivization was necessary'. In doing so he again shows a misunderstanding of the subject of my article, which was Stalin and not collectivization as such. I carefully made the point that non-Communists would have found some totally different solution; I also quite specifically left open the question of the possible viability of alternative policies. What I tried to do was to stress the considerations which led to the decision to impose collectivization, looking for the impersonal logic of events, noting that the bulk of the Communist Party, including former oppositionists, rallied round the Party in its campaign against the peasants. All this is relevant to the assessment of Stalin's personal role. I also noted that voluntary collectivization was a non-starter in the circumstances, and that in those same circumstances forced collectivization would be associated with excesses. The actual methods used, not without a great deal of personal encouragement from Stalin, led to excesses and brutalities on a vast scale. What happened then is not part of any model for underdeveloped countries to follow. It is rather a terrible warning, and I never suggested otherwise.

Labedz roundly asserts that I deny any connection between collectivization and the great purge. Perhaps he would re-read my article, where I devote much space to establishing the connection between the harshness and brutalities of collectivization and the increasing intensity of police repression. But the events which followed Kirov's death, and especially the great massacres of 1936–38, were no *necessary* consequence of the events before 1934. Labedz seems to overlook the distinction between a causal connection and a necessary connection, though admittedly the distinction is never absolute, but is rather one of degree. *Of course* the events of 1929–34 were part of the essential background of the purges. But was it a logical consequence of collectivization for Stalin to massacre the majority of the members of his own faction, the very men who carried collectivization through? Is there not some evidence for the proposition that this massacre followed an attempt by his colleagues to restrain Stalin's growing arbitrariness and blood-letting? True, the earlier events created an atmosphere in which a mass purge became possible. However, as recent Chinese experience suggests, disastrous 'leaps forward' can sometimes be followed by a sinking of differences in an effort to put matters right, rather than by mass shootings.

Labedz would seem to ascribe to me the belief that I accept only economic and social logic, and not a political logic of events. This is surely not the case. The desire of the Communist leadership to maintain itself in power was an essential element in the choices which they made, including the decision to collectivize. The relative importance of this aspect of the decision is a matter on which legitimate disagreement is possible, but I nowhere denied that this was a significant factor. Did the events of 1936–38 follow from political necessity? If they did, and I failed to allow for this, I am guilty of error. However, despite carefully reading Schapiro's book, I still believe that what I called the 'whole hog Stalinist terror' was primarily aimed at securing the absolute dictatorship of Joseph Stalin, over the Party and everyone else. (Schapiro's chapter on the purges is entitled: 'Stalin's Victory Over the Party'!) I say this while entirely accepting the proposition that political logic led to toughness and to numerous restrictions on human freedom. It is true that the power manoeuvring of Stalin did indeed have its own logic and its own 'regularities'. However, since my paper was concerned with identifying Stalin's personal role, I naturally treated actions in furtherance of Stalin's career as attributable to Stalin rather than to the impersonal logic of events. I am surprised that Labedz should be so insistent on historical inevitability and the inexorable march of History, etc., etc. On other occasions he and those who think like him seem to take a somewhat different view of the role of personality.

A. Nove

2. *The uses and abuses of Kremlinology**

The object of this article is to discuss the relative significance of various methods of studying the Soviet Union, and it is convenient for this purpose to use 'Kremlinology' as a peg on which to hang the discussion. By 'Kremlinology' I mean the method of analysis which lays great stress on a careful study of the promotion, demotion and interaction of personalities, and also on the exact wording of pronouncements of certain conventional or formal kinds. On the whole, I take the view that this can be greatly overdone, and once gave a talk under the title of 'Down with Kremlinology'. However, it must be emphasized that 'down' does not mean 'out', but rather 'down to the second division', to use footballing language. It is certainly useful to study the sort of things which Kremlinologists study. The problem is—how useful, relative to other things.

A critique of Kremlinology involves two important points of principle. The first is the role of personality in history in general, in Soviet history in particular. The second relates to the validity of the technique of Kremlinology as a guide to personality struggles or to policy clashes. The two points are to some extent independent of one another. Thus one may well hold the view that the decision about who is to succeed Khrushchev is of vital importance to the entire world, and none the less argue that we cannot discover who will succeed him by watching the careers of the supporters of Brezhnev, Polyanski, Kozlov or other possible contenders, or the precise wording of *Pravda* editorials. We will discuss later on the extent to which the traditional methods of Kremlinology are helpful even within the narrower confines of power-struggle analysis. But, first, what is the case for the Kremlinological approach?

On a naïve level, it consists of variations on the theme of the well-known generalization, 'history is about chaps'. The biographies of politicians, on this view, *are* political history. It

* From *Survey*, January 1964.

would not then matter particularly whether two (imaginary) comrades named Bushkin and Kukushkin stand for different policies. A conflict between them, if such exists, is by definition both relevant and important. Such an approach is common enough among diplomats and newspaper correspondents, and rightly so. It is an essential part of their jobs to report the rise and fall of personalities. The promotion, demotion and ambitions of politicians must be reported, whether or not there results any change of policy. This is at least as true of the Soviet Union as of any other country.

But the Soviet Union is a special case, argue the Kremlinologists. Political strife does not take place there in the open, it is conducted behind the scenes, and little hints appear in obscure ways. These may be connected with the rise and fall of individuals in the hierarchy or with significant policy shifts. Hints may be found in obscure paragraphs or in some peculiar rewording of certain formal statements. This is the bit of the iceberg that shows above the surface. Rumours of conflict within the leadership are always denied even when the political battle is in full swing, as it was on the eve of Malenkov's fall and in the struggle with the anti-party group. Yet acute observers did spot some tell-tale signs. Then it is also argued that policy issues in the USSR are in a special way subordinated to the power struggle, that it shows a misunderstanding of Soviet political realities to study issues in themselves. This view can readily be supported by evidence which shows that pronouncements on policy, ideology and philosophy have been repeatedly used as missiles in political in-fighting. It is also said, again with justice, that the penalties of defeat in Soviet politics have been exceptionally severe, and that this has affected the behaviour of the actors on the political stage. It is also undeniable that the decisions of politicians affect many more aspects of the lives of the people in the Soviet Union than is the case in Western countries. It may also be legitimately argued, though this point is often pushed too far, that in the Soviet Union politics control social-economic reality, making nonsense of any analysis based on economic determinism. Thus, for example, forcible collectivization and the first five-year plan represented a politically-inspired attempt to change drastically the then existing economic and social milieu; these policies could hardly be regarded as a reflection of the class structure of Soviet society in 1928. All this does seem to add up to a powerful case for Kremlinology. The more intelligent practitioners of the art would presumably not deny that many things happen in the Soviet Union which have no causal connection with the power struggle, or that real problems do not exist. They would surely also agree that the power of the Soviet totalitarian state is not absolute, that it is limited not only by physical fact (a quart will not go into a pint pot, in Moscow as in London) but also by certain social and economic realities. In fact, the discussion between sensible Kremlinologists and their sensible opponents is concerned with emphasis. Neither side would assert that the preoccupations of the other are nonsensical. Both would admit that it is possible to go too far in either totally ignoring the power struggle or in considering nothing else. In the one case one abstracts from an important aspect of Soviet political life, in the other the analysis becomes one-sided and superficial. It is likely that we would all agree that the emphasis which one places on Kremlinological analysis is partly related to time-scale. The more one is concerned with 'micro-history', the greater the role of the manoeuvres of individual politicians. Conversely, developments over a longer period tend to have causes of a less personal kind.

What weaknesses are there in the Kremlinologists' case? In the first place, I feel that they tend to over-estimate some of the differences between Soviet and Western political systems. No one would deny that there are important differences, but in virtually all countries politicians are ambitious men who intrigue against one another, who in the course of their intrigues do not always say what they mean, and are known to adopt policies with one or both eyes on the consequences of these policies to their political ambitions. An unambitious politician would probably be in another profession. A desire for power and a capacity for intrigue are a common denominator. As I am reading these words, I have in front of me an article by the *Evening Standard*'s political correspondent, published on June 25, 1963, which contains the following words: 'It is a truism that politics is concerned with power. Equally its motive force is ambition to wield that power, directly or indirectly.' It is sometimes necessary to remind over-enthusiastic Kremlinologists that such words as these can be used, as they were used, about Great Britain as well as Russia. It follows from the above that politicians, in pursuit of their own ambitions, may adopt policies which are suggested to them by circumstances, in which case it is the circumstance rather than the ambition which explains the course of events. Thus Disraeli extended the franchise to the urban artisans in 1867, 'to dish the Whigs', as he himself said. One notes this fact, but presumably no serious historian would assert that the extension of the franchise in the second half of the nineteenth century was 'caused' by Disraeli's understandable desire to carry out a political manoeuvre. One could assert with some justice that the pursuit of greater power is for politicians what the pursuit of profit is for the business man, a motive for action which causes men to take opportunities, but which is common to so many men that it ceases to be an underlying cause of events. Of course differences of setting and opportunity make for wide differences of tactics and throw up quite different kinds of politicians in different countries. Mr Maudling and Lord Hailsham do not strive for success by methods which served Beria and Malenkov, and it would not have occurred to George Brown to have his rival Harold Wilson arrested for counter-revolutionary activities even if he controlled the police. However, reasons for such striking contrasts in political behaviour must be sought in impersonal factors—institutions, traditions, political atmosphere, etc.

Are real issues and doctrinal arguments in the USSR subordinated to the power struggle in some special sense which does not apply elsewhere? That they are mixed up in varying degrees with the power struggle is not denied. The problem is of finding a method of analysis which most usefully enables us to see the causes of events. Let us take some examples. Malenkov's fall was preceded by politically inspired attacks on his alleged economic heresies. He was accused of doctrinal error in overstressing consumers' goods as against producers' goods. The arguments were put in the official and technical press in a dogmatically one-sided way. There was no debate in any serious sense. This was part of the process of removing Malenkov from the premiership, conducted in a certain conventional manner. Yet, underlying the formal verbiage there were some very real problems. Malenkov's abandonment of traditional priorities led to some confusion in planning, since shortages persisted. He had demagogically reduced retail prices, lowered taxes, halved forced savings, increased wage levels and peasant incomes, a policy which adds up to inflation. There was also a conflict with those who, like Khrushchev, desired a substantial increase in investments in agriculture. We may be sure that these things were debated behind the scenes. Issues and personal conflicts were intermingled, as they nearly always are, but the economic problem was quite plainly present, and it is wrong to treat this as a mere by-product of the power struggle.

Yet, from another standpoint, it was just such a by-product. There is no need to overstress the purely economic aspect of the story. It is not my purpose to argue for economic determinism, but rather to stress the importance of issues, circumstances, the logic of events. This logic may or may not relate to economic factors; the point is that it is impersonal. Kremlinologists seem to overlook even the logic of the power struggle itself. Let us take the position at Stalin's death. His successors faced a longing for relaxation of terror, an urgent need of agricultural reforms, an immense desire for more houses and consumers' goods. *Any* successor was likely to compete for support by adopting policies which reflected this situation. The danger clearly existed that competitors for the leadership would try to outdo one another, to go beyond the possible in efforts to achieve popularity. Even Beria was reportedly aware of the need to act on these lines, Malenkov certainly was. One could treat this as a distant Soviet relation of a British 'election budget', but because of the much greater economic powers of the Soviet state the dangers of such a policy are greater there. There was an immediate need for deflationary measures in 1955. The immediate cause of these measures must be seen as the overstrain which had to be remedied. In other words Khrushchev's economic policies of 1955 should not be explained *directly* by the power struggle. But it is true that the logic of the succession problem was itself part of the explanation for the overstrain.

While the above analysis is to some extent independent of any particular personalities (save that the situation might not have arisen if Stalin were immortal), it is not argued that all the leaders would adopt the same policies or that their decisions are at all times situation-determined. No one can assert such things about many important elements of Stalin's career, for instance.

Some leaders can and do adopt drastic policies from which some of their colleagues would have shrunk. Others can commit grave errors. We must at all costs avoid a 'what happened had to happen' approach. Or perhaps not quite at all costs, since to find the rationale of what did happen is usually a more fruitful way of writing history than attributing major events to the power struggle or to accidental decisions of great men. At any given moment the past is past, and the men at the top have before them a range of choice which may be small or more considerable. Sometimes the general lines of policy are indicated by the already existing circumstances. It is a myth that the choice of the Soviet ruling group is infinite. It is circumscribed not only by the objective situation but also by the ruling group's own thought patterns. This remains the case despite the lack of institutional checks on the exercise of power. Political scientists sometimes overstress the importance of institutional factors in decision-making. After all there are many things which a Conservative or Labour government in this country would not do which it would have the *power* to do. But the role of an individual leader remains great in Russia, and consequently some decisions and reorganizations bear the imprint of Khrushchev's personality. Thus his attempts to overcome inefficiencies in economic planning are greatly influenced by an oversimplified picture of party trouble shooters, a picture which is quite irrelevant to the solution of the real problems. Thus we have here an important personal element. Yet any serious analysis would have to take account of three things:

(*a*) The problem of industrial planning is real and has a life and logic of its own, independently of Khrushchev's view of it.

(*b*) Khrushchev's view of it is itself a product of his experience of party life in the last thirty years.

(*c*) Because his solution is no solution, the problem will continue to plague him and his successors, compelling them to try out other ideas, which are being actively discussed.

Economic organization is an area where policy, efficiency, ideology and power considerations overlap and interact. The Sovnarkhoz reform of 1957 was both a genuine effort to correct real defects of planning, and a blow dealt by Khrushchev against his enemies. The precise shape of the reform was certainly affected by Khrushchev's political position (such things are, of course, not unknown in other countries!). Thus, to take one example, the number of Sovnarkhozy was much too large for economic convenience and must have been influenced by Khrushchev's need to secure support from Obkom secretaries, and this led him to preserve in most cases the existing administrative boundaries but the reform had causes and logical consequences which transcended the power struggle and which made it unavoidable that Khrushchev would make further changes. Thus the built-in tendency towards 'localism' on the part of Sovnarkhozy made recentralization the only alternative to a kind of decentralization (to market forces) which neither Khrushchev nor the party machine is yet prepared to contemplate. The inevitable recentralization placed impossible burdens on Gosplan and this led to the multiplication of state committees and other co-ordinating bodies. Whatever Khrushchev's intention was, effective central control could not be exercised by local party organs because these inevitably identified themselves with economic interests of their locality, i.e. with obtaining maximum investment resources from the state and fulfilling local plans regardless of the effect on others. The small size of the Sovnarkhozy led to experiments with co-ordinating committees and large regions. There was plenty of evidence of stresses and strains, which had a reality quite independent of the will of particular politicians and which called for urgent remedial action. Early in 1962, the author of these lines wrote an article (published in July) which forecast imminent changes. When these changes came, the pattern of reform was again affected by the political interests of individuals and of groups. (There is urgent need for studying interest groups and the extent to which they find voices speaking for them within the party machine.) We should not imagine that the leadership sits in the clouds immune from the influence of their surroundings. Khrushchev tried in November 1962 to strengthen centralized party control, while weakening the position of the Obkom secretaries. The solution adopted in March 1963 may be a compromise, since it differs in several significant respects from the ideas submitted to the November 1962 plenum. Of course, different leaders may have had different ideas about just what should be done. It would be amazing were it otherwise.

The point is that the problems these men dealt with are complex, intractable and have a logic and reality of their own which should be analysed as such. Economic organization and the political aspects of planning also no doubt enter into the power struggle.

In fact it is possible to forecast with some confidence that there will be a political and personal conflict on this very issue. It may already be in full swing. It is possible to interpret the otherwise obscure elements in the industrial reorganization of March 1963, and in particular the appointment of Ustinov as a planning overlord, as evidence of just such a conflict. Perhaps this explains the otherwise peculiar outburst of Khrushchev in his speech to the ideologists in June 1963, in which he sought to assert the superiority of the party over the planners; the context was most unsuitable, and he seemed to be arguing with someone, whose opinions have not so far been reported. Far from denying the power struggle, it may be asserted that the adoption of reforming ideas by power-seeking persons or groups is a vital part of reality, but the issues here help us to explain and even forecast what the struggle is likely to be about.

It may not be unfair to assert that Kremlinologists are quite ready to see impersonal logic of events when they write about the sector of Russian life which they themselves know. Thus, Robert Conquest is able to see the logic of Socialist Realism in the general context of the totalitarian system established by Stalin, and I feel sure that he would not attribute the repressive policies of the period in any fundamental sense to the personalities or ambitions of Shcherbakov or Zhdanov. He would doubtless agree that the two above-named comrades, as well as their views on art and their means of enforcing these views, were an integral part of the Stalin system. Similarly, while he and other Kremlinologists may note that Kozlov seems to be associated with a tough cultural line in 1963, they would doubtless admit that the hesitations of the leadership over the consequences of cultural liberalization have a very real objective basis. What he does seem to overlook is that virtually every separate sector or aspect of Soviet reality has its own inner logic, and that the role of the power struggle as an explanation of events is generally greatest in the spheres of which the given analyst is most ignorant. Whether one discusses the general pattern of Soviet diplomacy, the quarrel with China, legal doctrine, fuel policy, or whatever it may be, almost every expert on *that* sector will tend to devote his serious work to analysing the circumstantial logic of events, and while the decisions of politicians must be fitted into the pattern, they will only occasionally emerge as a decisive part of the explanation. Thus Kaganovich may have favoured the steam locomotive, and it may have delayed the introduction of diesel and electric traction on the Russian railways, but no one writing on transport would take very seriously a Kremlinological explanation of the advent of diesels and electrification.

In recent years Kremlinological methods have also suffered a blow from the gradual erosion of certain conventional procedures. The names of the leaders are generally in alphabetical order, though indications of relative status do continue to appear occasionally, as, for instance, in lists of localities wishing to adopt a given leader as a candidate for the Supreme Soviet. The absences of individuals from official functions are no longer an indication that anything is afoot. In 1953 the Kremlinologists rightly noted the significance of Beria's absence from an operatic performance. It was indeed a sign of his downfall and could not possibly mean, within the then existing conventions, that he did not like opera or even that he had a cold. Lists of leaders attending formal functions were a signal, read and understood as such by local officials. Presumably if a leader really did have a cold, his name would still have appeared as attending the Bolshoi Theatre to avoid confusing the local comrades. But in recent years we have had repeated instances of prominent leaders absenting themselves, without any significance attaching to their absence. Similarly, it is no longer true, though it once was true, that a critical or unusual statement by a scholar or technician is likely to be officially inspired. Under Stalin statements which diverged from the official line involved so much risk that they would only be made with powerful political backing. Therefore even the opinion of an expert on a technical matter could be an important indication of changes in policy or the relative positions of politicians. Quite plainly this is no longer the case. As Herbert Dinerstein rightly put it, 'It seems that discussion . . . does not necessarily indicate a dispute over policy in the party. A debate may be just what it purports to be, an expression of differences of opinion by experts who hope that the cogency of their arguments will compel party leaders to retain or modify official policies.'[1]

Similarly it is no longer possible to assert that a public criticism of a Minister is necessarily the reflection of the power struggle. It may be, but more often not. For example, while agriculture is certainly an area in which Khrushchev's personal policies have played a most important role, analysis of the careers of and political attacks on successive Ministers of Agriculture would tell us very little about anything. It is not enlightening as a guide to agricultural policy or to the power struggle. One could write a long and detailed work on the many serious problems of collective and state farms without mentioning the name of a single Minister. This is not to deny for a moment that the deliberate weakening of the Ministry of Agriculture was a political act, and the obscure episode of the creation and apparent abandonment of an all-union state committee on agriculture in 1962 (and the fall of Ignatov) has real political as well as Kremlinological significance. This seems to be part of a struggle over the role of the party machine in which Khrushchev himself is heavily involved. It could be objected that Ministers of Agriculture are relatively poor and insignificant creatures, so that their replacement has no major political effects. However, several very prominent leaders have been retired from political life in recent years, and this too seems to have made no appreciable difference to anything. What about Kirichenko, Aristov, Belyaev? Whom or what were they plotting against, or for? With what issues were they associated? In what respect did their rise or fall affect Soviet policy on farming, China, culture, the cold war, investment priorities or even posts and telegraphs? It the answer is 'we have no idea', then how does their demotion matter, except to themselves, their friends and their relations? Admittedly this is putting it a bit strongly, but it is surely reasonable to ask of any analyst of the Soviet scene that he explain the practical value of his researches in terms of explanations of the past or prediction of future events, and not just political biography. To repeat, it clearly does matter to the world who will succeed Khrushchev. If, as seems to be the case, Khrushchev suffers from some loss of coherence and confidence, if on various issues he appears to

[1] *Soviet Doctrine on Developing Countries: Some Divergent Views* (Rand Corporation, 1963).

be in conflict with colleagues, these are matters which must be watched and studied. If we can find indications as to the views on significant questions of Brezhnev, Polyanski, Kozlov, then their changing relative positions in the succession stakes would be a really important political indicator. Yet, while not for a moment denying the importance of personalities, and without subscribing to determinism, it is again worth emphasizing that choices by politicians are often much more limited than we suppose. Kremlinologists have been known to argue that the fact that politicians have adopted their opponents' policies after achieving power lends support for their viewpoint. On a superficial level it could be said that such behaviour proves the primacy of the power struggle, but on reflection it is as likely to prove the opposite, that after all perhaps there was only one thing to do.

3. *The politics of economic rationality: Observations on the Soviet economy**

The object of this paper is to consider the growing importance of economic rationality in the affairs of the Soviet Union, and to express a few ideas about the possible political implications of such problems. But first, what is 'economic rationality'?

Some economists equate it with what they call 'consumers' sovereignty', a state of affairs they believe to exist in Western countries. This belief seems odd when, as in Great Britain, about 36 per cent of the national income is expended by the state, but in any event there is no necessary connection between consumers' sovereignty and rationality. All that is meant here by 'rationality' is the following relatively simple proposition: that the economic purposes of society, whatever these may be *and* whoever decides them, are achieved with maximum economic efficiency—or alternatively, that maximum results are achieved at minimum real cost. Theoretically all the aims of economic activity could be decided wholly by planners (God forbid that it should be so! But theoretically it is possible), and an economically rational arrangement would then consist in achieving these aims with the greatest possible efficiency in the use of available resources. Involved in the problem of rationality is the linked question of so arranging the economic structure of society as to make possible its measurement, that is, the objective determination of the most efficient way to proceed. It also means that economic policy must, to some major extent, conform to the requirements of rationality, rather than be based on arbitrary or non-economic criteria.

It must be clear that economic rationality is by no means the highest good to which human society can aspire. Nor has its

* From *Social Research*, Summer 1958, without any 'modernization'. Of course, the Soviet discussions have gone much further and deeper since that date.

importance been always appreciated in human history. For example, efficiency and growth were not regarded as of particular importance by the thinkers of mediaeval Christendom. Their aims, and their society, were concerned with something else. Even if it had been possible to make St Thomas Aquinas understand that a rate of interest is necessary to achieve the optimum distribution of economic resources, he would hardly have been converted to the view that interest is a good and necessary thing. Nor are considerations of efficiency likely to be very important in a serf-owning society. For instance, it would be easy to demonstrate that the existence of serf labour on the landlords' farms renders calculations of costs and productivity impossible (for reasons that have much in common, statistically, with those that now render so difficult similar calculations on collective farms). But few Russian *dvoryane* in 1820 were likely to draw practical conclusions from this or other samples of economic analysis. It will be recalled that Pushkin's Eugene Onegin 'read Adam Smith'. It is hardly a historical accident that, as Pushkin says, 'his father could not understand' about commodity production and exchange, and indeed Onegin's own behaviour does not suggest that his studies of Adam Smith affected him in the least. (Note the contrast with Tolstoy's Levin in *Anna Karenina*, who takes much interest in farm economics; but by then serfdom had ended.)

More recently we have had the experience of a war economy that was everywhere accompanied by the subordination of purely economic calculations to general priorities determined by the exigencies of war. No country was willing to pay the high social price of waging war by free-market methods. Everywhere there was rationing, price-fixing, direct allocation, attempts at more or less arbitrary central planning, and so on. Needless to say, this did not mean that efficiency was not desired. Of course it was desirable to achieve maximum military results for a minimum expenditure of resources. But in practice economic considerations tended to be thrust into the background, and the war economy was conducted on lines far removed from traditional notions of rationality. Even now, in time of peace, there are numerous departures from the principles of rationality: monopolies, rings, the price policies of most nationalized enterprises, import duties, and so on. Let us not imagine that efficiency and rationality are present in pure form anywhere on the globe.

I

Stalin's Russia had much in common with a war economy, and not only because it used military 'campaign' terminology. His policy when he launched his 'second revolution' in 1928 was not the result of the operation of the forces of economic rationality. On the contrary, it was an essentially political matter, one of deliberately tearing asunder the existing pattern, disregarding or crushing the existing economic arrangements and the various forces they represented. Purely 'rational' considerations argued for gradualism, for a Bukharinite or even menshevik approach. This, however, was a time of the primacy of politics, the coercion not only of economists but also of economic life.

It is true that theory, dogma, helped in the process. It is the traditional view of most Marxists, beginning with Marx himself, that market forces, the 'law of value', will wither away under socialism. The point was well made by Ostrovityanov in a recent issue of *Kommunist* (No. 13, 1957). He pointed out that Marx, in his *Critique of the Gotha Program*, held that 'in a socialist society the principle of distribution according to work done will operate without trade and money, with the aid of chits on which will be marked the number of hours worked'. Plekhanov, in the same tradition, remarked that trade under socialism is as much use as 'fried boots' or 'a fifth wheel to a cart'. Lenin's almost ludicrous underestimate of the complexities of economic administration, in *State and Revolution*, is typical of this kind of approach. There is a constant tendency to believe that the planners, in their ultimate wisdom, are able to *replace* the normal measuring rods of economic activity by a new 'socialist' form of calculation, conducted merely in terms of quantity and time. The superiority of the planner over 'blind' economic forces, over the elemental pressures of the market, was somehow deemed to be part of the transition from the realm of necessity to the realm of freedom. To be sure, Lenin and Stalin at times spoke about the importance of statistics, and they preferred efficiency to inefficiency. But the whole mental atmosphere hardly predisposed them to pay much attention to economic rationality.

More important, perhaps, than any theory were the realities and logical consequences of Stalin's policies themselves. Top priority was granted to heavy industry, and everything was sacrificed to this, as non-military needs are sacrificed in a war economy. Since no one could possibly pretend that this pace and direction of industrialization reflected any measurable profitability, 'economic' criteria were barely applicable, and so they were not applied. Indeed, it is arguable that no 'deliberate' industrialization programme—such as that being attempted today in India—can obey the traditional laws of economic rationality. The authors of such programmes generally base their thinking on some kind of long-term calculation, and indeed may be right to do so, but their essential decisions are political, or based on a political interpretation of long-term economic desiderata.

Then, too, Stalin's régime (unlike the Indian Government) paid a great deal of attention to so arranging the economy as to achieve certain ideological and political objectives, and this was often given priority over elementary efficiency considerations. The most obvious example is agriculture. Collectivization, control over peasants, repression of private-property instincts, were of great importance, as was the squeezing of produce out of the villages to feed the growing towns. As for efficiency, it was very largely ignored, a fact that was reflected in the total neglect of problems of costs of production in agriculture until well after Stalin's death.

Much more could be said about the economic policies of the Stalin epoch, but I am confining myself here merely to emphasizing the elements in these policies that helped to produce a climate in which economic rationality did not prosper. It is true that Stalin himself—in 1941 and again in 1951–52—drew attention to the 'law of value' and its significance in Soviet society. But he appeared merely to be warning his subordinates that some attention must be paid to objective reality, that not everything was wholly under control. For instance, he 'discovered' that peasants who were offered excessively low prices for cotton, in relation to bread, would probably produce less cotton. Yet he left unchanged the monstrously unfair prices at which the villages had to deliver produce to the state. This was typical: whatever may be the dictates of the 'law of value', priority was nevertheless given to the politically determined task of exploiting the peasantry to the uttermost in order to maximize resources for the expansion of heavy industry.

So much, then, for Stalin's epoch. What has changed since? A whole paper could be devoted to this question alone. Little more than a bare enumeration of the relevant factors can be attempted here.

First of all, underlying the whole problem, is the frequently repeated aim of Soviet economic policy: to overtake the West in economic might at the earliest moment. This is, of course, a *political* aim. It is connected directly with power in the international sphere, with attracting the uncommitted countries by the allegedly superior efficiency of the Soviet system. It is also relevant to the internal position of the régime, in that 'overtaking the West' is used as a slogan to mobilize behind the régime's policies the dynamic elements in Soviet society, and especially the technical and managerial personnel, whose support is necessary to make the system work. This must be stressed at the outset, because some critics have doubted whether efficiency as such is of importance to the Soviet Government. Such critics are likely to stress instead the 'realities of the power struggle'.

It is not the intention of this paper to deny in the least such realities as these. But the Soviet leaders, in their pursuit of power, are not so shortsighted as some of these critics imagine. It will be argued here that they now feel that they *need* economic rationality *because of* (not despite) their power ambitions, and in a way that did not apply to the Stalin régime to anything like the same extent. (It is not argued that they are attracted by rationality *per se*.)

A key element in the situation is the apparent effect of the death of Stalin on the system of priorities. A war economy, or a Stalin economy, can run more or less effectively *provided* the priorities are few and clear. This, in turn, means that there must be important sectors that can be neglected with impunity. In Stalin's time, for instance, agriculture and housing suffered, and in suffering provided a 'cushion', which could absorb errors of planning without disorganizing the priority sectors. But since Stalin's death it has been found necessary to launch major campaigns to improve agricultural production and to build houses. A number of concessions have been made to the consumers.

Hours of labour have been reduced. Workers are no longer forbidden to leave their jobs. The forced-labour population has greatly diminished. Various commitments have been undertaken to satellites and underdeveloped countries. There is urgent need to expand investments in the overloaded transport system. The development of new raw-material bases in remote areas requires heavier investments per unit of future production. All these things represent additional calls on resources. To make matters worse, a major 'resource'—labour—is rendered scarcer by reason of the delayed effect of the catastrophic decline in births in the USSR during the war.

This bare recital of some of the important facts leads inevitably to the following conclusion: the economy is strained by very numerous calls on scarce resources, and the dilution of the old 'Stalin' priorities greatly complicates the task of planning, indeed virtually makes it impossible to plan in the old way. One example will serve to illustrate this: at the end of 1956, major errors and strains arose, and nowhere more so than in the building industry. Materials were scarce, many construction projects could not be completed. The traditional way out was to cut housing and deliveries to the villages. But in fact we have seen a marked acceleration of the housing programme and an increase in direct and indirect investments in agriculture (for example, for cowsheds and refrigerated meat storage). This cannot but pose problems to those who have somehow to maintain the tempos of growth of heavy industry. It also leads to trouble on the political level: thus it is known that arguments about the investment programme of 1957 played an important part in the December 1956 plenum of the central committee of the Party.[1]

The essential point is this: the leaders find it very hard indeed to find the resources for all their various purposes, and so they are seeking ways of using them most efficiently. Therefore the inefficiencies that were tolerated in the past become intolerable. Terror is simply irrelevant in this situation. It may be true that deviationist literary productions can be prevented by the shooting of a couple of writers, but by no stretch of the imagination can the rational functioning of the economy be assisted by the execution of a batch of managers and planners.

[1] See, for instance, a pamphlet by Kulev, *O dalneishem sovershenstvovanii planirovania* . . . (Moscow, 1957).

II

What is it that is irrational in the Soviet system? On this there is now abundant evidence, because Soviet economists have been allowed, indeed encouraged, to discuss the existing weaknesses as part of the drive to correct them.

First of all, the absence of a logical price system makes it impossible for the central planners to choose wisely between alternatives. It became quite fashionable, in fact, to fix prices to make a given policy *seem* profitable. Thus machinery prices were low 'to encourage mechanization', the freight rates for Moscow basin coal were artificially lowered 'to encourage its use', and so on. As has been pointed out by Soviet economists,[1] this meant that the planners were often unaware of the loss caused by their own acts. Some investment decisions are now recognized to have been almost absurdly uneconomic; for example, the steelworks at Cherepovets and Rustavi, remote from sources of materials, produce at two or three times the average cost.

Then there have been serious distortions in the carrying out of plans at enterprise level. The vagaries of the price system have made it impossible to let profits serve as the guide to managerial behaviour. Plan targets are set in terms of money or quantity. Whenever the commodity is not homogeneous, this encourages the managers to distort the output assortment in order to fulfil the plan. Thus they tend to use expensive materials if the plan is in rubles, heavy materials if it is in tons, and so forth. Innovation is not properly rewarded, because innovation involves risk, and there is in effect no reward for risk-taking at the level of the enterprise. The following comment is taken from *Zvezda* (No. 5, 1957): 'The system of innovation is bad. Innovation involves risk, and, like all gambling, also capital. A risk means the possibility of loss, does it not? But if a manager is granted capital, let him try to risk and not win? . . . No, a manager must not take risks.'

The preoccupation with plan fulfilment up and down the various economic hierarchies causes many departures from elementary commonsense, not least in the procedures of deciding what the plan should be. Repeatedly the managers try to conceal

[1] For instance, Malyshev in *Voprosy Ekonomiki* (No. 3, 1957).

their production possibilities, to facilitate overfulfilment and the consequent bonuses. As Nikolaeva wrote in *Oktyabr* (No. 7, 1957), a wise manager aims at achieving 105 per cent of plan, not 125 per cent, for in the latter case he will be set an impossible target for the year following.

These problems, too, can be the subject of a long paper to themselves.[1] Their existence is universally admitted in the USSR itself. The discussion as to what to do about it forms part of the argument on the role of the 'law of value', prices, and the market in the USSR. Other difficulties are also involved, and raise not dissimilar problems bearing on the price structure.

Thus the very inadequate organization of retail trade in general, and of the disposal of peasant surpluses in particular, is directly connected with insufficient incentives to efficiency in the trade network. Nor is there the necessary link between the desires of consumers and the pattern of production. This is due to the peculiar effect of turnover tax. For most commodities this tax is a so-called 'difference', that is, it consists of the difference between the supply-and-demand retail price and the cost of production (with allowance for a profit margin and trade margin). Thus if a given type of cloth is in heavy demand, it is possible that the retail price will be high in relation to costs, but there would be no greater profit in making it, since turnover tax would absorb the difference in price.

Curiously, this state of affairs was well described before the war, by Oskar Lange, as follows: 'One may well imagine a system in which production and the allocation of resources are guided by a preference scale fixed by the central planning board, while the price system is used to distribute the consumers' goods produced. In such a system, there is freedom of choice in consumption, but consumers have no influence whatever on the decisions of the managers of production and on the productive resources. There would be two sets of prices of consumers' goods. One will be the market price at which the goods are sold to consumers; the other, the accounting prices derived from the preference scale fixed by the central planning board. The latter set of prices will be those on the basis of which the managers of production would make their decisions. However, it does not seem very probable that such a system would be tolerated by the citizens of a socialist

[1] See 'The Problem of Success Indicators in Soviet Industry', in this volume.

community.'[1] All except the last sentence applies in every particular to the USSR.

Why should this bother the authorities? For one good reason. Numerous concessions in recent years suggest that they are seeking to satisfy to some extent the urgent demands of the citizens. Their motives are immaterial. What matters is this: granted that this is so, it is obviously in their interest to do so with the minimum diversion of resources to consumption. Or, to put the same thing in another way, it pays them to maximize the satisfaction that can be provided by whatever is available to the consumer. It is therefore conspicuously wasteful to use cloth and timber to make dresses and furniture in unpopular styles. This, too, leads to a reconsideration of the role of prices, profits, 'value', in the economy.

The recent reorganization of industrial planning and administration does not help to overcome the inadequacies of the present price system. On the contrary, these inadequacies become more glaring. While it is true that the increasing size and complexity of Soviet industry demand greater devolution of decision-making powers to the men on the spot, the lack of economic criteria for decision deprives these men of a guide to action. The Minister in Moscow may have had his views distorted by narrow departmentalism, but at least he was able to look at things on a national scale. The chairman of the *sovnarkhoz* at Omsk cannot see beyond the confines of the Omsk province. Whenever he has choices to make he cannot, with the best will in the world, take the national interest properly into account. The necessary link is—once again—a price system that provides a calculus of rationality, an objective basis of decision. Therefore, as Gatovski and other Soviet economists have pointed out (*Kommunist*, No. 9, 1957), the reorganization makes it all the more important to devise criteria for action in the new regions. Exactly the same kind of problem has arisen in agriculture. Here too there have been decisions to permit the farms a wider range of choice. They are urged to act so as to 'maximize output per hectare'. Unfortunately, with farm prices in their present confused state, it is quite impossible to compare different assortments of products, or to decide (for example) whether it is worth buying fodder rather than growing it on the farm. This is obviously quite unsatisfactory.

[1] Oskar Lange, *On the Economic Theory of Socialism* (Minneapolis, 1938), p. 96.

III

Thus on all counts the USSR needs a big dose of economic rationality. This is far from being mere theory-spinning by an incurable bourgeois; it is well understood by numerous Soviet experts. It is enough to read the specialized press, and also economic articles in such party organs as *Kommunist*, to be convinced that they know it themselves.

But while there has been much talk, there has been relatively little action. This also is hardly surprising. For what kind of action does the situation demand? Surely the cure involves: first, a price system responsive to the supply-and-demand situation; second, the use of this price system as a guide to action; third, much greater freedom to managers of enterprises to respond to price-and-profit stimuli; fourth, and above all, a great restriction of the everyday role of arbitrary political decision in economic life. Economic calculation, 'the law of value', material interest, should to a much greater extent be the mainsprings of action. The cost of not acting on these lines is continued inefficiency. But the political and ideological obstacles to such actions are formidable, and must now be examined.

Let us turn first to ideology, though it may not in itself be of key importance. In the first place, Marxist economic theory, especially as traditionally interpreted in Russia, remains an obstacle to progress. Even original and critical thinkers, such as Strumilin, are sidetracked into recommending a criterion for price-fixing totally unconnected with changing patterns of demand; in Strumilin's model (*Planovoe Khozaistvo*, No. 2, 1957) value and price bear a constant relationship to labour cost, to which he adds a species of tax burden corresponding to the proportionate cost of accumulation and all unproductive services (thus investment costs, military expenditure, and the like would be divided among all products in proportion to the wages paid out in producing them).

All this is derived from Marx's view of value as equal to 'socially necessary labour', a view that leaves utility out of account (except in so far as a totally useless article has no value). Yet the logic of the situation clearly requires a price system that is responsive to relative scarcities and changing use-values, for only such a system would 'transmit' the shifting pattern of demand to the producing enterprises. Thus the USSR needs a new theory of value, or some drastic reinterpretation of the Marxist canon. This question is close to the theological core of Marxist-Leninist 'political economy', and therefore needs rather careful handling.

A politico-ideological argument now being raised against the more radical critics concerns the so-called 'regulatory' role of the law of value. This is linked with the controversies on this same subject in Yugoslavia and Poland. In these countries economists have been advocating a free market, and in the case of Yugoslavia some action has followed the words. Autonomy of enterprises in the face of a market is connected in these countries with the idea of workers' control. All this is, in orthodox Soviet eyes, dangerous 'revisionism', and has been criticized as such in authoritative Soviet journals. Thus both Gatovski and Ostrovityanov (*Kommunist*, Nos. 9 and 13, 1957) have warned Soviet economists against taking a necessary reform too near to the heretical ideas of such revisionists as the Polish Professor Brus. It is less clear just what kind of half-way house can be discovered between arbitrary planning and a genuine market system. But more of that anon.

A more important obstacle than any ideological formulation is the vested interest of the party machine. It is, most of all, the *party* which, by its decisions at all levels, replaces the operation of economic forces. At the top levels it launches campaigns that in varying degrees reflect its arbitrary judgment. While of course these party decisions are not taken in the void, they are none the less taken by the political arm, and the choices between alternatives are all too often made for political reasons. For example, the meat and milk 'campaigns' now being waged under Khrushchev's leadership do not cease to be politically motivated if we appreciate that more meat and milk are needed.

Indeed, these campaigns are the most recent example of the primacy of political decision over economic rationality, and Khrushchev himself has admitted that he disregarded his own economists' advice. The leaders, and especially Khrushchev, like to be able to direct economic life, and do not take kindly to limitations on the power of arbitrary decision on any issue. Below the top level the party officials' interest in preserving their power over economic life is even more evident. A *raikom* secretary, for instance, spends most of his time telling the farms what they should do. If the farms were really to take their own decisions by reference to objective criteria, then most of the powers of the *raikom* secretary, and the bulk of his staff, would be lost. The secretary is as unlikely to countenance this as any other bureaucrat in any other country in a similar situation.

The party's vested interest, therefore, would seem to be inconsistent with economic rationality. In *this* context, the so-called 'anti-party group' can have differed little with Khrushchev. While disagreeing with the actual policies advocated by him, it seems most improbable that Malenkov, Molotov or Kaganovich held the view that the party's right and duty to take economic decisions should be limited by 'the law of value' or principles of rationality.

It might appear from the above that rationality is bound to be defeated by the combined forces of party interest and party doctrine. Yet the situation is by no means so clear. Let us now turn to those forces that tend toward reform.

One of these has already been analysed. It is that the rational use of resources is essential if the aims of the party's own policies are to be effectively realized. Thus the party has, in this connection, a split personality. It cannot wholeheartedly man the defence lines against those who are usually party members, act in the name of the party's aims, and do so in the profound conviction that they act in the party's best interest. Increasingly, the party's appeal to the educated public, to the 'intelligentsia', stresses the alleged superiority of the Soviet way of utilizing resources, the superior rate of growth of material production, and so on. There is little or no reality in the slogans about the transition to communism. Therefore the party's ideological-political position cannot be allowed to contradict too obviously the commonsense of political economy.

Then we must consider the interests of the managers. The more extensive the role of economic forces (as against those of party and state officials), the greater is the freedom of the manager. Conversely, no major devolution of power to managers is consistent with efficiency unless prices are such as to provide objective criteria for managerial decision. The point is clear enough, and there is ample evidence that the managers understand it. They do not like the arbitrary interference of officialdom. They consider that they know their own business best, and in this they are generally right. Therefore their self-interest is allied to a strong feeling that any arbitrary interference is positively harmful to efficiency. They naturally see advantages in a much wider freedom to negotiate contracts with other managers. In this they are often joined by technicians, such as the engineer who wrote an article in *Znamya* (No. 2, 1957), pointing out the harm done to technical progress by the present system of financial controls over managerial initiative and urging a more direct connection between use-value, price and profit. It is not suggested that there is a 'managers' party' in the USSR, or that managers are a united pressure group. But it is clear enough on which side, in the present context, their interests lie.

Another group, less important politically, is already tending to provide a theoretical basis for reform: this group consists of the more go-ahead economists. This, too, is natural. As soon as discussion centres on the problem of objective criteria for economic decisions, economists are bound to have a predisposition toward advocating a rational price system and all that goes with it. The logic of their science *and* their professional interest point that way. Those who have not lost the faculty of independent thinking do in fact argue on these lines; anyone who reads, for instance, Malyshev's article in *Voprosy Ekonomiki* (No. 3, 1957) can satisfy himself that this is no mere theoretical hypothesis.

At this point someone is likely to object: this is all very well, but the party leaders have always pursued maximum power, and are most unlikely to be deflected from that course by talk of economic rationality. It must again be emphasized that this objection is both real and important, and no 'historicist' forecast is here intended about the triumph of rationality over the party. Such a triumph is indeed impossible without a political revolution.

The point is rather this: the party must seek somehow to *reconcile* its power functions with efficiency, and must therefore initiate discussions and reforms *in order* to make its power position more consistent with the practical aims pursued by its economic policies. It is facing a dilemma. It cannot simply oppose the tendencies toward reform. It is typical of the complexities of the situation that the party itself initiated the discussions among economists in which the formulations of men like Malyshev emerged. The most orthodox of the party's own economists, while stopping short of 'revisionism', urge important changes in the present system, in the direction set out above. If one wishes to express the point in 'militant' language, the fifth columnists of rationality have already penetrated into the minds of many of the general staff of the party, weakening their will to fight.

It is also worth considering whether one should, in the present context, speak of a 'party' united in its interest and attitude. This problem is related to the possible role of the party and its leadership in a more rationally organized Soviet economy, and leads one straight to the argument advanced by Djilas. His view, it will be recalled, is that the party has an objective function in the period of industrializing a backward economy, but that in due course it becomes a mere parasite, a class deriving its prosperity from its control over the instruments of production. There is certainly some truth in the Djilas case, and indeed the argument of the present paper is in some respects similar to his. But Djilas, and many Western critics, seem to underestimate the necessary economic role of a party in Soviet society. The word 'necessary', it must be emphasized, has no moral connotation at all, and does *not* mean 'desirable'. Let me spell out this thought.

Suppose we assume that the most radical of the reformers has his way. Suppose there is a fluctuating price system based on supply and demand, with freedom of contract between enterprises, with profitability as the essential criterion of managerial decision. The central Government will still retain quite vital economic functions. It will have to decide about investments, because, with all industries nationalized, the necessary transfer of resources to new and developing economic sectors will require deliberate decision at the centre; so will financial policy and distribution of resources between investment and consumption. Then there are all the numerous economic questions that keep the Government busy enough in so un-Soviet a country as Great Britain. Many of these decisions have an important political aspect, and cannot be taken by mere civil servants. Thus the political leaders, which in Soviet conditions means the party or some alternative to the party, will have essential functions to perform in the economic field.

During a recent 'Third Programme' talk in Britain, Professor

Ely Devons, in a stimulating phrase, contrasted the apparent macro-economic chaos and micro-economic order of capitalism with the macro-economic order and micro-economic chaos of the Soviet system. The phrase, like all generalizations, does not entirely fit. Thus the errors and confusion at enterprise level in the USSR are often accompanied by wrong decisions at the centre, because the measuring rod (prices) used by the centre is itself affected by the arbitrariness that prevails below. Nonetheless, the idea is a very interesting one. It could be adapted to our present purpose as follows: the reformers wish to create order at the micro-economic level and to provide objective macro-economic criteria. But, whatever these criteria are, the macro-economic decisions in a state that has nationalized the means of production must be very largely taken at the centre, and depend a good deal on the judgment of political men.

And if this is so, the reforms do not threaten the functions of the party at the centre nearly so much as they affect the powers of local party organizations. It is the *oblast* party secretary and those beneath him whose *raison d'être* very largely consists in interfering with economic processes. It is true that the party at the centre is also guilty of 'objectively unnecessary' interference, but at least at the centre it could refrain from such interference and still retain essential economic functions. Let us take some examples: to develop agriculture in the Asian steppelands, an industrial centre in North Kazakhstan, or the output of synthetic materials there *must* be a decision at the centre, just as in Great Britain the Government decides to build (or not to build) a system of super-highways or to raise money to expand nuclear generation of power. But what would a local party secretary do if farms and workshops in his area functioned free of his control (as they should)?

Therefore we must expect the strongest resistance to change to come from the party's local functionaries, and of course from those at the centre whose mentality reflects their interests and who love to interfere personally in detailed economic problems. Khrushchev would seem to be just such a man. Yet the recent agricultural reforms he has initiated show that he is aware of the dilemma. Efficiency considerations demanded the elimination of the Machine Tractor Stations (MTS), although these were centres not only of state but also of party control over the collective farms. Indeed, the number of local party officials has been sharply reduced as part of this reform. A major change in the price system is in active preparation at the time of writing, affecting not only farm produce but also a wide range of capital goods used in agriculture. This, in turn, must surely bring nearer the day when a more logical price system is introduced for capital goods in general. Needless to say, the principle of party control over agriculture is far from being abandoned; the reform must be seen as part of the necessary effort to *reconcile* the requirements of efficiency with control in essentials. In any event, the problem is bigger than Khrushchev, and will outlast him.

We can expect the search for new forms of economic planning to continue. There is likely to be a gradual tendency toward a less irrational price structure, more freedom of contract between enterprises, more direct links between user and producer throughout the economy. All this will call for considerable changes, in planning practice, in contract law, in economic theory, in the powers of enterprise managers. Such problems are being talked and written about, and probably more is going on under the surface than is visible to Western observers.

It may well be that the recent industrial reforms, the creation of *sovnarkhozy*, will unintentionally serve to speed up the process, because of the confusion that must result from arbitrary interference by *sovnarkhozy* with contractual ties between enterprises situated in different economic regions. We may anticipate a period of trial and error. There is as yet no properly worked out 'model' of a reformed Soviet economy. Marx and Lenin are barely relevant in this situation, and it must be admitted that the various 'socialist' models constructed in the West—by both sympathizers and critics—are also of little help. The search must go on. The pressures toward reform are strong, pressures of interest and necessity. Resistance to major changes is strong too, on grounds of self-interest and of ideology. In all these circumstances it would be foolish to forecast anything, except perhaps that conflicts over these questions will be a feature of Soviet history in the years to come.

II. INDUSTRIAL GROWTH AND PLANNING

4. *Prospects of Soviet economic growth**

This is not an easy paper to write or to deliver. The only possible reason for asking me to deliver it is that I happen to be in America this year and you may want to see a new face. Among the participants at this conference are many who are eminently qualified to give a paper on this very subject. Worse still, some of them have in fact done so, and many of the participants, myself included, have had the benefit of reading their work.

The title of the paper might suggest that its author has special qualifications as a crystal gazer. Nothing is further from the truth. Fortunately he shares this defect with all his colleagues. Even if we ignore the possible direct impact of nuclear weapons on the productive capacity of industrial nations or the effect on output of the continuation or cessation of the arms race, there remain a large number of unforeseeable developments which could occur in the next decade in science and technology and also in economic and political organization, within the Soviet bloc and elsewhere, which defy prophecy. However, the Soviets have declared it to be their aim to overtake America in economic might within ten years or so and have indeed published a number of detailed targets for industry and agriculture through 1970 and even 1980. To some extent, therefore, it behoves us, who claim to possess some information on the Soviet economy, to become part-time reluctant crystal gazers. The interested non-specialist is entitled to some kind of answer to such questions as: Are the declared aims of the Soviet leaders in the economic field within the realms of possibility? With what obstacles will they

* From the *American Economic Review*, May 1963.

have to contend? By what criteria can one measure their progress toward their declared goals? How useful or misleading can such criteria be? Is it the case that the present organization of Soviet economic planning favours, or on the contrary restrains, the rapid growth envisaged by the plans? The observations that follow might be of interest, if only as an attempt to analyse some of the unknown factors relevant in considering answers to the above questions.

A few basic statistics related to Soviet performance and plans are given in the table below. These are deliberately confined to the present decade. Figures for so remote a year as 1980 seem to me hardly worth detailed discussion.

GROWTH OF USSR ECONOMY
SOME OFFICIAL SOVIET DATA
(Growth per annum, per cent)

	1954–61	*1957–61*	*1959–65 (Plan)*	*1961–70 (Plan)*
National income*	9·7	8·3	7·2	9·2
Gross agricultural production	6·0	3·1	8·0	9·6
Gross industrial production	10·1	10·2	8·6†	9·6
Steel	8·0	7·8	8·3‡	8·2
Oil	15·4	14·7	11·2‡	10·1
Electricity	11·7	11·3	12·3‡	12·8
Cement	15·6	14·9	12·9	10·2
Cotton fabrics	3·3	3·8	4·4	—
Wool fabrics	6·9	5·8	7·8	—
All fabrics	—	—	—	7·5

* Soviet definition ('material production').
† Implicitly revised upwards, though no new figure available.
‡ Upward revision of original targets for 1965 (steel from 88·5 to 96 m. tons, oil from 235 to upwards of 240 m. tons, electricity from 510 to upwards of 520 billion kilowatt-hours; some of these and other figures are midpoints of ranges).

All figures on past and present performance in the above table represent official claims. There is a wide consensus in favour of the proposition that they are a reliable guide to growth rates of industrial commodities in physical terms, but that agricultural statistics have been or may have been inflated on an increasing scale in the last few years. For familiar reasons, aggregate percentage indices of national income and industrial production should be regarded with varying degrees of suspicion, although it is accepted by most critics that the amount of exaggeration has somewhat declined compared with the period before

1950. This is not the place for a detailed discussion of statistical reliability; nonetheless, it is relevant to any real or implied extrapolations which might be involved in thinking about the future. For example, in the above table it appears that the growth plan through 1970 for Soviet industry implies a slight decline in tempo compared with that achieved in the last five years. However, if, as is widely believed, output indices for past years are somewhat exaggerated and if indices reflecting output plans for the future do not suffer from this defect, what looks like a slowdown may in fact represent acceleration. This seems a reasonable conclusion, on the admittedly imperfect evidence available, because the principal causes of exaggeration—essentially the effects on methods of aggregation, statistical reporting and certain production choices of the desire to show success in terms of high growth rates—ought not to be operating when planners make forward projections. But, of course, we will never be in a position to prove our point with official statistics when the future becomes the past.

It is tempting to substitute for the official figures a recomputation of the relevant magnitudes by Western scholars. However, it is not to a discussion of the intricacies of interpreting statistics of the past that this paper is to be devoted. I will confine myself to the following generalizations, which most specialists would probably accept. Plans for the rest of this decade call for increases in industrial output at a rate slightly exceeding that genuincly achieved in the recent past; agricultural production is to advance at a spectacular rate never hitherto achieved in Soviet (or, one suspects, anyone else's) history; at the same time, the trade and miscellaneous services sectors are to grow relatively more rapidly than ever before. It is common ground between Soviet planners and Western scholars that this extremely ambitious programme cannot be achieved without much greater efficiency in the use of resources.

It is to this question of efficiency, and the related questions of organization and growth measurement, that much of the present paper will be devoted. If most of the space will be given over to industry rather than, for example, agriculture, the reason lies in the fact that some particularly interesting problems arise in assessing the ability of the USSR to reach its industrial goals, whereas there is an understandable and well-founded unanimity among all Western commentators concerning the unrealistic nature of the agricultural plans for 1965 and 1970.

To sustain an annual growth rate of 9.6 per cent to the end of the present decade, Soviet industry will require a vast increase in the flow of materials and fuels. A very rapid rise in labour productivity is envisaged by the plans, for otherwise labour will be a bottleneck, the more so as the intake of young workers is now adversely affected by the low birth and survival rates of the war and early postwar years. This will require substantial investments. These facts are, of course, well known to Soviet planners, who seem justified in their confidence that the necessary minerals and fuels can be provided, while synthetics could provide alternatives to materials of agricultural origin. It is true that new areas may have to be developed, with consequent expenditures on social overhead capital. However, this may well increase the capital-output ratio only in the short term, as some of these new sources of minerals, notably in the East, should prove economical to work. One recalls that the Kuzbas, though costly to bring into operation, has for many years been providing some of the cheapest coal and steel in the Soviet Union.

However, organizational inadequacies and irrational investment choices would quickly lead to shortages. They would express themselves by the emergence of bottlenecks, in shortages of labour, of capital, of this or that material.

Soviet economists and planners are well aware of this, also. Never has there been such widespread and frank discussion of the defects of the planning system. To an even greater extent, Soviet economists express the view that a new stage has been reached, that the old methods of planning cannot any more cope with the problems of an increasingly mature and sophisticated industrial system. The pages of *Pravda* and of the specialized press are filled with debates on radical reforms. It is clear that these are needed if the economy is to cope with the demands made upon it and that drastic changes cannot be long delayed. In the words of Academician Berg, 'We cannot permit ourselves the luxury of wasting time, if we soberly consider the tasks that face us and also the difficulties which we must overcome as quickly as possible.'[1] The drastic changes in party and state organization announced in the November 1962 plenum—and

[1] *Pravda*, October 24, 1962.

indeed the fact that so fundamental a discussion of the very bases of Soviet planning has been openly raging in the party's own press—clearly show that the political leadership is deeply concerned with remedying existing defects. It also follows that these matters are in the highest degree relevant to our assessment of the growth prospects of the USSR.

A number of economists in the East and West have at various times in the past few years echoed similar sentiments to those cited above. Oscar Lange, in his lectures in Belgrade in 1957, contrasted the 'highly politicalized' system of the crash industrialization period, which he likened to a war economy, with the needs of a more developed and settled economic and political order, in which efficiency considerations become vitally important. With increasingly diversified needs, with more complex and less easily defined priorities, new methods are being sought, a fashioning of new planning instruments, new theories. There is a search for efficiency in the use of resources scarce in relation to needs, including the need to increase living standards.

All this is familiar enough in the form of generalizations. It is necessary to examine the nature of the actual defects from which their economy suffers and relate them, and possible means of correcting them, to problems of growth.

The present difficulties of Soviet planning relate both to the position of the planners and to the behaviour pattern of enterprises.

There is ample evidence that the planners are overwhelmed by the complexity and burdens of planning both output and inputs of many thousands of enterprises. As the size of the economy increases, so the number of planned interconnections increases much more rapidly. The key problem in operational planning is what in Russian is called *uvyazka*, or ensuring consistency of different portions of the plan. Yet the sheer volume of work requires it to be divided between different institutions, or different offices within the same institution. The supply plans often fail, at micro level, to match with another or with the production plan, creating headaches and holdups at enterprise level for which the planners are responsible. Plans for costs, labour productivity, profits, calculated in yet other offices, may not match output or supply plans, or one another. Investment plans, a vital aspect of the long-term growth plan, are not properly geared in to the current production and material allocation plans, so that machinery is not ready for installation, building materials fail to arrive, and there is an alarming rise in unfinished construction. All this is complicated by the fact that the leadership is pursuing several objectives at once; so that the priorities have become blurred or at least difficult to enforce. Thus planners find it remarkably difficult to give priority treatment to the list of 'especially important investment projects' which they themselves have drawn up. For example, in the Russian republic in the current year the entire investment plan has been 89 per cent fulfilled, but the percentage for the 'especially important' projects was 83.[1] There are bitter complaints from below concerning 'the endless musical chairs' of repeated changes in the plan through the year to which it is supposed to apply, a consequence of the desperate attempts by planners to cope with an impossible task. Thus the investment plan for the Tatar ASSR was amended 'almost 500 times' during 1961.[2]

While centralized planning overburdens the organs charged with carrying it out, decentralization—the obvious remedy—proves completely unworkable so long as planners' instructions are the principal criterion for local decisions. The modest attempt to devolve authority to territorial economic organs, in 1957, was inevitably followed by renewed centralization. Within the system as it is, only the centre is in a position to know the needs of industry and of society at large, since these are not transmitted by any economic mechanism to any territorial authority. The latter is therefore unable to foresee the effects of its decisions on the economy of other areas, and, in the circumstances, decentralized decision making must lead to intolerable irrationalities. The consequent recentralization went so far that an official of the Estonian (republican) regional economic council complained in 1962 that the seventeen commodities planned by Estonian officials represented 0.2 per cent of the industrial output of that republic, and that 'all the rest is decided by the USSR Gosplan', which now plans production and distribution of close on 19,000 commodity designations.[3] Thus decentralization is both indis-

[1] *Ekonomicheskaya gazeta,* November 17, 1962, p. 5 (the figures relate to the first ten months of 1962).

[2] *Ibid.*, p. 6.

[3] *Ibid.*, November 10, 1962, p. 8.

pensable and impossible. Recentralization led to errors, confusion, overwork.[1] As a result of the reforms at present being implemented, the work may be redistributed, but without curing the diseases necessarily associated with centralization.

Planners are also handicapped by inadequate criteria for decision making. This applies most clearly to the much discussed problem of choice between investment variants. It applies also to the placing by the planners of production orders with different enterprises; as a Soviet critic pointed out, the officials in charge of this task do not even conceive it as part of their duty to know the relative costs in different enterprises; they are busy enough simply distributing the various production tasks to be performed.[2] These are direct consequences of quantitative administrative planning.

Obviously, if planners are to perform their tasks effectively, all this must be changed radically. Two approaches to reform may be observed. They have in common the belief that the central planners, expressing the will of the Communist party leadership, must decide the basic pattern of investment and production, as well as the basic 'proportions' of the economy (i.e. allocation of resources between consumption and investment, industry and agriculture, and so on). However, one group of would-be reformers envisages a high degree of centralization, hoping that new planning techniques, and especially the electronic computer, will make it work effectively. The other lays much greater stress on enterprise initiative, on freely negotiated inter-enterprise contracts and supply arrangements, which would free the central planners of much of the detailed operational work which at present threatens to overwhelm them. Neither species of reform would be practicable without a major overhaul of the price system. Thus Berg, in his already cited article, points out that 'the task of optimal and continuous planning cannot be carried out satisfactorily without a reform of price fixing. Can one speak of any optimum if the criterion of its determination is unclear at existing prices?' He advocated the creation of 'a mathematical economic model of the economy' in which with the aid of input-output balances, it will be possible to 'correct the sins of pricing'.

[1] See A. Nove, 'The industrial planning system—reforms in prospect,' *Soviet Studies*, July, 1962 (reprinted below).

[2] I. Borovitski, *Pravda*, October 5, 1962.

Nor do the advocates of decentralization deny the need to use mathematical techniques in central planning. One of the best-known of the 'mathematical' reformers, Novozhilov, has emphasized that the proper use of computers and the efficiency prices which would emerge would make possible effective decentralization by providing proper price criteria at enterprise level. Nonetheless, despite some similarities and overlaps of ideas, one can discern two different kinds of outlook about the matters with which central planners, as distinct from productive units, ought to be concerned. One could perhaps add a third view, apparently held by Khrushchev, to the effect that proper party leadership can solve all problems. In itself such a view is naïve and irrelevant: 'party leadership' cannot provide rational choices between investment alternatives, or match supply plans with production programmes. In sanctioning or tolerating open debate of basic planning problems, and indeed in his own not unfriendly comments on some of the radical reform proposals, Khrushchev has shown himself aware of this. Yet his own predisposition towards party-enforced priorities and administrative solutions leads him to lean towards the centralizers.

We have so far been concentrating on planners' problems. However, as recently published debates in the Soviet press have underlined, much that goes wrong does so in the microworld of enterprises. It is only in the imagination of model builders, not in reality, that Soviet enterprises are passive and obedient executants of plans passed down from above. In varying degrees, enterprise management is able to adapt its behaviour, and the product mix, to the often ambiguous process of measuring the fulfilment of plans. Since, for reasons already given, the various plans it receives are frequently inconsistent with one another, it can and indeed must manoeuvre to fulfil some plans at the expense of others—and its principal guideline, despite efforts to change this deeply ingrained habit, remains the fulfilment of output goals in tons or in rubles. Since rewards are related to the fulfilment of plans, managements are encouraged to conceal production possibilities, to hoard, to refrain from doing too well in case the plan for the next period is made too 'tight'. New production methods, new designs, impose disproportionate risks upon management, with few compensatory rewards. 'Plans are fulfilled at any price, to the detriment of quality, reliability, durability.'[1] The orders placed by the trading network, which do on occasion reflect consumer demand, are too frequently ignored by industrial enterprises, partly because the required product mix does not fit plan fulfilment indicators, partly because of the inflexibility of plans for material supplies, costs, prices. This applies in at least equal measure to the problem of adapting production to the requirements of other industrial enterprises. It is worth emphasizing at this point that, whatever may be the value of computers to central planners, they are very largely irrelevant to the solution of 'microproblems' of this type.

As is well known, reform proposals designed to provide a rational basis for choice at microlevel have been put forward by the professor from Kharkov, Liberman, in the pages of *Pravda* and elsewhere. By basing incentives on profits, following a drastic change in the price system, 'the proposals would free central planning from detailed supervision over enterprises, from wasteful attempts to control production not by economic but by administrative methods', as Liberman put it.[2] Nemchinov, another vigorous advocate of similar reforms, would like to see planners planning only final output, leaving intermediate stages essentially to interenterprise arrangements; he would 'convert the material allocation system into state trade, cease distributing commodities through an endlessly complex system of material allocations'.[3] These proposals, which would have the effect of relieving the planners of much detailed work, have run into heavy opposition, but experiments are proceeding. It is true that they seem to be very different in spirit to Khrushchev's re-emphasis on party control. Yet Khrushchev's latest moves may seriously disorganize the planning organs and may have the possibly unintended effect of speeding up the adoption of such proposals as Liberman's. In any event, the growth prospects of the USSR must surely depend in some considerable degree on the extent and the success of the various reforms now being implemented or discussed.

It may be objected that all this analysis is exaggerated, that the very impressive growth of the Soviet economy proves that all is basically still well—though this would be a criticism which

[1] Borovitski, *Pravda*, October 5, 1962.

[2] *Pravda*, September 9, 1962.

[3] *Pravda*, September 21, 1962.

would apply as much to the Soviet planners as to the author of this paper.

The answer to such an objection falls into two parts: The first concerns the relative impact of the defects of the system on different sectors of the economy. The second relates to the statistical reflection of the defects themselves.

Some activities lend themselves more easily than others to centralized planning. For some, indeed, it is decidedly advantageous. If output is relatively homogeneous, if inputs are few in number and relatively easy to determine in quantity and quality, if the flow of information to the central authorities gives them reasonably sure data on which to base decisions, then the planning system works reasonably well. These considerations apply, for instance, to pig iron, steel, aluminium, cement, electricity, coal, oil and gas. Electricity is the perfect example of a homogeneous commodity, producing only kilowatt-hours of current. In many Western countries its output is nationalized. Whatever may be the inefficiencies of Soviet electricity generation, they cannot be ascribed to the nature of the planning system. In fact, it is noticeable that the bulk of the commodities listed above are controlled by very large enterprises or by monopolies or are nationalized in Western countries. This suggests advantages of scale, of the possibility of planning output, research and investment. So far as investment is concerned, future demand in the USSR is largely a function of the planners' own decisions, and consequently investment planning is facilitated: the quantities required in 1965 are more or less known already in 1962. This has not prevented expensive errors in choice between investment variants, but this raises rather different questions. It is also the case that some of the microproblems of planning arise in much less acute form in the industries listed above than elsewhere in the Soviet economy. Output is easier to measure; distortions of the product mix are less likely or less harmful; the rewards for success (in increasing output or productivity or reducing costs) are easier to determine. It is surely not a coincidence that few of the vast numbers of complaints printed in the USSR about the operation of the planning system relate to production in and supplies to these particular industries. Steel works are efficiently run; they receive the planned amounts of coking coal and iron ore; they overfulfil output plans. This is partly due to the high priority they enjoy, but a part of the explanation is to be found in the relatively simple process of planning the operations of and supplies to this type of industry. In typically colourful fashion, Khrushchev put it this way to the November 1962 plenum: 'Steel production is like a much-used track with deep ruts; even a blind horse will not lost its way.' By contrast, the high priority chemicals and some of the machinery industries have run into many troubles. It is true that military weapons and rockets seem to be efficiently produced, but this is a branch of activity where, in all countries, decisions on output and exact technical specifications are centralized, and no one doubts the ability of the Soviet system to ensure the production of any clearly defined piece of hardware to which high priority is given.

It is worth noting that the top priorities of the Stalin era, basic heavy industries, related to the most easily plannable part of the Soviet economy, are the most amenable to centralized decision making. It is perhaps not a coincidence either that these basic sectors are still showing the most impressive increases in production. But now other sectors, in which output—and therefore inputs—is very varied, have acquired much greater importance: machinery and metal manufactures, chemicals, consumers' goods of many kinds, and so on. It is essential not only to simplify the tasks of the planners but also to enable the requirements of the users to affect the behaviour of producers and distributors, without giving the central planners the impossible job of incorporating these detailed requirements into their instructions.

A few words are now needed concerning a difficult but vital question: the statistical reflection of irrational production or investment decisions. It is far too easily assumed that these slow down measurable growth. But do they necessarily do so?

Of course, some do. Unfinished investment projects, which lock up resources and delay the flow of output, or production holdups due to non-arrival of materials, reduce growth rates. However, a whole range of 'irrationalities' have no such effects and may even speed up growth as this is statistically measured. A few examples will illustrate the argument.

According to a leading Moscow dental surgeon, Soviet dental fillings remain in Soviet teeth only a very few months; this seems due to poor-quality materials used in making fillings ('cement').[1]

[1] *Ekonomicheskaya gazeta*, September 29, 1962, p. 39.

statistics reflect unnecessary production of fillings and also very frequent visits to dentists. The effect of a switch to the production of a more durable, but apparently not much dearer, amalgam for filling teeth would cause a decline in net output and, to the marked satisfaction of all concerned, the USSR would fall 'further behind America' in this sector of economic life. Similarly, Soviet tyres, television tubes and a long list of other goods wear out more quickly than might be expected in the current state of knowledge and technique. Of course, it is true that American output of certain consumer durables 'benefits' from planned obsolescence and deliberate avoidance of durability. However, in the Soviet case, which extends over a much wider field, the cause of the trouble lies precisely in an overconcentration on fulfilling output targets; i.e. on the adaptation of the product mix to the statistical measurement of growth. The same point arises when one considers quality of consumers' goods, the range of choice, and the differences between consumer demand and what is actually produced. In terms of welfare or usefulness, it is obvious that in such circumstances statistics of gross or net output can be misleading, the more so if, to repeat, there is an inbuilt tendency to produce for output statistics rather than for need. It therefore also follows that remedial measures may slow down statistical growth rates, even while welfare can benefit. For example, to increase the range of shirts or trousers available for sale is inconvenient from the standpoint of maximizing production in terms of either thousands of garments or rubles. It must not be forgotten that Soviet prices do not, as a rule, reflect degrees of scarcity, quality or need, and tend to be changed by a very clumsy procedure at infrequent intervals—all of which tends to accentuate the extent to which aggregate statistics can mislead.

Irrational decisions on investments, location and production may also be consistent with high growth rates. Of course, in these and in other respects there is an opportunity cost: resources cannot be devoted to other potential uses if they are wastefully deployed on irrational projects. Yet it does not necessarily follow that they could or would be used to greater statistical advantage. Let us take two different examples. Suppose a steelworks is located far from sources of materials, so that large additional transport costs are incurred, as has in fact happened in the case of Cherepovets. Or that agriculture is supplied with equipment so inefficient that its use actually raises the cost of production. The net output of the steelworks and the farms is adversely affected. But in both the examples, costs consist of unnecessary goods and services (freight transport, wagons, locomotives, rails, tractors, steel for all the above, fuel, etc.). These are part of the national product on any definition. True, the output of end products of consumers' goods is less than it otherwise would have been. The effect of the inefficiencies mentioned above is to increase unnecessarily the volume of intermediate products, of 'producers' goods'. In fact, this may be one of the explanations for the striking contrast between growth of aggregate output in the USSR and the much more modest growth in living standards.

Of course, it does not follow from all this that the vast bulk of Soviet output is either useless or defective. Wasteful or uneconomic practices are, in any event, common enough in Western economies. The point is that the Soviet economy was organized for rapid growth, particularly of heavy industry, and that the incentive system was deliberately related to measurable growth as a prime objective. But, since there is an unavoidable element of artificiality in measuring growth of varied assortments of products, this led to a sizable disparity between the growth of useful output and the growth of output as measured by statistics.[1] However, the Soviet political leadership and planners are increasingly aware that growth as such is a misleading criterion and that many highly desirable objectives of domestic and foreign policy require the elimination of waste, even if this waste does 'count' statistically as output. Or, to put it another way, there is consciousness of the high opportunity cost, in terms of planners' preferences, of present inefficiencies.

Let us now draw a few conclusions from the arguments set out above. Soviet industrial planning has run into heavy weather, and everyone knows it and is busily engaged in seeking remedies, suggesting new courses and reforms. It is by no means clear whether they will be able to find the desired balance between central planning of essentials and the local operational initiative which they are seeking. These are matters in the highest degree

[1] To this extent there is value in M. Polanyi's 'Theory of conspicuous production', *Soviet Survey*, October–December, 1960, though he seems to me to go much too far. See also the penultimate item in this book.

relevant to the assessment of Soviet performance in the next decade. We may see a period of experiment which could lead to increased confusion. In the short run, we may be seeing a victory of the 'conservatives'—an attempt to maintain tight centralization, with the computer used to facilitate more speedy working out of consistent material balances and production plans. This may do no more than enable the planners to keep pace with the constant increase in the volume of work which they have to perform as the economy grows. It is hard indeed to imagine how any form of centralization can eliminate the major inefficiencies of the present system, but we would still see impressive increases in industrial output in terms of percentages or tons or metres which can be used to substantiate the claim that America is being overtaken and the long-term plans fulfilled. In particular, the seven-year plan, due to end in 1965, may even be declared fulfilled in 1964. Yet these figures may be misleading, for reasons already discussed. Some of the output will be a consequence of inefficient resource utilization. In any case, the volume of production of basic commodities or aggregate indices expressing quantities are becoming increasingly irrelevant as a guide as to whether or when America is being overtaken. Soviet planners know this, too. Thus V. Dymshits, the rising star among industrial planners, expressed this thought when he said to the November 1962 plenum: 'It is time to take seriously the economy and rational utilization of timber. Of course the question is not one of overtaking America in the volume of timber-cutting, but of using the timber better than in America.' These considerations apply, in even greater measure, to consumers' goods and services.

However, it seems hardly likely that major decentralizing changes in the planning system will be avoided for long. Let us suppose that the Liberman proposals or some variant of these are adopted, and that much greater flexibility is introduced into the economy through the use of incentives based on prices and profits. The net effect should be to make production much more responsive to demand and eliminate inefficiencies of many kinds. However, this could have two adverse effects on growth—one apparent and one real. In the first place, insofar as production geared to growth statistics is replaced by production for need, the statistics of growth may show a slowdown contrasting with the increase in the relative usefulness of what is produced. It is hard, indeed, even to attempt to quantify this proposition; yet the point is surely not an insignificant one. The second adverse effect concerns the likely drift of resources into non-priority sectors, which do not promote rapid growth. This is the great fear of the conservatives—the source of much of their opposition to the Liberman and Nemchinov proposals. On both counts the effect might well be a rise in real consumer welfare and probably also a decline in the ratio of producers' goods to consumers' goods in industrial production (an excessive production of intermediate goods is a direct consequence of many of the present inefficiencies). The effect on growth rates is hard to forecast, since among the unknowns are the extent of the micro-inefficiencies and underutilization of resources which the reforms might correct and also the strains and confusions which may follow from them. However, statistical success is certainly possible.

The national income targets through 1970 seem somewhat less realistic than the industrial output goals for the same period. The principal reason for scepticism relates to the nature of the plan for agriculture. A number of analysts, including the present speaker, have written at length about the difficulties which beset Soviet agriculture, and there is neither space nor the time to repeat these arguments now. Even according to the official statistics, farm output has increased very slowly since 1958 and is very far indeed behind plan. Four main causes may be distinguished: unfavourable natural conditions, inadequate incentives, excessive centralization and insufficient investments. One might add the complex of problems connected with the troubled relationship between the authorities and the peasants and the grossly excessive size of most farms. Unfortunately, centralization, which does so much harm in agriculture, has been somewhat reinforced during 1962. However, one must expect vigorous efforts to improve matters. For example, there is to be a substantial rise over the next few years in the output of fertilizer and in the production of much essential equipment, and for these and other reasons one must suppose that the rise in agricultural production will be resumed, perhaps amounting on average to some 3 per cent per annum through 1970. However, this is only a small fraction of the planned rate. Since in 1960 agriculture was, according to Soviet official statistics, responsible for just under 21 per cent of the national income, this in itself will cause a significant shortfall in the latter.

Other spheres of what is known in the Soviet Union as material production will hardly be in a position to make up the difference. The volume of construction will of course increase, though probably not as fast as industrial production. The relative contribution of freight transportation to the national income ought to diminish somewhat with the elimination of unnecessary cross-hauls resulting from an improvement of the planning system and economy in the transport of bulky, solid fuel by rail. On the other hand, the relative importance of trade is expected to increase, as the plans envisage substantial improvement in the still primitive system of distribution. The labour plans as published imply a substantial relative increase in the numbers engaged in trade, and also in so-called 'non-material' services, ranging from hairdressing and laundries to education and health. This presupposes considerable release of labour from agriculture, and a comparatively small addition to the industrial labour force, i.e. would be conditional upon a major improvement in productivity and efficiency. Failure in these respects would express itself in acute labour shortage in relation to the plan objectives, just as shortages of various materials are and will be indications of defects in planning.

This brings us yet again to the problems of the organization of the economy, price system, centralization and decentralization of decision making, investment criteria and the rest of the now familiar headaches of the Soviet planners. Here, in my view, lies the main bottleneck, the principal unknown, in the assessment of the Soviet economic performance in the immediate future. I do not think any confident forecast can be made either about the pattern of reforms or their consequences. In all probability we would be no better off even if we had before us all the information available to Soviet planners, as judging from the very frank discussions that have been published, they do not know the answer either.[1] It should be a very interesting decade for those who study the development of the practice and theory of the Soviet planning system.

[1] Anyone who can read Russian is urged to read the debates in *Ekonomicheskaya gazeta*, November 3 and 10, 1962.

5. *The problem of 'success indicators' in Soviet industry* *

Critical analyses of planned economies have tended to concentrate on such problems as rational investment choices, or the proper basis for planners' decisions. These are indeed matters of great importance, to which the experience of the Soviet Union is highly relevant, but it is not to them that the present paper is devoted. Let it be assumed that the decisions of the central planning authority about economic behaviour in all its aspects accord with ultimate wisdom, however this may be defined. There remains the problem of having these decisions implemented at the level at which production takes place, for it remains true, in Russia as elsewhere, that planning authorities produce only official documents. The actual work must be done within an enterprise or firm, under the authority of a director. The director is told from above what he should produce, and what he is told accords with the plan, so on the face of it there is no problem, so long as he does what he is told. However, the situation is much more complicated in reality, and it is my belief that much goes wrong precisely at this stage.

A director of a state enterprise in the Soviet Union owes his position to the Ministry or regional authority which appoints him to manage state property, and he is bound by the orders he receives from his superiors. Failure to obey can result in dismissal. He is under orders to implement the plan. Many of the basic materials and components necessary for the productive process are allocated to the enterprise by decision of superior authority, and he must dispose of the product through official disposals agencies, at prices fixed from above. Yet despite all these things, the director is constantly presented with a range of alternative decisions. Let us briefly examine in what they consist.

In the first place, only the man on the spot is likely to know

* From *Economica*, February, 1958.

the precise possibilities of the plant under his control, and so he is bound to be involved in the elaboration of the production plan for the enterprise. The planning authority depends, therefore, on his positive collaboration at that stage.

Secondly, the large majority of commodities are not homogeneous. Listed or implied in the plan must be a variety of different types, models, sizes. Then, of course, many enterprises produce more than one commodity. The director is constantly involved in choices as to exactly what to produce, either because the plan does not itemize the variants in detail, or because it is found necessary or convenient to fulfil part of the plan at the expense of another.

Thirdly, it is vital to the central planning authority, and to the Soviet state, that enterprises produce goods with a minimum expenditure of resources. It is clear that economical operation must depend to a large extent on the management on the spot, and cannot just be prescribed from above—though efforts are made to lay down various 'norms', for instance for the utilization of certain materials.

Fourthly, the development of new production methods, or of new variants and designs of the product, depend to a large extent on the initiative of those in charge of particular enterprises, or on their willingness to utilize positively the ideas and initiative of others.

Fifthly, despite the existence of central allocation schemes, for a number of materials, the director can, and does, exercise choice. He can, within fairly wide limits, decide what materials to indent for, he can take the initiative in seeking out suppliers and enter into contracts with them, he can try to use his own resources to make on the premises such components as he finds it difficult to obtain from outside sources.

The above list is by no means exhaustive, but should suggest to the reader that it is important for the Soviet economy that managers should use their powers in the desired direction. Mere orders, threats, 'terror', cannot do the job. This is not to say that straight coercion has not played an important role in Soviet economic history. Obviously, it has. However, coercion is not a means of ensuring efficiency, indeed, it is often directly destructive of efficiency. It is effective in ensuring that a few clearly defined priority objectives are met, *at any cost*. With the growing complexity of the economy, and with the emergence of more and more competing pressures for limited resources, the cruder methods of the 'thirties become less and less satisfactory. As the leaders strive after their basic objective—defined repeatedly as 'catching up the most advanced capitalist power in the shortest possible time'—they are driven to consider more carefully the relative scarcity of resources. They are compelled more and more to make economic calculations, to count the cost. This has led to much discussion in print of how best to ensure the efficient operation of enterprises, especially in 1956–57, which has made possible a clearer view of the practical problems involved, and has contributed much of the raw material of the present paper.

The planners, then, must so stimulate the behaviour of plant managers as to achieve efficiency. This can only be done by rewarding 'desirable' behaviour, either in cash or in increased esteem, improved chances of promotion, the issue of Orders of Lenin, or some other form of incentive. These rewards, in their turn, must be associated with some definable achievements. The management must know in advance what it must do to qualify for rewards. Therefore it becomes necessary to define what I have called 'success indicators' (in Russian, *pokazateli*) under various desirable heads, such as volume of output, reduction in costs, labour productivity, and so on. In a number of respects, which may not be obvious at first sight, many of these indicators have operated in ways which cause managements to deviate from the pursuit of efficiency, and have largely defeated their own ends. The rest of this paper will be devoted to considering these difficulties.

The criterion of success most familiar to us is that of profit. Enterprises are encouraged to make profits in the USSR, and derive material advantages from so doing. A part of the planned profit, and a much larger proportion of any in excess of plan, is used to create a so-called 'fund of the enterprise', formerly known as the director's fund.[1] Part of this money may be

[1] Usually from 1 to 6 per cent of planned profits, plus 20–40 per cent of any additional profits, subject to a maximum of 5 per cent of the given enterprise's wages fund. The higher percentages apply to enterprises expected to make small profits. Those expected to make losses are rewarded by the transfer of part of any saving on cost of production to their Fund of the enterprise. Any profits remaining after allocations to this fund are transferred to the state budget, apart from amounts retained for purposes specifically authorized—e.g. an approved investment project.

devoted to expanding productive capacity over and above the authorized investment plan, part for housing and amenities, part for the payment of bonuses. There is thus an interest in increasing profits. Managers are also interested in avoiding losses, since these are likely to lead to difficulties with the State Bank and attract the unwelcome attention of inspectors from various supervisory agencies. However, profits have not served, so far, as a major criterion of success, and the reasons for this are not far to seek.

The basic difficulty has always been the absence of any objective criterion for price-fixing, and the lack of any logical relationship between prices, profits and the desired assortment of production. Indeed, one critic has rightly argued that this makes the present rules governing allocations to the 'Fund of the enterprise' highly unfair, precisely because 'it is clear that in the Soviet economy, profit is not the aim or the regulator of production', so that a reward related to profits does not reflect real efficiency.[1] Another Soviet critic draws attention to the 'enormous range of profit rates as between different sectors and between different products within the same sector'.[2] This is a consequence of arbitrary and centralized price-fixing. While it is no longer the normal practice of Soviet planners to fix prices below the prime cost of production, for many products they barely cover average costs for the given industrial sector. This inevitably leaves a large number of enterprises working at a loss, and indeed their financial plans envisage a deficit. Even now, 'in the extractive industries about 25 per cent of enterprises make planned losses', and 10 per cent of engineering ('machine-building') enterprises are in the same position.[3] The importance of the concept 'profit' is necessarily affected by the existence of so many enterprises which make losses through no fault of their own. In any case, the measurement of profit under Soviet conditions is economically misleading, even if one leaves out of account the illogicalities of pricing. There is no interest payment on basic capital, and the

[1] Karagedov in *Finansy SSSR*, No. 6/1957, pp. 36–7.

[2] Kulikov in *Voprosy Ekonomiki*, No. 9/1957, p. 80.

[3] Kisman and Slavnyi: *Sovetskie Finansy v pyatoi pyatiletke* (Moscow, 1956), p. 63. The data relate to 1956. For a valuable survey of relationship of prices to costs in the last thirty years, see Lynn Turgeon in *Soviet Studies*, October, 1957.

depreciation allowances are much too low.[1] There is no land rent, with all the complications which must follow from its absence in the agricultural sector and elsewhere. Profits are expressed not in relation to capital but as a percentage of gross turnover. Under all these circumstances, profitability could not and cannot possibly be used as the basic criterion for economic decision. If managers were allowed to pursue maximum profits, it is clear that their choices between alternative inputs of materials and output of commodities would be highly irrational in relation to the requirements of the economy—unless and until there is a major overhaul of the theory and practice of pricing.

We will return to these problems later on. It is sufficient at this stage merely to note that profits have not been the dominant 'success indicator' to which the operations of Soviet enterprises could be geared.

The primary, essential success indicator has been *plan fulfilment* in quantity terms. Other indicators of considerable importance have concerned labour productivity, costs per unit, economy of materials, economy of wages, and the list could be prolonged. In each case, achievement of the plan is rewarded, failure leads to loss of bonus and/or administrative reprimand. Rewards are often very substantial indeed. For example, a manager in the oil industry may receive a bonus of 42 per cent of his salary for fulfilling the output plan, plus 4½ per cent for every 1 per cent overfulfilment.[2] There is abundant evidence that it is on plan fulfilment that the credit of a manager with his chiefs primarily depends. A whole complex range of problems and distortions arises in connection with the rewarding of plan fulfilment, and these must now be considered.

The first problem arises at the stage of deciding what the plan should be. The director knows that a large bonus awaits him if he exceeds 100 per cent, and the smaller the '100 per cent' is, the easier it will be to exceed it. The more honest he is about production possibilities, the higher will be the target set him, the more difficult will it be to win the bonus on which, *inter alia*, his wife's promised fur coat may depend. As has been repeatedly pointed

[1] Their extreme inadequacy is strikingly illustrated by Safrai in *Voprosy Ekonomiki*, No. 7/1957, and by many others.

[2] *Spravochnik po zarabotnoi plate v neftyanoi promyshlennosti* (Moscow, 1956), p. 192. (Note: no longer applicable. A.N.)

out by Soviet writers, honesty is thus penalized, and deceit rewarded.

Then, once the plan has been decided upon, it is often best to avoid overfulfilling it by too wide a margin, for fear of inciting the authorities to make an excessive upward adjustment in the year following. Several sources make this point: a wise director fulfils the plan 105 per cent, not 125 per cent.[1]

However, a more serious problem is how to define what the plan is. In some industries, of course, this is not difficult. Thus, electrical energy can be conveniently defined in kilowatt hours. But most enterprises produce many varieties of articles, whether these be machine-tools or cloth, toys or building materials. Success, to be rewarded, requires a definition, a target figure of some kind. It can be in weight, length, numbers, money or some other suitable unit. In almost every case, distortions and illogicalities result in the course of plan fulfilment at the level of the enterprise. On these there is now quite an extensive literature in Soviet periodicals.

When the output target is in tons, then any shift to a less heavy variant will be avoided by the enterprise whenever possible. It does not 'pay' to make lightweight rolling mill products, small cement blocks, and so forth. For example, a certain metal works increased its output of roofing iron in a five-year period by 20 per cent in terms of tons, but by only 10 per cent in square metres; the plan, of course, was expressed in tons, and the enterprise reached its output target by an economically and technically unnecessary increase in weight.[2] Needless to say, there would be an equally 'logical' tendency to avoid making the heavier kinds of roofing iron if the plan were in square metres. A long catalogue of examples of this kind can readily be assembled from the Soviet specialized press.

More common, on the whole, is a measure of success in money terms, by the value of gross output. For many years this 'success indicator' has discouraged the production of cheap clothing, since the cheaper is the material used, the harder—other things being equal—it must be to fulfil the plan. For the same reason there has been a marked reluctance to use any but

[1] For example, Nikolaeva in *Novyi Mir*, No. 7/1957, p. 74, and also *Kommunist*, No. 1/1957, p. 49, and so on.

[2] *Sotsialisticheskii Trud*, No. 1/1957, p. 50.

the dearest kinds of steel in tool-making.[1] Again, examples can easily be multiplied, and there seems no doubt that substantial distortions have been introduced into the economy by what one critic has called 'the cult of gross output' (*kult vala*).[2] Then, because gross output includes any increase in the carryover of uncompleted production, there is also a tendency for the management to aim at having an unnecessarily large amount of work in hand at the end of the plan period, exclusively to be able to score a 'statistical' success.[3] A more serious, though less obvious, consequence of the use of gross output as an indicator of success is a shortage of spare parts, which for long has been a notorious source of weakness in the USSR. At first sight this may appear strange, since it seems that a sparking plug worth 10 roubles would 'count' equally whether it is sold separately or placed in a completed tractor. However, in a tractor this sparking plug is combined with goods and services purchased from *outside* the given enterprise. Suppose, to take a simplified example, half of the completed tractor consists of components bought from other factories. Then its total value will be equal to twice the value of parts which *are* made in the given enterprise. But then it follows that the sparking plug will be worth twice as much, in terms of plan fulfilment, if it is in a completed tractor than if it were sold separately.[4]

Of course, it has not escaped the notice of Soviet economists that gross output can be a misleading criterion of success, because of the effect on the end-result of purchases of goods and services. Some have argued for the use of value-added as a truer measure. Indeed, from 1957 the 'cost of work done' in the enterprise, and not gross value, has become the basis for measuring plan fulfilment in the clothing industry.[5] However, the net output principle is also open to grave objection, in that it encourages maximizing of work carried out within the enterprise, discourages rational forms of inter-enterprise co-operation and sub-contracting. These arguments were made in a vigorous discussion on this

[1] *Sotsialisticheskii Trud*, No. 1/1957, p. 52.

[2] Kondrashev: *Tseno-obrazovanie v promyshlennosti* (Moscow, 1956), p. 32. This writer is among the more radical advocates of price reform.

[3] Antonov in *Planovoe Khozyaistvo*, No. 5/1957, p. 83.

[4] Similar cases are discussed by Antonov, *op. cit.*, and by Kontorovich in *Planovoe Khozyaistvo*, No. 3/1957.

[5] *Vestnik Statistiki*, No. 3/1957, pp. 74–75.

question, and the conclusions seemed on the whole not to favour a change to net output.[1]

Another weakness of plan fulfilment as a major success indicator is the influence of the calendar on economic activity. Targets have necessarily to relate to some date, and so the activities of the management inevitably concentrate on the task of recording the appropriate achievement by the date prescribed, which is by no means the same thing as acting in the most rational manner. This explains the marked tendency towards so-called 'storming' (*shturmovshchina*): a mad rush occurs towards the end of every plan period, followed by a lull and then another mad rush. There is an extensive Soviet literature on 'storming', with many an official condemnation of the practice. Yet it goes on, which suggests that it is actively stimulated by the planning system.

The measurement of success over time also introduces the complication of deflating value figures for price changes, a process made difficult by the introduction of new products or variants. The attempt to express output in terms of 'unchanged plan prices' has at times led to major distortions of both output and statistics, which it is impossible even to begin to discuss here.[2]

It has already been noted that the management is rewarded not solely for raising output, but also by reference to a whole number of other success indicators. However, far from correcting the deviations listed above, these other indicators either exercise a distorting pull in the same direction or introduce new distortions of their own. Some of the clearest examples concern the rewarding of increases in labour productivity. Since this is calculated, in most cases, by dividing the labour force into the *gross output*, there is just the same interest in inflating the latter to any possible extent. Almost every example of the distorting effects of endeavours to fulfil the plan recurs repeatedly in discussions about the measurement of labour productivity. For instance, in one such discussion it was pointed out that output and productivity in the case of wool cloth are both measured in linear metres, with the consequence that its width averages 106 centi-

[1] Though on the discussion of measuring labour productivity, reported in *Vestnik Statistiki*, No. 3/1957, it was well argued that, for this purpose at least, net output is less misleading than gross.

[2] For a survey of the distorting effects of the use of so-called 'unchanged prices of 1926–27', see Nove ('1926–27 and all that') in *Soviet Studies*, October, 1957.

metres, against a technical optimum of 142 centimetres, as this is the easiest way to be rewarded for success under both these heads.[1] Indeed, many are the contrivances by which the management seems able to affect the statistical expression of productivity without any real gain in efficiency, and one wonders whether direct rewards for increases in output per head are a useful way of stimulating the rational use of labour.

Serious difficulties also stand in the way of finding some means of rewarding the management for reducing costs of production. These are mainly connected with changes, real or potential, in the assortment or type of product. Thus one Soviet critic has pointed out that such rewards can incite the management to reduce quality, a tendency which can also be encouraged by rewarding economy of materials.[2] Then there is the question of comparability. A Soviet economist has shown that 'in order to provide effective checks on cost reduction, the greatest possible number of products are considered to be comparable', even though the design may have been appreciably altered.[3] This affects not only the validity of aggregate output statistics, but also the pattern of production. The same economist added: 'The question of comparability is often in conflict with the improvement of the quality and range of output of the enterprise, and sometimes acts as a direct obstacle in the path of introducing new and better types of products', because the enterprise will tend to avoid making 'those products which will be deemed "comparable" if the change in design involves increased costs per unit'. No one likes to lose their bonus. So here again the success indicator stimulates a departure from the path of economic common sense.

The 'success indicator' system has a negative effect in two other ways. It fails to provide any encouragement for innovation, and it does not reward quality or, to put it another way, it does not provide the necessary link between the producer's behaviour and the user's requirements.

First, the question of innovation. The Soviet régime has devoted much effort to the encouragement of inventors, and whole sectors of its industry have certainly been equipped with excel-

[1] *Sotsialisticheskii Trud*, No. 1/1957, p. 50 (note: square metres now used).
[2] Kondrashev, *op. cit.*, p. 32.
[3] Vainshenker in *Vestnik Statistiki*, pp. 20–21.

lent machinery. However, much of this occurs on the direct order or instigation of the central authorities. Initiative at the level of the enterprise is, unintentionally, somewhat discouraged. There is no disposition on the part of superior authority to tolerate a halt for retooling, which is involved in a change of production method or design, since it would affect the current output plan. Nor is there any reward for risk-taking, though there is generally some risk if a manager takes it upon himself to try something new. The difficulty has been well stated in a literary periodical: 'The introduction of a new method involves risk and, as in all gambling, capital is needed. Risk involves the possibility of loss, does it not? Yet even if a director is given the capital, just let him take a gamble and not win! . . . No, it does not behove a director to take risks. . . . The trouble is not so much that a few millions might be lost but, God forbid, the quarterly output programme might be threatened. Then the department concerned will appear in an unfavourable light in the statistical board's report.'[1]

Secondly, a few words about quality and the demand pattern. Here the problem is intimately connected with the inadequacy of the price mechanism. Clearly, so long as the primary object of the management is to strain to achieve plans expressed in quantitative terms, quality will suffer. So long as the goods conform to some minimum standard, they will count for purposes of measuring gross output. If the user's preferences—be that user a citizen or another factory—do not fit into the various success indicators, they tend to be disregarded. Since prices are decided centrally, and cannot be varied (save in a very few instances) by agreement between supplier and recipient, an essential economic link is missing. The consequences have been much commented upon in articles published recently in the USSR. A Soviet technician argued that the managerial incentive system leads to failure to adapt civil aircraft to the needs of the *Aeroflot* line, and adversely affects the durability of such commodities as rubber tyres and electronic valves by providing no reward for quality.[2] An economist pointed out that engineering factories are often 'uninterested in improving their machines, as this might lead to a worsening of their economically-measurable activities' (i.e. would affect the

[1] Lebedev in *Zvezda*, No. 5/1957, p. 155.

[2] *Znamya*, No. 2/1957. This technician had no doubt that the 'comrade economists' should devise a connecting link between use-value and profitability.

success indicators).[1] Another economist criticized the repeated failure of the consumers' goods industries to respond to consumer demand. Requests from the retail trade network are often rejected 'because a change in output would lead to the non-fulfilment of the gross output plan' by the manufacturers.[2]

The tendency to distort the output assortment is, of course, limited by certain specifications in the plan itself. One reason for the excessive centralization and great detail of planning, which has been the subject of much criticism, has been precisely the need to combat the tendency to distortion inherent in the 'success indicator' system. However, there is ample evidence to show that those items which fit most easily into plan fulfilment indicators are produced in excess of the plan, while others remain relatively scarce. Nor can all variants be separately prescribed from above.

In theory, the supervisory organs are supposed to prevent the deviations which have been here described. Among them, the most important are the local Communist party organizations and the immediate superiors of the enterprise (i.e. a department of the economic ministry or, under the recent reform, the appropriate department of the regional economic council). Unfortunately, all these bodies are interested in just the same success indicators as the enterprise. Their credit depends in large part on the plan fulfilments in their area of responsibility. It is Khrushchev himself who has been urging the need to relate even the salaries of party officials with the economic success indicators of their areas. Therefore, far from checking these undesirable tendencies, the 'supervisors' connive at, or even encourage them, judging from the indirect evidence available.

Before turning to a brief discussion of what can be, or is likely to be, done to correct these deficiencies, a few other remarks would be in order, if only to ensure a due sense of proportion. In the first place, it must be emphasized that the paper is concerned with an aspect of Soviet micro-economics—or should it be micro-planning—and not with the more general question of the relative strength and weakness of the Soviet economic system as a whole. This system grew up as part of an attempt by an authoritarian régime to maintain ultra-rapid tempos of industrialization and to

[1] Ganshtak in *Finansy SSSR*, No. 6/1957, p. 19.

[2] Lokshin in *Voprosy Ekonomiki*, No. 5/1957, p. 132.

build up military might. To the extent to which these objectives were achieved, it would be foolish to speak of 'failure'. Perhaps if the highest priority is maximum growth of heavy industry at almost any cost, in conditions of relative abundance of labour and a lavish supply of untapped natural resources, there is some logic in a system which provides the highest rewards for those who produce more. The student of the British war economy will have little difficulty in finding parallels for many, if not most, of the distortions listed in the preceding pages; the problem of how to stimulate and reward desirable activity by firms was a very real one. It is possible, therefore, that the harmful effects of 'success indicators' are an inevitable part of the cost of running an economy dominated by a few priority objectives determined by politicians.

Then it should not be thought that, so far as the USSR is concerned, the distortions discussed here are in any sense new. There is ample evidence that they existed also in the 'thirties.[1] The new element in the situation is the effort now being made to probe the sore as part of an attempt to find cures for the disease. For reasons too complex even to touch on here, there is now much less willingness to pay the price, in terms of waste of scarce resources, involved in the highly centralized system of 'priority' planning of which the success indicators are a part.

Soviet economists have approached these problems on a number of different levels. Some have gone no further than pointing out ways of improving the existing success indicators—and it is certainly true that some indicators are less unsuitable than others. However, the more thoughtful members of the profession see this question as part of a more fundamental one: the role of the 'law of value' (i.e. prices, profits, market forces, rationality) in the Soviet economy. Two national conferences, in December 1956 and May 1957, have been devoted to 'the law of value',[2] and the specialized press has been publishing articles on related topics throughout 1957.

A key element in any such discussion must be the relationship

[1] See, for example, D. Granick's *Management of Industrial Firms in the USSR* (Columbia University Press, 1955). A new book by J. S. Berliner, *Factory and Manager in the USSR* (Harvard, 1957), also deals with these topics, using largely materials relating to the 'thirties, but this book was not to hand at the time of writing.

[2] Reported in *Voprosy Ekonomiki*, Nos. 2 and 9/1957. Also a similar discussion among statisticians is related in *Vestnik Statistiki*, No. 4/1957.

between the central plan and the actual operation of the economy. It must therefore be mentioned that, while the economists argued, the Soviet leaders introduced an important new element into the situation by a radical reorganization of industrial planning and administration. By a new law, which came into operation on July 1, 1957, the USSR has been divided into 105 economic regions. Most industrial ministries have been abolished. Each regional authority now plays an important role in directing the operations of industrial enterprises within it and for drawing up plans, subject to the authority of the centre. The reform has many aspects which cannot be discussed here, but in one respect it is most relevant to the problems with which we are concerned. A planning authority with *regional* responsibilities is in quite a different situation from that of the central planners. The latter can, at least in theory, estimate national need in quantitative terms. A planning chief located in Kursk or Archangel cannot do so, and indeed cannot even know the direct consequences of his decisions on enterprises located outside his own area of responsibility. No doubt each region will work to a plan prescribed from above, but there are bound to be decisions to be made at regional level—the more so as one object of the entire scheme is to ensure a much needed increase in local initiative. But what are to be the criteria underlying regional decisions? There are signs that the regions are being provided with success indicators of their own, and of course the obvious one, already in use in 'inter-regional competitions', is gross output in monetary terms. This suggests that all the distortions which have been noted at enterprise level will operate in the new regional structure, only on an even larger scale. Thus the creation of regional planning bodies, far from simplifying the relationship between planners and producers, has introduced a new complication, and has made the search for more satisfactory economic criteria more urgent than ever.

These problems must lead to a reconsideration of the role of market forces, of profitability as the irreplaceable all-in criterion of success and of action. Once the economy grows too complex to be controlled effectively from the centre, it is increasingly difficult to avoid using the market mechanism, with a flexible price system responsive to supply and demand. There are signs that some Soviet economists see this clearly enough; thus I.

Malyshev has argued for a recognition of the logical connection between rationality and profitability.[1] A leading 'official' economist, Gatovski, has also spoken up in favour of a more logical price system and a more extensive role for the profit motive.[2] However, there are serious obstacles in the way of an explicit recognition of the needs of the situation.

One such obstacle is Marxist theory. It is not enough to advocate a more rational price system, it is also necessary to define some means of deciding what a rational price is. Turning to Marx, Soviet economists find themselves saddled with a definition of value in terms of 'socially necessary labour power'. This has caused a number of them to criticize the existing price system by reference to the Marxist concept of value; values and prices should, they argue, equal wages of labour plus the 'surplus product' created by the workers.[3] Certain exceptions are admitted, e.g. in the case of such interchangeable fuels as coal, oil and natural gas—but this approach involves basing prices on some version of factor *cost* (though there is disagreement about how cost should be defined for this purpose), while almost entirely disregarding use-value, demand. Under such a price system, at best the management will be *indifferent* on whether to produce article A or article B, even though the user would prefer A. Such a theoretical approach as this leaves no place for market forces. It is an interesting question whether Marxist modes of economic thought can be adapted to serve as a basis for necessary reform. The economist Kulikov, in his contribution to the discussion of December 1956, brought up the point that an unsaleable commodity fails to achieve 'social recognition', i.e. that the labour used in its production is misapplied. Marx did, of course, recognize that a *useless* object has no value. Perhaps someone will have

[1] *Voprosy Ekonomiki*, No. 3/1957, and again in *Planovoe Khozyaistvo*, No. 7/1957. In the latter (p. 63) he urged the need for some objective basis for choice between alternatives at the level of the enterprise.

[2] *Kommunist*, No. 9/1957, and also his contribution to the discussion in *Voprosy Ekonomiki*, No. 9/1957.

[3] In pure form this somewhat scholastic approach may be found in Strumilin's contribution to *Planovoe Khozaistvo*, No. 2/1957. Variants of the same idea are put forward by Kondrashev and Kronrod, and even Malyshev is not free of it. In Strumilin's version the price of any one product should in principle be equal to wages paid out in its production, plus that fraction of society's total expenditure on accumulation and services which is represented by the enterprise's wages bill in relation to the total wages fund.

the sense to see that some commodities, though not useless, are less useful than others. Then perhaps there will be forged the essential link between 'value' and utility, by the recognition of 'degrees of social necessity' or 'degrees of social recognition', thus bringing the operation of market forces within the verbal framework of Marxism (e.g. 'A is more wanted than B, and therefore, *ceteris paribus*, the labour expended on A is socially more necessary. . . .').

However, there is little doubt that the principal obstacle is not theory, but rather the conviction of the political leaders and planners that *they*, and not any 'law of value', are the regulators of economic life. Their function, indeed, does to a large extent consist in replacing the operation of economic laws by political decision. This attitude is expressed by official economists by denying to the 'law of value' a regulatory role under socialism. The contrary view is denounced as 'revisionism'. Professor Ostrovityanov put the point this way: 'The idea is widespread among foreign economists . . . that output should be regulated by the free fluctuation of market prices . . . under the influence of supply and demand. Such ideas involve the unleashing of elemental forces and would cause anarchy in production, contradicting the very essence of the socialist planned economy.'[1]

It is important to distinguish two strands in the debates now going on in Russia. One line of argument is primarily concerned with *criteria for planners at the centre*. It is admitted by everyone that the importance of economic calculation was underestimated, that planners' minds were confused by an illogical price system, and that in consequence expensive errors were made, particularly in the planning of investments. It may well be that, from the point of view of central planning, a system of values and prices based on some concept of factor cost could serve as a useful criterion. But this paper has been concerned with a rather different (though related) question; not with planners' decisions (be they sound or unsound), but with behaviour at lower hierarchical levels. It is on these levels that the success indicator system has so clearly shown its inadequacy, and official thinking has not yet advanced much nearer to the only possible solution. There is evidence that some Soviet economists have been advocating the

[1] *Pravda*, April 26, 1957. The 'foreign economists' are, principally, Poles and Yugoslavs.

D

'market' idea,[1] and many managers of Soviet enterprises must surely support it, since it is not only conducive to greater efficiency but also enhances their powers. However, it remains politically very difficult to pursue this line of argument.

The orthodox theoreticians, and also the Soviet leaders, face a dilemma. They need efficiency, they are in no mood to tolerate the irrationalities of the over-centralized planning mechanism inherited from the Stalin period of industrialization, they repeatedly stress the need for reform. Yet ideological principles and political interests cause them to shy away from a consistent approach to the problems they wish to solve. Marx has said nothing which can help them, but it must also be admitted that they would derive little aid from studies of planning by Western economists, as these have dealt almost entirely with the behaviour of a central planning agency. Little has been done to consider the position of the productive units within a planned economy, in relation to the planners and to the incentives provided. It might be useful to compare the position of a Soviet enterprise to that of an autonomous division of a great Western monopoly, where we also find the need to reconcile central control with initiative, the stimuli of market forces with the headquarters plan. British nationalized industries are another fruitful field of comparative study—though they mainly operate in sectors where the problem of choice between variants of output scarcely arises. (It might be said in passing that the price policies of our nationalized industries should remind us that irrational pricing is no monopoly of the Soviet world.) It would be useful to examine the experience of Yugoslavia, where market relations have to some extent been restored in recent years, and to consider the discussions which have raged in Poland. The 'success indicator' problem is part of a neglected study—the micro-economics of planning. We could spare a sympathetic thought for the Soviet economists who, in not altogether favourable circumstances, are cautiously seeking ways and means of tackling it.

[1] Ostrovityanov, in *Kommunist*, No. 13/1957, p. 99, claimed that the heretical arguments of certain Poles, who had been advocating a free market, were rejected by 'the overwhelming majority' of Soviet economists. This means there was a minority which accepted them. The tone of the articles against 'revisionism' certainly suggests that Soviet economists have been straying from the path of orthodoxy in these matters.

6. *Soviet planning: reforms in prospect**

Five years have passed since the *sovnarkhoz* reform of 1957. Already the system then introduced has been significantly modified. It is a virtual certainty that further modifications are imminent. There is evidence of stresses and strains, and patchwork efforts to put right particular weaknesses have led to new administrative headaches. The object of the present article is to analyse the weak spots and assess their importance. But first it is necessary to list briefly the changes which have occurred since 1957, and to indicate the probable reasons for these changes.

Firstly, the number of industrial *state committees* has greatly increased. The most recent move in this direction was the setting up of state committees for metallurgy and the fuel industries in 1961 and for timber and paper in January 1962.[1] Presumably the object was to ensure that the special technical and planning problems of the industries so covered received due care and attention. However, 'operational' plans remain the responsibility of *Gosplan*, perspective plans of *Gosekonomsovet*.

Secondly, in 1960 *Gosplan* was split at all-Union level into a current planning body (still called *Gosplan*) and an organization responsible for perspective planning and also for considering problems of planning methodology (*Gosekonomsovet*—Economic-scientific council). With the adoption of 'continuous planning' (i.e. five years ahead in every year), Gosplan appears to be responsible for the plans for periods up to and including five years.

Thirdly, in 1960 the three biggest republics (RSFSR, Ukraine,

* From *Soviet Studies*, July, 1962.

[1] Such committees (affecting industry only) are as follows at the date of writing: Aviation technique, Defence technique, Radio-electronics, Shipbuilding, Chemical industry, Automation and machine-building, Electronic technique, Metallurgy, Fuel industry, Atomic energy, Timber and Paper (see list in *Pravda* April 26, 1962). Also relevant are the state committees for the sale of agricultural machinery, for the co-ordination of research and for construction, and *Glavgaz.*

Kazakhstan) set up *republican economic councils*, nominally for operational control, co-ordination and material supply arrangements, leaving the republican Gosplans the task of current and perspective planning.

Fourthly, in 1961 it was decided to divide the USSR into seventeen big regions, ten being in the RSFSR and three in the Ukraine. Kazakhstan became a 'big region'. The Baltic states, the Central Asian republics and the Transcaucasian republics each form a region covering respectively three, four and three Union republics. Finally and oddly, two republics (Belorussia and Moldavia) joined no big region. The new regions have co-ordinating functions and can make recommendations to the all-Union Gosplan and also to the republics and *sovnarkhozy*. It is not clear on present evidence what (if any) actual powers are vested in them.[1] The reasons for setting up these regions are rather obvious; indeed, some *sovnarkhozy* had been conferring informally with their neighbours for some years. Clearly, the *sovnarkhozy* were and are too small to be natural economic administrative units.

Fifthly, at some date probably in 1960—I have failed to find any decree to that effect—some large part of local industry formerly administered by *oblast* soviets, including the former producers' co-operatives, were transferred to *sovnarkhozy*.[2] Presumably this was to avoid overlaps and confusion arising from the co-existence of two economic authorities, each with enterprises of its own, in the same area.

Sixthly, there were significant reductions in the range of allocation and investment decisions which could be taken at local level. The most important examples concern forbidding the distribution of 'funded' products by *sovnarkhozy* without an allocation certificate (*naryad*) obtained from higher authority (1959),[3] and the drastic reduction in decentralized investments imposed in 1961.[4] Both reflect the dangers which decentralization brings

[1] The decision was reported in *Ekonomicheskaya gazeta*, May 28, 1961. Reports of the work of co-ordination appeared in *Ekonomicheskaya gazeta*, e.g. on January 15, 1962, pp. 24, 25.

[2] For references to the transfer, see E. Kudryavtsev, *Ekonomicheskaya gazeta*, January 22, 1962, p. 45. However many small workshops remain under local control (see arguments against further transfers, *Ekonomicheskaya gazeta*, April 2, 1962, p. 10).

[3] I. Baranov and F. Liberman, *Planovoye khozyaistvo*, 1959, No. 9, pp 39–40.

[4] V. Garbuzov, *Pravda*, December 7, 1961.

with it in a Soviet-type economy. The same trends have been visible in Soviet agriculture and in Czechoslovak industrial planning. More will be said about this later on.

Several commentators, including myself, have discussed certain familiar distortions engendered by the *sovnarkhoz* reform, such as 'localism' (*mestnichestvo*). The trend towards stricter centralization is part of the reaction to these distortions. But several other weaknesses do not seem to have received sufficient attention. They are closely interconnected.

The first of these is the nature of the change in supply arrangements to which the 1957 reform and subsequent amendments have given rise. The essential point is this: under the ministerial system, enterprises were administered and supplied by 'their' ministry. The ministerial *snab* department was the body responsible for supplies of all major materials and components to that ministry's enterprises; in so far as the materials came from other ministries, it fought the necessary battles at the central planning level. So the enterprise had a clear boss who told it what to produce and laid down the various indicators (the ministerial *glavk*), and a single agency responsible for its supplies (the ministerial *snab*). It is true that this system led to various kinds of ministerial empire-building and cross-hauls with which students of the 1957 reform are familiar. But at least it was reasonably simple to operate administratively.

The present situation on the supply side is far more complex. At the all-Union level there are a number of departments within Gosplan for particular materials, machinery, etc. Suppose an enterprise requires for its production three 'allocated' materials. There would now be three *snab* organizations concerned, one for each material. This immediately complicates the problem of ensuring consistency in allocation. But more serious is the fact that some of these materials may be allocated not by the union but by the republican organs, and some more minor (but possibly essential) ones by the *sovnarkhoz*. The enterprise thus faces a complicated situation, and the chances of a bad supply planning correspondingly increase.

The situation should be improved, theoretically, by the fact that there exist production plans with which these multi-level supply plans must be co-ordinated. At all-Union level these production plans are elaborated within Gosplan's numerous specialized production divisions, and possibly also in the relevant state committees. Production plans emerge also from republican and regional organs, of which more later. But in actual fact there is abundant evidence that we are here at the weakest link of the planning chain. For it is precisely the failure to ensure consistency between production and supply plans which is the source of widespread complaint. The 'ministerial' system concentrated *snab*, production-planning and operational control within the same ministry; in other words, from the enterprise's point of view its hierarchical boss was responsible for ensuring its supplies. True, many discrepancies could arise because some of these supplies had to come from other ministries, and precisely this weakness stimulated ministerial autarky which the 1957 reforms were intended to combat. But the present situation, seen from the enterprise's point of view, is surely very confusing. Who is its effective 'boss'? The apparent answer is: the *sovnarkhoz*. But this answer would be quite misleading. It would depend on who plans production. Often the all-Union or republican Gosplan—or rather its appropriate production division—is the effective body so far as output planning is concerned. Particularly is this so if important products at important factories are concerned. Yet a great many enterprises produce more than one commodity, and so find themselves subject to several bosses, none of whom are responsible for the production programme or the economy of operation of the entire enterprise. Two examples of this can be cited. One relates to the Kirov factory in Leningrad: the party secretary of Leningrad, Spiridonov, complained that, while its output of heavy machinery is under the all-Union Gosplan, its other production (mainly metal and metal goods) has no chief in Moscow, that it is 'an orphan'.[1] The other is worth citing in detail. The author of the remarks to be quoted is the director of the Tula farm machinery works. He writes: 'The multiplicity of planning organs, the absence of agreement among them, have become a brake upon the initiative of the director. The basic plan for farm machinery for the Tula combine factory (row harvesters) is decided by the USSR Gosplan; to this Gosplan RSFSR adds hemp and reed cutters; VSNKh,[2] *Rosselkhoztekh-*

[1] *Pravda*, June 23, 1960.

[2] The Russian republican economic council, referred to above. (Note: now known as the RSFSR *Sovnarkhoz*; the name VSNKh now has another meaning; see p. 117.)

nika[1] and *Soyuzavtoselmash*[2] send us plans for motor vehicle spare parts and farm machinery components; and on top of this the *sovnarkhoz* gives us a variety of tasks for the manufacture of metal parts, units, sections and machines for the chemical, electrical, metallurgical and other industries of its economic region. The party *obkom* in its turn compels us to prepare, for the needs of the *oblast*, battery holders, manure spreaders, silage combine-harvesters, spare parts for farm machinery and tractors, etc. As a result the factory is overburdened, but for some reason everyone considers that it is working at half-pressure and throughout the year gives us additional tasks.'[3] How can anyone be responsible for the factory in these circumstances? Is it likely that the *material supplies* plan will coincide with this conglomeration of production plans devised by different bodies at different hierarchical levels for a variety of unco-ordinated purposes? So of course the author goes on to complain that the output plans, which are repeatedly amended, are inconsistent with the supply plans, and that the department of machinery and metal goods of the Tula *sovnarkhoz*, the nominal superior of the enterprise, can do little to help. One result is that plans frequently exceed practical possibilities, because the organ which decides the plan is unaware of the given factory's situation and has no responsibility for the enterprise as a whole. Thus, reports the same director, in 1962 the factory must deliver to other factories 394,000 hinges, though it cannot possibly produce more than 250,000 and asked to be freed from the obligation to produce even these hinges, because it requires space for other urgent tasks. 'But neither our requests, nor the danger of breakdown in supply co-operation, bothers the planning organs. In the last analysis, we will be held responsible for the underfulfilment of the hinges plan, while the planning organs will be out of the line of fire.'[4]

It is surely sufficient to ponder over this state of affairs to see that something is seriously awry in the planning arrangements. It is true, of course, that there is no simple solution to the problems raised by administrative planning of production and supply

[1] The Russian republican agricultural machinery department, set up in 1960 as intermediary between farms and industry.

[2] All-Union body in charge of farm machinery and rural lorries, presumably within Gosplan.

[3] V. Pushkarev, in *Ekonomicheskaya gazeta*, January 15, 1962, p. 8.

[4] *Ibid.*

in a complex industrial economy. There is certainly no need to imagine that there were no acute difficulties of co-ordination under the ministerial system. There were plenty. Whatever organizational variant is used, any production decision affects inputs (both in the producing and in the user enterprises) in other industries and in other areas. Yet the present system is peculiarly confusing, and becomes more so as the need to patch and improvise brings into being additional overlapping organizations, both at the centre and in the republics. This emerges again and again in articles in the press. Here is another director, this time of a heavy machinery works in Irkutsk, contributing to the same issue of the same journal:[1] 'The tasks of planning and supplies were badly carried out in the former ministries, although within the same organ. Now, however, the productive activities of the enterprise are supposed to be controlled by the *sovnarkhoz*, while planning and supplies come under Gosplan RSFSR. In these conditions, the director usually gets left out of the process of decision-making, while the planning organs often fail to take into account the conditions and requirements of production. . . . In practice the country's heavy machinery factories, including our own, receive plans only for the following year, and that only in October-November. Their applications for materials, finally collated by the *sovnarkhoz*, are submitted in the middle of the year, i.e. long before the production plan is received. Hence flow thousands of misfortunes and directorial worries. The finally-confirmed output plan for 1961 was received by our factory in March of the same year. When we set about fulfilling it, we discovered a mass of unforeseen miscalculations. For example, we were to receive sheet steel from Chelyabinsk, but the production unit whence the metal was to come had not even been completed. Nor were the Magnitogorsk and Tagil works able to send us metal: they received allocation orders for much more metal than was to be produced under their output plans. But this is not all. During the course of the year Gosplan RSFSR, VSNKh, and on occasion also the *sovnarkhoz*, utilizing their rights, told the factory to produce items not provided for in the plan and often unsuitable for it. In 1961 alone directions were received to produce for enterprises of the Irkutsk *sovnarkhoz*: automation control equipment, three lots of large metal decking, specialized

[1] N. Baibuzenko, in *Ekonomicheskaya gazeta*, January 15, 1962, p. 11.

equipment for an aluminium works and several other orders. To fulfil them the factory had to take the metal assembly shop off the work of fulfilling the state plan for a month and a half. . . . We cannot expect anything better in 1962. The output plan was received only in November, but the material supplies for the year were decided already in July. And even at the end of December it was not known at the factory what should be made, and when, for the priority construction projects of 1962.' This story relates to heavy machinery, which has a long production cycle. It helps to explain why difficulties arise in completing investment projects; but more of this in a moment. A very similar picture emerges from an article by the director of the famous *Uralmashzavod*.[1]

The number of overlapping organizations and the consequences of such overlapping on production, supplies and investment can be illustrated by summarizing another article from the same issue of the same journal—and suspicious readers can rest assured that other issues are full of supporting evidence on this and many other matters. The author, V. Dykin,[2] describes his efforts to discover why, among a myriad of other 'supply' complaints, the allocation certificates for phenol issued by the department of chemicals and rubber of the material supplies division of VSNKh RSFSR were not honoured; deliveries could not be made, output was halted at user factories. The head of the department, besieged by representatives of *sovnarkhozy* and enterprises, complained that he did not know this year, and did not know in previous years, what proportion of his allocations would be covered by actual production. He admitted in particular that a Saratov factory was to have delivered phenol which it was not yet able to produce, and referred complaints to *Rosglavkhimsnabsbyt*; this apparently is also within VSNKh RSFSR, duplicating in some measure the VSNKh division referred to above. There a planner admitted that they knowingly allocated nonexistent Saratov production of phenol and blamed *Soyuzglavkhim*, a division of Gosplan USSR. There in turn it was stated that they knew of the situation, and in fact had reported to 'the department of aggregate balances and material requirements of Gosplan USSR' the need to reduce the output plan in respect

[1] *Ekonomicheskaya gazeta*, December 18, 1961, p. 8.
[2] *Ibid.*, January 15, 1962, pp. 11–12.

of some chemicals in which phenol is used. They also blamed Gosplan RSFSR for planning 'fictional deliveries'. The next stage was to blame the department of chemical industry (i.e. the production department) of Gosplan RSFSR. The official there declared: 'You will never find the actual guilty person. It will be necessary to analyse the question in *Rosglavkhimkomplekt* of VSNKh (an organization responsible for equipment for chemical factories), Gosplan USSR, and a mass of other organizations. I can assure you that if anyone said he was responsible for the muddle and should be punished, no one would believe him.' The head of the department of chemical industry (the production department again) of Gosplan USSR blamed Gosplan RSFSR. There it was confirmed that the Saratov plant should have been producing phenol in 1960. The necessary shop should have been started in 1957, but the state committee for the chemical industry (at last *it* puts in an appearance!) altered the investment project, and building only began at the end of 1960; errors in investment plans led to further delay. Then it was found difficult to place the necessary orders for equipment, and by the end of 1961 only 35 per cent of the projected work had been completed. Enterprises located in twelve *sovnarkhozy* failed to obtain the phenol provided for in the supplies plan. And so on. The author makes it quite clear that phenol is one small example, 'taken at random'. 'This kind of planning has nothing in common with the kind mentioned in the Programme of the CPSU.' No indeed.

So far we have been concerned with the situation of enterprises which are formally subordinated to *sovnarkhozy*. It may be thought that, despite the difficulties described above, some advantage does accrue from having all but the purely local enterprises within a given region under one organizational umbrella. At least there is joint planning, the possibility of redeploying resources within the region. But even this does not appear to be the case, at least for certain industries. Thus the chairman of the Altai *sovnarkhoz* complained that, 'from January 1960', the timber industry in his region is divided between the *sovnarkhoz* and a totally different organization, the *Glavleskhoz* (chief timber department) of the RSFSR. In the case of prefabricated cement parts, of Altai's twenty-three enterprises only six are under the *sovnarkhoz*; eleven are under *Selkhoztekhnika* (the agricultural machinery administration) (!?), and the remainder are divided between the *krai* soviet, the (all-Union) Ministry of transport construction and the RSFSR Ministry of procurements. 'Brickworks are under the *Altaitselinstroi* trust, the *sovnarkhoz*, the *sovkhoz* department and other departments of the *krai* soviet, the *krai* branch of *Selkhoztekhnika*, the Ministry of transport construction and the Ministry of communications. In all these offices—this is in one economic region!—there is a separate administrative apparatus. Is this perhaps why the capacity of brickworks in Altai is utilized only 65–70 per cent, and the costs of red brick not infrequently exceed the plan by two and more times?'[1] Finally, there is ample evidence that within the *sovnarkhozy* there is often much confusion and overlapping between the functional and industrial-sector departments; the latter indulge in empire-building of their own, hoard materials, fail to collaborate with factories in the same *sovnarkhoz* but under a different sector department, establish direct links with the sector departments of republican planning organs, bypassing their own *sovnarkhoz*. Thus, 'despite the prohibition of the Government, in June-July 1961, when the plan for 1962 was being formulated, hundreds of officials of the sector departments of *sovnarkhozy* were at the (Ukrainian) Gosplan and the Ukrainian (republican) *sovnarkhoz*'.[2] There is much discussion in the press about streamlining the *sovnarkhoz* administrative machine, but no action yet, except that small sector departments in a few *sovnarkhozy* have been abolished or amalgamated.

Among the organizational peculiarities to which critics frequently draw attention is the duplication in the big republics between the republican *sovnarkhoz* (VSNKh in the RSFSR) and the republican Gosplan. One is indeed at a loss to account for the structural change which brought these republican *sovnarkhozy* into being. One's sense of puzzlement is in no wise reduced after perusal of the explanation of his own activities advanced by S. Afanasev, chairman of VSNKh RSFSR. His account emphasizes, indeed, the important role of his organization in production planning. He himself admits that 'many well-founded complaints are heard from *sovnarkhoz* officials about the fact that on some questions there is no clear division of functions between

[1] V. Kargopolov, *Ekonomicheskaya gazeta*, March 19, 1962.

[2] I. Kuzmenko, *Ekonomicheskaya gazeta*, April 2, 1962, p. 8; and see also P. Nosev in *ibid.*, p.9.

Gosplan RSFSR and VSNKh. Naturally this complicates planning and control of industry, and in a number of cases causes an unjustified parallelism.'[1]

A strong attack on this 'parallelism' was launched by the chairman of the Buryat *sovnarkhoz*, A. Davydov, 'Two-step planning, Gosplan plus VSNKh, calls for double negotiations, frequently leading to red tape and confusion. As a result the *sovnarkhoz* had not even received the full plans for 1962 by the end of January, and once again there are serious errors in material supplies and capital construction. The reconciliation of plans for 1962 between the *sovnarkhoz* and VSNKh, on which so much time was spent, became a useless operation, since most of the agreed figures, confirmed by the deputy-chairman of VSNKh, were pitilessly eliminated by Gosplan and by numerous departments of the VSNKh itself.' The author further raises the point that detailed financial control exercised by organs of the Ministry of Finance is carried out without due regard to the realities of economic planning. Major reorganization is urged at republican level to correct these and other defects.[2]

His criticisms were promptly taken up by the chairman of the Tambov *sovnarkhoz*, G. Mylnikov.[3] Gosplan RSFSR contains within itself many departments which fail to co-ordinate their activities, he argued. Thus one Tambov factory received from the *sovnarkhoz*, in agreement with a (the?) 'functional department of Gosplan', an output programme for washing-machines: 30,000 units. But 'the department of electrical industry and equipment of Gosplan, which determines the washing-machine production plan, decided on 46,000. This figure was rubber-stamped by the collation department (*svodny otdel*). However, the material balances department allocated enough stainless steel for only 25,000 machines, explaining this by the fact that the department of ferrous metallurgy planned insufficient stainless steel. . . .' Mylnikov insists that, despite all this, the 1957 reform has led to a substantial improvement. However, 'can one really say that the reconstruction [of the administration of industry] has been completed?' While at Gosplan RSFSR there is a failure to achieve a necessary interlinking of the separate decisions of

[1] *Ekonomicheskaya gazeta*, January 1, 1962, p. 5.
[2] *Ibid.*, February 5, 1962, pp. 5, 6.
[3] *Ibid.*, February 19, 1962, p. 14.

various sector departments, further and unnecessary troubles arise from duplication with VSNKh. 'Its structure resembles Gosplan's like two drops of water. . . . VSNKh, as well as exercising control over *sovnarkhozy*, has taken over planning functions. Now plans are drafted in parallel in Gosplan and in VSNKh. In real life the result is this: before, the *sovnarkhoz* got one document, from the RSFSR Council of Ministers. Now it gets another one from the VSNKh. Before, officials of the *sovnarkhoz* had to visit sector and collation departments of Gosplan and its materials disposal divisions, to agree the plan. Now the process begins with the sector departments of VSNKh. Then come its collation departments and territorial department, which, as a rule, cannot decide all the questions arising. And then the officials of the *sovnarkhoz*, together with the appropriate officials of VSNKh, repeat all the "technological operations" in Gosplan and in the disposals divisions. This doubles the number of stages to go through.'

VSNKh, obviously, is not a very successful institution. But surely at bottom the error consists in imagining that it is possible to divide planning and operational control between two different bodies. The processes overlap so substantially that VSNKh, called upon to exercise operational control, unavoidably 'invaded' the area of planning ostensibly reserved for Gosplan. It should not be overlooked that the plans finally agreed at republican level have still to be amended by Gosplan USSR, and that not a few complaints, before VSNKh existed, pointed to a needless parallelism between the republican and all-Union Gosplans.[1]

The perennial problem of an excessive 'spreading' of investment resources (*raspyleniye sredstv*) is also affected by the present confusion of planning, although it would be misleading to pretend that it was not causing trouble also under the ministerial system. In fact great practical difficulties have always arisen in ensuring that the necessary labour, materials and equipment are available to complete quickly the large number of factories and other capital projects. Partly this was and is due to the tightness of planning, which results in shortages which delay completion. Partly the explanation lay, and lies, in a quite unavoidable multiplicity of agencies whose decisions and activities must be combined if the job is to be done: investment planning must be

[1] For example, see I. Kulev, in *Kommunist*, 1959, No. 9, p. 24.

geared in with the current 'operational' plan (to provide the building materials and machines needed to continue or complete the investment project in the given period), the construction enterprise must co-ordinate its work with that of a quite different enterprise (in a different ministry or *sovnarkhoz*, as a rule) which makes the equipment, and the necessary finances must be advanced by the investment bank, which must receive the sums from the state budget or other sources of financing. Still another aspect of the problem is that, because investment grants from the centre are 'free' and non-returnable, planning and territorial authorities tend to overapply for investment funds, and, if short of these, are tempted to start projects which they know they cannot finish, in the hope that it will be easier to persuade the centre to supply the money if the work is actually in hand.

All these difficulties are not new. Yet there has been a big wave of complaints, even larger than usual, on this issue, suggesting the possibility that more has been going wrong than was the case in previous years. It is true, of course, that the mere appearance of a larger volume of criticisms in print is not proof that matters are getting worse, but sometimes merely means that someone is intending to take remedial action. For example, the appearance in 1957 of articles on the weaknesses inherent in the MTS-*kolkhoz* relationship showed most of all that reform was in the air, not that their relationship had grown particularly bad in 1957. None the less, in the present instance the evidence suggests that things *have* been getting worse. Thus severe criticisms have in fact been followed by organizational decisions which bore every sign of being reflections of an actual emergency or at least of an accumulation of intolerable troubles. The first of these, announced in the 1960 budget speech, concerned the creation of a list of top-priority investment projects to which special attention was to be directed. The second, reported in 1960, forbade any territorial state organ to submit an investment project for approval without the authorization of the appropriate party committee.[1] Finally, as already mentioned, decentralized (unplanned) investments were severely cut in 1961. These 'centralizing' measures, limiting the rights of local organs, were no doubt designed to combat *raspyleniye sredstv* and also 'localist' tendencies on the part of *sovnarkhozy*. They seem likely to have undesirable effects, and even unwittingly

[1] I. Bocherov, in *Planovoye khozyaistvo*, 1960, No. 12, p. 60.

to stimulate *raspyleniye*, as we shall see. Evidence is cited by well-qualified Soviet writers to the effect that the volume of unfinished construction has grown faster than the volume of investment.[1] Let us see to what causes this is attributed.

The obvious reason is simply that 'planning organs, *sovnarkhozy*, enterprises, construction trusts, do not satisfactorily link investment plans . . . with material supply plans, and particularly with the plans for producing and delivering equipment. As a result of such defects in planning and organization of construction, *more building projects are in hand at any given moment than can be supplied with metal, cement and equipment*.'[2]

These generalizations were given detailed illustration in an article by a senior official of the Tatar *sovnarkhoz*. He asserted that, despite every effort to concentrate investment resources, his *sovnarkhoz* is put in an impossible situation. Construction plans arrive late, are repeatedly amended during the year. 'The "spreading" of investment resources is in reality built into the plans themselves. The responsibility for this lies less on the construction organizations than on planning organs and contractors. . . . The completion of this or that industrial plant is envisaged, yet the financing of all the work is not provided. Yet the work is completed, and exceeds the amount covered in the annual plan. Where did the money and materials come from? *At the expense of other construction projects, which had to surrender some of the missing money and materials*. They, of course, were sufferers from this. . . . So it was two years ago. So it was again last year. It is too early to speak of this year's plans, so we still do not have them in final form [In February! A.N.]. But extracts from the plans yet to be confirmed by Gosplan RSFSR and VSNKh lead to the conclusion that the *raspyleniye* will be still greater than last year.'[3]

It is interesting to note the frequently-repeated complaint that the financial allocation is inadequate to complete the planned investments, though at least equally common is its opposite: that the money cannot be used because the necessary materials or equipment do not arrive. This is a reflection, of course, of the

[1] V. Smekhov, *Ekonomicheskaya gazeta*, January 29, 1962, p. 10.

[2] V. Dymshits (deputy chairman, USSR Gosplan), *Ekonomicheskaya gazeta*, December 18, 1961, p. 6 (Emphasis his.)

[3] S. Dongaryan, *Ekonomicheskaya gazeta*, February 5, 1962, p. 17. (Emphasis his.)

planning defects already analysed in earlier pages. As a result, it is pointed out, allocation certificates are not honoured, and again one hears of republican *snabsbyt* organs issuing allocations certificates which relate to non-existent output.[1] It is also difficult to obtain regular deliveries, there being a strong tendency to receive the necessary materials and components towards the end of each plan period. Obviously, faced with shortages which prevent them from completing a given building project, conscientious local planners and building organizations carry on working on other projects for which the necessary material resources do exist. Thus even in the absence of any 'localism' the volume of uncompleted production can show an upward trend.

Efforts are being made to ensure the co-ordination of plans to provide for the necessary materials and equipment for important factories currently under construction. Typically, this takes the form of *ad hoc* bodies charged with this particular task, the *Glavkomplekty*, of which we have already encountered one (republican *Glavkhimkomplekt*) earlier in this article. While they have existed for some years, these organizations are being strengthened. In 1962, 476 projects are to be treated as 'especially important', and the necessary work, and relevant production and delivery arrangements, are to be planned on a long-term basis. The all-Union *Glavkomplekty*, attached to the USSR Gosplan, will supervise the equipment needs of a major portion of the list of 476, the less important coming under analogous republican organizations. The same source gave particulars of a new and more highly centralized procedure for reviewing and approving all construction plans and investment lists (*titulniye spiski*). For example, no investment worth over 2.5 million (new) rubles can be included in the plan without the approval of Gosplan USSR. The investment bank, *Stroibank*, is to have wider controlling functions and has been taken out of the Ministry of Finance, achieving equal status with *Gosbank*. The state committees for industrial sectors, and also Gosplan, are to have a tighter grip on project makers' plans and designs.[2]

All these measures, along with the cuts in permissible decentralized investment, could result in some improvements. However, the effect of a list of key construction projects is sometimes

[1] For instance, Dongaryan's article just cited.

[2] V. Dymshits, *op. cit.*, pp. 6, 7.

to denude others of materials, and to introduce into investment planning acute forms of 'storming' methods. In just such a context, it is relevant to cite the case of the Lipetsk metallurgical plant. The work has been progressing in discontinuous rushes, with repeated delays due to the absence of the necessary blueprints and failure to place orders to receive supplies in time. In an effort to achieve success 'regardless of cost, towards the end of the year a large part of the necessary equipment was taken away from the other construction sites, to deliver it to Lipetsk by redistributing other already-allocated materials, at the expense of the reserves of the Council of Ministers of the RSFSR. This equipment came from thirty-two economic regions, in express trains, by air, it was brought in motor vehicles from Kharkov, Leningrad, Cheboksary. . . . The number of building workers rose to double the planned amount. They were transferred from other construction sites, including those which were due to be completed, although there too things were none too good. As a result, costs of construction rose higher and higher.'[1]

Here one sees a clear cause of delays in completion of a large number of other investment projects: labour, materials, machines, rubles, were removed to complete a super-priority objective. Yet the old-fashioned term 'shock-work construction' (*udarnaya stroika*) has been revived and is prominently featured in official statements.[2]

Other evidence shows that the *Glavkomplekty* themselves are unhappy about their own activities. An article by the head of *Soyuzglavmetallurgkomplekt*, the all-Union body responsible for ensuring supplies of metallurgical equipment, is highly critical of the existing arrangements. 'Building sites require complete deliveries of equipment. Precisely here occur numerous breaches of state discipline.' He cites several instances of failure to deliver, or long delays, even where priority construction projects are concerned. These failures are attributed to the behaviour of the republican Gosplan, VSNKh and *sovnarkhozy*, as well as to the enterprises concerned, since the suppliers are themselves victims of supply failures, notably of equipment necessary to produce the required equipment and components. The greatest difficulty is encountered in the placing of orders for non-standard equip-

[1] A. Kozhin, *Pravda*, January 20, 1962.

[2] For instance, see *Pravda* editorial under this very title, January 11, 1962.

ment; among the examples he cites is a special oven intended for the new Lipetsk steelworks, whose supply problems have been mentioned already. 'The delivery of non-standard equipment for especially important construction projects was planned on a reduced scale for last year. Despite this, the plan was only half fulfilled.'[1]

More articles on the same theme, many of them under a common banner headline, 'Capital construction—the key question', make similar points. The secretary of the Chelyabinsk *obkom* of the party complains: 'Briefly, not a single priority construction project received its equipment on time. This was last year. What can we expect in the present year? So far there is insufficient clarity: whence and when will we obtain the equipment for very important ferrous metallurgy plants?'[2]

The planners admit that they are failing to cope, but claim that they are victims of a clumsy system. Thus an official of VSNKh pointed to the multiple-stage system of planning deliveries of capital goods, which in the end makes it impossible for his department to satisfy the requirements of construction sites. Delays were such that 'at the beginning of 1962 *sovnarkhozy* had no allocations of a number of types of equipment and materials (diesels, transformers, cable, etc.) and their delivery in the first quarter was in effect rendered impossible'. He cited an instance in which, on the insistence of the all-Union *Glavkomplekt*, VSNKh was forced to allocate so many transformers to super-priority projects of all-Union significance that it had to cut deliveries to republican priority projects and to reduce sixfold the number of transformers allocated to *sovnarkhozy* for their almost-completed capital work.[3]

It seems very likely that further reforms in the structure of planning will be attempted in the very near future. The patchwork of state committees, VSNKh, *Glavkomplekty*, new territorial planning agencies, plus some *ad hoc* bodies and no doubt also improvised party supervision of priority projects, will have to be reviewed and revised. But how? In Krylov's famous fable, some animals sought to play a quartet, but, wherever they sat, the music was no good. Can any reform based upon so high a

[1] V. Novakovski, *Ekonomicheskaya gazeta*, February 26, 1962, p. 20.
[2] V. Petrov, *ibid.*, p. 22.
[3] M. Bezzabotnov, *ibid.*, April 2, 1962, p. 20.

degree of administrative control of resources produce better results? Will there not always be a considerable degree of inefficiency and waste associated with planning output and supplies in government offices, rather than leaving much more to be settled by direct contract between enterprises? In principle, the desirability of a move in this direction is widely recognized among Soviet economists. But what further changes would be required if enterprise directors are to be given more scope for initiative? Is not price-flexibility an essential part of a solution which is effective? How far would the widespread application of mathematical techniques, and of the prices, real or 'shadow', that go with them, provide a way out? These and many other questions cannot be discussed here. The evidence suggests that the still-rapid advance of Soviet industry is accompanied by alarming symptoms of operational inefficiency, that the enormous and growing complexity of the Soviet economy can no longer be effectively handled by the traditional methods. But there is also evidence that these traditional methods cannot easily be discarded, on grounds of practice as well as of ideology. The point is that piecemeal reform is liable to be self-defeating, as has been shown by the results of attempts at regional devolution of authority in industry and agriculture alike. The answer therefore seems still to be sought in renewed centralization, and it must be surmised that a reorganization of central (and to some extent republican and big-region) planning and supply organs will occur, possibly even by the time this appears in print. Logically a return to economic ministries is probably called for. However, for obvious political reasons they cannot be called ministries. Therefore we should expect a strengthening and reshuffling of Gosplan and the state committees at the centre, with more of the former ministerial power exercised within these bodies, including above all greater central responsibility for supplies (*snab*) and for the production pattern of at least those factories or industries which are of special interest at the all-Union level. One consequence of such selective centralization has already emerged: local planning organs switch productive capacity under their control to what is needed to fulfil priority plans imposed by the centre, and therefore reduce the output of unplanned consumer goods. Thus, despite a decree forbidding just such action, several *sovnarkhozy* have been cutting out production of miscellaneous household goods, toys, chessmen and so on, to the marked inconvenience of the local population.[1]

The more drastic reform, of prices, incentives and planning, which alone would make possible the much-needed genuine decentralization, seems still far away, the more so as the simultaneous pursuit of rapid growth and increased welfare now has to 'compete' with an expanded army programme, which must contribute to strains and shortages.

* * *

The 'reforms in prospect' were in fact promulgated in two slices, in November 1962 and March 1963. The second was in a sense the implementation of the first, but there were some important differences between November and March, a full discussion of which would require another long paper. This short addendum is only intended to draw attention to those major features of the reforms which affect the situation described in the pages above.

The following are the principal institutional changes:

(*a*) *Enlargement of sovnarkhozy*. Their numbers have been reduced to forty-seven. By making *sovnarkhozy* larger, fewer natural economic regions are broken up by administrative boundaries. Whether the new *sovnarkhozy* are to have more or less *power* is far from clear. The fact that their boundaries will hardly ever correspond with those of a Party *obkom* may strengthen them *vis-à-vis* the local party secretaries, but the fact that the party's functions in industry have been widened may mean that the *sovnarkhozy* will be often by-passed. One exceptional feature of the new arrangements is that one *sovnarkhoz*, for Central Asia, will group the four Central Asian republics.

(*b*) *Elimination of 'local' industry*. This has now been wholly placed under the *sovnarkhozy*.

(*c*) *Construction* enterprises are no longer to be even nominally under the *sovnarkhozy*. The reform envisages a new hierarchy of control under, at the top, a strengthened State Committee on Construction (*Gosstroi*). This committee is to play a key role in authorizing (or stopping) investment projects, along with the appropriate state committee and other central planning agencies.

[1] *Pravda*, August 9, 1960, and *Ekonomicheskaya gazeta*, January 22, 1962, p. 45.

(*d*) The number of *industrial state committees* has been further enlarged, and the list now resembles that of the former ministries. The committees are to have more effective control over product design and over investment plans. Most of the committees have ceased to be known as '. . . of the Council of Ministers of the USSR' and are now 'attached to (*pri*) Gosplan' or in some cases to one of the other reorganized co-ordinating bodies (see below). For list see supplement to *Soviet Studies*, April 1964.

(*e*) *Plan co-ordination at the centre* is to involve four reconstructed institutions:

(i) Gosplan, now concerned with perspective planning and the co-ordination of current plans, but without operational powers. (Head: P. Lomako.)

(ii) The USSR Sovnarkhoz, a new body which, as announced in November, was inheriting the operational powers of 'the committee on current affairs of the Council of Ministers'. Its task is to implement plans, and presumably it is in charge of materials allocation at the centre. This reproduces at the all-Union level the division between planning and execution of plans, which worked so badly in the RSFSR. (Head: V. Dymshits.)

(iii) *Gosstroi*, already mentioned. (Head: V. Novikov.)

(iv) The state committee on co-ordination of science. (Head: K. Rudnev.)

(*f*) *Co-ordination of the co-ordinators* is to be through a new body, announced in March 1963, the Supreme Economic Council (VSNKh SSSR), headed by D. Ustinov, with powers to give orders to all other economic planning and administrative bodies. It is not made clear whether this will at least partly supersede the operational powers which, in November, were to be granted to the USSR *sovnarkhoz*. (There may well be some important power-conflict reflected in Ustinov's appointment.) Certain industrial state committees, notably those concerned with armaments are placed directly under VSNKh USSR. Most of the others are attached to Gosplan; those concerned with building are under Gosstroi. Retail trade is under the USSR *sovnarkhoz*.

(*g*) *Republican powers* are supposedly to be considerable. However, the various plan-co-ordination organs are now 'union-republican', which means that (for instance) Gosplan USSR can give direct instructions to Gosplan Ukraine, Gosstroi USSR to the construction chiefs of Georgia, etc., etc. Since resource allocation, especially in the investment field, has been greatly tightened up, and since there is no sign of any serious devolution of authority in materials allocation or production planning, despite pious sentiments about the role and rights of republics as initiators of plan projects, the keynote is centralization.

(*h*) Enforcement of rules and combating breaches of law are prominent among the functions of a new *party-state control* apparatus, under A. N. Shelepin, one-time security chief.

(*i*) *The Party's* role in industrial planning and administration is to increase. The party is divided into industrial (including construction and transport) and agricultural sections at all levels; only at the very top is there to be an effective all-party all-purpose presidium (in republics there are to be presidia, but they are enjoined not to interfere with the separate industrial and agricultural bureaux). However, the functions of provincial party officials are adversely affected by increased centralization (e.g. of investment), and also by the fact that each of the new *sovnarkhozy* usually covers the 'empires' of several industrial *obkom* secretaries. It could well be that the reform was intended to weaken 'localism', which provincial party secretaries supported or even represented.

On balance, the new proposals are of a centralizing character. In so far as investment is concerned, the battle against 'spreading' (*raspylenie*) of resources has been much intensified, but the consequences will surely be that orders will go out to stop 'non-priority' projects for which the necessary labour and materials happen to be available, and one can foresee many kinds of unnecessary losses. Other headaches of general co-ordination, which arise essentially out of the multiplicity of interconnected instruction-issuing from (necessarily) different offices, can hardly be cured by the latest measures. They could perhaps prove a stopgap only, designed to minimize confusion until the authorities decide on much more fundamental changes. We can therefore say: 'more reforms in prospect'.

7. Principal problems of Soviet planning*

Some years ago a distinguished participant in our discussions wrote a book entitled *The Soviet Economy at the Crossroads*. The Soviet economy is at the crossroads still, and an increasing proportion of Soviet economists are publicly expressing their awareness of this fact. Of course, this is no criticism of Professor Boettcher. Crossroads in history take many years to traverse. This one will be with us for quite a time yet.

This paper will avoid discussing organization as such, as this is being dealt with by another contributor. However, there is an intimate connection between organizational questions and planning problems, so that in a sense we will be discussing different aspects of the same general and basic problem: how to achieve greater efficiency in resource allocation.

It may be desirable to begin with the following question: Is there in fact a new stage, a new crossroads, in Soviet planning? Or is it simply that problems which have existed for many years are now more freely discussed? If there is a change, is it merely one of degree? And what is the basic cause of change? It is useful to begin by considering such matters, since such consideration will help to put the present situation into proper perspective.

Clearly, no one can deny that most of the problems which are now agitating Soviet economists have existed since the early days of the planning era. Misallocation of resources by planners, misleading success indicators at enterprise level, inconsistency of planning instructions, illogical prices, all these existed to a greater or lesser extent. What then distinguishes the present situation from that of, for example, 1936?

Certainly the Stalin terror atmosphere and the resultant censorship and timidity did have the effect of suppressing much of the debate among Soviet economists. We must certainly not forget

* Paper presented at conference on Soviet economy, Free University of Berlin, March, 1963.

that many of the ideas which are now being so vigorously discussed were originally put forward when Stalin was still on the throne, but were suppressed or ignored. Nonetheless, there were some weighty reasons why weak spots in the economy were regarded as tolerable, or were at least tolerated, until recent years. The following points seem to be relevant to any explanation:

1. The greater complexity of planning, arising simply from the greater size and complexity of the economy.

2. The greater complexity of planning arising from the dilution of priorities. This dilution may well be a consequence of the end of the Stalin terror. It is no longer possible to disregard the needs of the formerly expendable sectors of the economy. Yet, the Stalin material-balance methods required, to be workable, the enforcement of a few over-riding priorities. (Western war economies functioned because of the over-riding priority of the war effort, but the same methods could not possibly work under normal conditions.) The greater importance of agriculture, housing and consumer welfare has greatly complicated the task of planning.

3. Many authors have noted the similarity of the early stages of an industrialization programme and a military operation. One sees this point in books about economic development in non-Soviet countries too. Higgins makes it in many words. Hirschman speaks of a development strategy, Lange of a *sui generis* war economy, Stalin of 'fronts' and 'campaigns'. One recalls the old argument about 'genetic and teleological planning'. Choosing the second of these, i.e. choosing to alter rather than reflect existing economic forces and proportions, involved a disregard for criteria of efficient allocation. It was a kind of economy to which so-called rational economic principles appeared inapplicable, in that same sense in which these principles were not applied to the war economies of Great Britain or Germany. But the achievements of Soviet industrialization have removed most of the economic and some of the political justification of the old methods. Perhaps it is worth recalling Hirschman's phrase: 'It is the experience of unbalanced growth in the past that produced, in an advanced state of economic development, the possibility of balanced growth.'[1]

[1] *The Strategy of Economic Development*, p. 93.

4. Certain factors of production, notably labour, have become more scarce. This point was greatly stressed by Boettcher, and also in the past by the author of this paper. On reflection I feel that it is not in itself a vital point. Scarce in relation to what? In relation to the more varied needs which the Soviet system must satisfy. If one must pursue simultaneously rapid growth of heavy industry, agricultural expansion, a big housing programme, the nuclear arms race, external economic aid, etc., one becomes very conscious of the relative scarcity of resources. Greater efficiency in the use of resources, including labour, becomes essential. This is another way of saying that the increasing importance of non-priority sectors has added to the opportunity-cost (in terms of planners' preferences) of inefficiency in general and inefficiency in the use of labour in particular.

Anyhow, for all the above reasons, as well as because of greater freedom of expression for economists, the problems of the Soviet planning systems are being actively and publicly discussed in the Soviet Union. A great change has taken place in the entire atmosphere surrounding the economics profession. Presumably the participants of the present conference are aware of the general nature of the discussions. I conceive it to be my task to arrange some major problems in rough categories, and also to express some views about the practical possibilities and consequences of possible reforms.

A key problem beyond doubt is centralization and decentralization. This has many inter-related aspects. There is the whole question of the burden of detailed work at the centre, with consequent delays and confusions. This raises the question of the possible use of econometrics, linear programming, input-output, as a means both for reducing the burden of work and improving the economic quality of decisions. All this becomes intimately connected with the nature and role of prices, with the role of profit and other criteria at local level, and with the relative importance of administrative instructions and economic incentives in the functioning of the system. There is also the important organizational-political question of the relationship between the Party and the state hierarchy, but this is outside the scope of the present paper.

One point which is often overlooked should be made at the

start. Generalizations about the Soviet economy tend to leave out of account important differences which arise in the applicability of given planning methods in different sectors of the economy. Yet this is a vital question. Methods that can work quite well in one sphere may be totally unsuitable in another. Let us take two examples: electricity and textiles. Electricity is a homogeneous product, measured in kWh. Its output is thus easy to plan. Its distribution can be centrally organized, to the extent to which the power stations are interconnected in a centrally-controllable network. Inputs are few and predictable. Future needs, on which investment can be based, are forecastable with only a moderate margin of error. Of course there are inefficiencies in Soviet electricity generation, but these are generally the result of insufficient investment (e.g. in materials handling equipment), or simply insufficient capacity (e.g. to supply rural areas). They do not arise from the nature of the planning system. It is hardly an accident that electricity is in fact nationalized in a number of Western countries. When, for instance in Great Britain, there were a large number of competing electricity undertakings, this fact was never used to advertise the superior virtues of competitive private enterprise.

At the other end of the scale are textiles. The variety of possible output is immense. Each enterprise can produce a wide assortment of commodities. There are complicated relationships with wholesalers and retailers which do or should reflect unpredictable changes in consumer tastes. Inputs are also highly variable, depending on the chosen product mix. For the central planners to decide just what should be produced would require immense labour, and in the end their decisions may prove unenforceable. The author of this paper has had some practical experience of controls in the field of textiles, when he worked in the British Board of Trade just after the war, and is acutely aware of the difficulties.

It is impossible to conceive of some one optimum planning technique equally applicable to electricity and to textiles. From this point of view some industries are of the electricity type, other of the textile type, and there are some in between. One should not confuse this distinction with that between producers' goods and consumers' goods. Some consumers' goods, for instance bread, may be as 'plannable' as steel. By contrast, chemicals, many kinds of agricultural machinery, and also instruments, though producers' goods, are greatly varied in type and so may resemble textiles rather than electricity. For example, Khrushchev has told us that there are 125,000 varieties of machinery and tools in production at present.

In practice, efficiency in planning depends also on priorities. Given a constant degree of 'plannability', a high priority industry will generally be better planned. It will have more attention given to it by more qualified officials and managers. No one doubts the ability of the Soviet system to concentrate resources so as to produce efficiently any item, however complicated, which the central authorities judge to be particularly important. We can all think of examples of this. Nonetheless, the distinction between different sectors by reason of their being more or less amenable to central planning remains relevant, and we will return to it several times in the subsequent discussion.

It is also necessary to be clear about the nature of the task which is being performed. Some commentators, in the West and East, discuss the computer without making it clear what it is being used for. There is, to begin with, the task of making up consistent plans for future years, of working out the consequences of alternative central objectives, and doing it quickly. For this purpose the computer can indeed be brought into play along with input-output and linear programming techniques. Such techniques would be superior to the present system of material balances. It would be of great help to planners to have, for instance, an input-output table of 350 items, and much work has, in fact, been devoted to the creation of such a table. Among the many obstacles was the fact that statistical information currently available did not fit the purpose of the table, and so a sample survey had to be carried out. It is particularly important that the new techniques save time. Notoriously, Soviet plans tend to be prepared late, which causes major inconveniences and loss at operating levels. Shortage of time also frequently prevents the full working out of the consequences of 'current' decisions affecting the production or use of resources, or of changes in the plan, a fact which frequently contributes to stresses and strains in the economy. Indisputably the computer will help, and it is not surprising that a great deal of attention is now being devoted by Soviet planners to its potential uses. The surprising thing is that it took so long for them to get down to this job. No doubt the intellectual atmosphere of Stalinism was responsible.

But it is much less clear how the computer will solve the problems of centralized resource allocation, if this remains as centralized as it is at present, or how it will provide a basis for a rational set of operating prices. There is danger of being guilty of simplifying the problem, when the very essence of the problem is its complexity.

The all-Union Gosplan at present plans output and distribution of about 19,000 commodities. Since the reform announced in 1962, the task is presumably transferred to the new all-Union Sovnarkhoz, but this does not alter the situation. Needless to say, the total number of commodities planned at all levels is vastly in excess of 19,000, and, in addition, many of the planned designations contain within themselves a number of variants. There are even more items or sub-items capable of being produced if a decision to produce is made somewhere. At present, the planners are responsible not only for the production plans of thousands of enterprises but also for the supplies of many thousands of inputs and their distribution to these thousands of enterprises. These multiple millions of inter-connections grow with the size of the economy. The sheer volume of work causes it to be divided between different offices, and the various planning offices find themselves out of line with one another, and this leads to the issuing of inconsistent sets of instructions, which, by the time they reach the factory, fail to match one another. The result, as seen from the enterprise, may be illustrated by the following quotation from an article in *Pravda* by a factory director: 'The department of Gosplan which drafts the production programme for Sovnarkhozy and enterprises is totally uninterested in costs or profits. Ask the senior official in the production programme department in what factory it is cheaper to produce this or that commodity? He has no idea, and never even puts the question to himself. He is responsible only for the distribution of production tasks. Another department, not really concerned with the costs of production, decides the plan for gross output. A third department or sub-department, proceeding from the principle that costs must always decline and labour productivity increase, plans costs, wages, fund and labour on the basis of past performance. Material allocations and components are planned by numerous other departments. Not a single department of Gosplan is responsible for the consistency of these plans.'[1]

What is the relevance to these kinds of problems of a 350 × 350 input-output table, however brilliantly designed? Yet, given the present degree of centralization and the reliance on instructions as the basis of enterprise activity, these are essential aspects of the planning system.

The same is to some extent true of the relationship between the computer and price formation. In choosing between alternatives, the planners should certainly be guided by prices which reflect the scarcity of resources by reference to the objectives of the plan. An increasing body of opinion among Soviet economists recognizes this. The resistance of dogmatic ideologists, with their simplified arguments based on a misunderstanding of the Marxist theory of value, should not stand in the way of reform, provided that the practical usefulness of the new techniques is demonstrated. There is gradually developing 'the theory of planning prices'. These prices may remain shadow prices, or may be actually used in transactions, it does not matter which at the present stage of our discussion. I only want to raise one question at this point. What practical application can we imagine these prices to have? It may well be found that they will be valuable at the macro-economic level, at which planners discuss alternative patterns of development in general terms. At the level of aggregation which these techniques require, this may still be an effective way of using them. Their use in planning practice may be considerable in the case of commodities of the electricity type. But those analysts who see the task in terms of a model consisting of a small number of homogenuous commodities, simplify what is really an extremely complicated problem. How does such a price apply to the determination of a product mix? A shadow price may exist for, say, tractors or furniture. But no one buys just 'tractors' or 'furniture', no one produces such items in general. People buy or produce, for instance, a Belarus wheeled tractor with certain attachments and so on. It is no easier to use a centrally operated computer to price such items than it is to plan their output or the supplies necessary for their production. Again we return to the essential question of the conversion of centrally

[1] I. Borovitski, *Pravda*, October 5, 1962.

determined objectives into innumerable pieces of micro-economic reality.

One should not overlook the fundamental problem of defining what the objectives of the planners are. Hitherto, Soviet political leaders have been in the habit of affixing high political priority to the output of certain basic materials, i.e. to intermediate goods, rather than deriving the need for intermediate goods from the pattern of final output. No doubt, the official targets for steel, cement, fuel, and so on, were not taken out of the blue, they must have been in some degree related to potential use. However, the planners did not, in fact, start from a final bill of goods and work backwards to discover how much steel or fuel would be needed. In fact, the political priority of producers' goods over consumer goods was reflected in the priority of targets for raw materials, intermediate goods in general, machinery, and so on. Nemchinov has argued that this is all wrong, that it is a cause of serious waste, that central planners should plan final output, and that the operating units of the economy should then make contracts for the purchase of the required inputs. The output of intermediate goods would therefore become determined by the demands of enterprises, which would be interested in minimizing the cost of inputs. This is linked with the idea of eliminating the administrative system of material allocation, an essential decentralizing measure[1] (of which more below). The increasingly influential school of Soviet mathematical economists urge the use of mathematical techniques to discover optimum routes to the achievement of given goals. The search for such optima is impeded by the traditional method of planning by material balances. For example, if to achieve given objectives it is rational to substitute synthetics for metals, this cannot be discovered by officials busily engaged in making separate material balances for steel and for chemicals, in strictly quantitative terms. A similar objection can be made against the static input-output model. However, linear programming techniques could be used, within some limits, to find minimum-cost solutions, i.e. to identify the most economic of sets of alternative means to a given end.

All this sounds very promising as a model. However, in order for it to work one must define what the objectives are. What is being maximized? How can the parameters be defined? Some

[1] V. Nemchinov, *Pravda*, September 21, 1962.

analysts cite examples of successful application of computer techniques in private industry in the West. Examples do exist, for instance, in the oil industry and in shipbuilding. However, the objectives could be clearly defined and fed into the computer. In the case of the entire Soviet Union, one suspects that the objectives would either be too vague (e.g. maximizing the national income), or so precise as to prejudge the important issues. Even the finding of an optimizing pattern of material inputs to achieve given outputs may be impeded by the linearity of linear programming, i.e. by the assumption within particular processes of fixed technical coefficients. There is, it is true, talk of more advanced dynamic models of a non-linear kind. They may one day come, but do not yet exist. None of this is intended to deny that the computer will help the planners to do quickly and more accurately many of the things which they do much less well. It will certainly be an advantage to be able to present to political authority a number of alternative consistent patterns of development, among which the politicians can then exercise choice. There is real danger in regarding mathematical economics as a kind of panacea. However, we should remember that there exists in the Soviet Union a number of brilliant mathematicians and that there is great interest in devising new means of applying mathematics to the solution of problems of Soviet planning. We may, therefore, see in the near future substantial advances toward the condition which Peter Wiles has so aptly called 'perfect computation'.

However, the principal advocates of programming techniques are not concerned with using the computers to preserve the present degree of centralization. They advocate the preservation of central control over essentials, but urge a wide degree of freedom of decision-making for enterprises, based on more rational efficiency prices within a new system of optimization. We will now turn to a brief discussion of the practicability of such decentralization in the context of Soviet economy.

Soviet planners, economists and the political leadership are all well aware of the fact that there would be great advantage in giving greater initiative to the men on the spot, while freeing them from excessively detailed supervision. Statements to this effect have been made repeatedly. There is no need to doubt the genuineness of the intentions behind the 1955 decree enlarging the rights of directors, or the 1957 reforms, which granted on paper substantial powers to territorial authorities. However, little in fact changed in practice. At a recent conference it was sadly observed that 'restrictions on rights of directors were particularly intensified in the most recent period. Many amendments by many institutions had the practical effect of negating the direct and clear instructions of the Soviet Government in the well-known decree enlarging the rights of directors.'[1] The same trend towards recentralization followed the 1957 reform. The following quotation tells its own story: 'The *sovnarkhoz* is the basic organ for governing industry. And yet the Estonian *sovnarkhoz* is permitted to plan independently seventeen commodity designations. This represents 0.2 per cent of the total volume of output. All the rest is dictated by the USSR *Gosplan*. This characterizes the operational independence of the *sovnarkhoz*. It is not in a position to change anything.'[2]

The cause of these apparent moves back towards centralization is not, in my view, due to any special desire of the top party leadership to have everything decided in Moscow (although it is certainly true that the top leadership has on occasion interfered in matters of detail, and still does so). The essence of the trouble is the lack of objective criteria for local decision making, so that, with the available incentives, the men on the spot are hardly able to choose right. This is particularly obvious in the case of the *sovnarkhoz*. Almost any industrial enterprise under its nominal control draws some of its inputs from outside its area, while its output constitutes the input of numerous other enterprises in various parts of the country. The more powers are given to a territorial organ, the more likely it is to divert resources to local needs, to the detriment of outsiders, and thereby cause damage to the national economy as a whole. It therefore followed logically that, as part of its campaign against 'localism', the centre should restrict the range of permitted choice and should plan outputs and inputs of all important commodities, issuing instructions to enterprises about what to produce and to whom to deliver it. In order to carry out these tasks after the abolition of the industrial ministries, the various central and republican planning organs had to divide themselves into a number of dif-

[1] *Ekonomicheskaya gazeta*, January 5, 1962, p. 12.
[2] *Ibid.*, November 10, 1962, p. 8.

ferent offices, with the consequence, as has already been pointed out, that the instructions they issue are frequently inconsistent with one another. The relative powerlessness of the *sovnarkhoz* has meant that enterprises as such have no clear line of subordination. All this has put many enterprises in a difficult situation. As might be supposed, the difficulties have been very much greater in enterprises of the textile type than in those of the electricity type.

Choice at the enterprise level is necessarily limited by the fact that instructions (i.e. plans passed down from above, which must be fulfilled or overfilled) were and are the dominant criterion of enterprise activity. This system of instructions is a consequence of planning by material balances, of quantitative planning designed to maximize growth, while expressing administrative priorities. Prices were and are irrational, in the sense of not being determined with the object of calling forth the desired pattern of output. Indeed, it has been customary to deny to prices any allocative function. In these circumstances, the absence of sufficiently detailed instructions has tended to lead to a wrong pattern of production, while, except in the case of electricity-type industries, it is physically impossible for the central planners to issue instructions which are detailed, consistent and unambiguous.

In my view, territorial decentralization must lead to undesirable forms of autarky, and that consequently the only effective line of workable decentralization is to grant greater decision-making powers to enterprises, though in certain cases the smaller enterprises might have to be grouped for purposes of commercial decision. It is interesting to note that in a number of areas experiments of grouping enterprises into so-called 'firms', under a general director, are currently in progress. The undesirable effects of the present system, in stimulating the wrong kinds of initiative at enterprise level or failing to stimulate any initiative at all, while in effect rewarding concealment of productive potential, are too well known to require comment here. There is a wide concensus among Soviet planners and economists about the need for reform. The only problem is one of finding an effective solution. How are enterprises to be encouraged to aim high, to utilize their resources to the full, to seek to make better products, to provide the goods which their customers want, and at the same time act in accordance with the general intentions of the central planners?

How can one ensure that, in Liberman's phrase, 'What is in the interests of society shall be in the interests of the enterprise.'? If a solution of this problem can be found, the resulting devolution of decision-making powers to enterprise level would relieve the centre of a mass of detailed work, thereby simultaneously solving another major problem of present-day Soviet planning.

The most discussed reform project is, of course, associated with the name of Liberman. Presumably the participants are acquainted with his proposals. They have been vigorously discussed in the Soviet Union, and the argument continues. It is a most encouraging fact that the debate has been concerned very little with ideology, has been conducted in a business-like and open way, with genuine differences of opinion publicly aired. A comparison with the content of Soviet economic journals ten years ago should convince even the most sceptical observer that something has happened in Soviet intellectual life since the death of Stalin. The discussions have brought forth a number of comments and objections to Liberman, and the study of the debates can greatly add to our understanding of the real problems which face a centralized economy of the Soviet type. It is hard to know where to begin, but the following are some thoughts which these discussions have raised in my mind:

1. Who should decide just what particular enterprises should produce? Liberman is vague on this point and has been interpreted in a number of different ways. Thus Zverev, the former Minister of Finance, who is a strong opponent of the proposals, has argued that since the planners would determine the volume of production, the assortment of output, the suppliers of inputs and the consumers of the product, the proposed reform would not stimulate any widespread initiative anyway.[1] What Liberman apparently has in mind, judging from some of his contributions to discussions, is that the higher authorities should confirm output, assortment and delivery plans, but that these plans should be based on the proposals put forward by the enterprise itself, and these in turn should be based on contracts negotiated. The enterprises incentive bonus, calculated as a share in profits (the latter being expressed as a percentage of capital), would then be conditional on fulfilling these confirmed plans. But what would

[1] *Voprosy ekonomiki*, No. 11, 1962, p. 93.

happen in practice? Would not centrally determined output objectives be in fact passed down in detail until they reach the enterprise in the form of orders? (Administrative orders, not commercial orders!) It is not clear to me, any more than it was clear to many of the Soviet participants of the discussions, just what would happen.

2. Nemchinov has gone further, and has argued for the elimination of administrative allocation of inputs, urging the substitution of free purchase. He has argued, not without reason, that quantitative plans for the output and distribution of intermediate products lead to waste and to endless bureaucratic complications. The state, in his view, should plan final output. It would follow that the production plans of enterprises making intermediate goods would be determined by the orders placed by other enterprises in the process of carrying out the state's plan for final outputs. Nemchinov envisages the central planning organs as playing a major role in placing commercial orders for the goods they want, while enterprises competed among themselves to obtain orders. Among other things, this would enable the state to choose the cheapest producer. All this would represent a major change in the present system. Not only would allocation be largely replaced by commercial relations between enterprises, but, as already pointed out, some of the state's traditional priority targets would cease to be planned as such. Nemchinov also strongly advocated making a capital charge a part of costs. It is not at all clear how far Liberman supports Nemchinov's views. Would he favour the retention of the materials allocation system? Judging from some of his past articles, probably not. Presumably he is finding it diplomatic not to be quite frank at this time.

3. For a number of excellent reasons, Liberman would leave the enterprise free to make its own wages, costs, profits and labour plans, and a considerable part of the total investment in the country would be financed out of enterprise profits which would be retained in the incentive fund he proposes. Yet he also advocates that there should be national plans for these items, as indeed there clearly must be. These plans should be sent down as far as the economic regions, but apparently no lower. But what would happen if the independently concocted plans under these various heads are inconsistent with central intentions, or with

available resources? It would be miraculous if it all added up right.

There well may be something in the fears of cautious officials, like Zverev, to the effect that the planning principle itself would be threatened. For example, such vital items as the total wages bill, budgetary revenue from profits and turnover tax, and above all the investment programme, would become in some significant part the consequence of a very large number of essentially decentralized and uncontrollable decisions. Hence his cry of distress at one of the discussions: 'Planning is one of the main achievements of the October revolution. Why abandon planning?'[1] Another cautious ex-official, Plotnikov, now Head of the Institute of Economics of the Academy of Sciences, particularly stressed the importance of centralized control over investment. And indeed already now the economy suffers from an excessive number of investment projects, which result in the freezing of substantial resources in unfinished construction. Tighter central control seems to him the only way out, otherwise confusion would get worse. In Liberman's proposals the profits plan is drafted by the enterprise itself, the size of its retained profits would depend on performance, and so the central planners who will still be responsible for the essential 'proportions' of the economy will in fact be unable accurately to forecast, let alone control, one of these proportions. These objections may not appear convincing to one who is drawing up a static model of a Soviet type economy, but they do have some basis in the context of an extremely ambitious programme of economic growth, with full commitment of resources and therefore some stresses and strains. It will be much harder for the centre to prevent resources from moving in directions which it regards as undesirable or of a low degree of priority.

4. Liberman and all other reformers strongly favour a more rational price system. Indeed, irrational prices could and would confuse any conceivable solution to Soviet planning problems. Discussions on prices and the law of value have gone on for years among Soviet economists, and there is not the time and the space to trace the various arguments here. I will confine myself to noting the logic, in respect of prices, of the Liberman proposals. It is self-evident that the use of profitability as the dominant criteria for enterprise activity presents the price system

[1] A. Zverev, *Ekonomicheskaya gazeta*, October 13, 1962, p. 6.

with qualitatively new tasks. So long as it is imagined that allocation, largely in physical terms, is a matter for the administrative authorities, it could be argued that prices have essentially the role of facilitating accounting and checking. This is the role granted to prices within the state sector by Stalin, when he denied the applicability of the law of value to transactions within the state sector. It is true that Stalin has been dead for ten years and that this particular theory of his has been dropped. Nonetheless the practice of price formation has changed little since his day. The Liberman plan, by substantially enlarging the range of choice at enterprise level and basing this choice so largely on the profit motive, requires prices to reflect in some significant respect both relative scarcity and relative need. The econometricians have argued, as we have seen, that prices which emerge from a programming exercise would have these necessary characteristics. However, as we have also seen, it is not so easy to envisage how programmed prices of this kind can be applied within the micro-world of enterprises producing a wide assortment of products. It may not be coincidental that Liberman does not in fact refer to the econometricians. (Nemchinov does do so.) Liberman states that he believes that prices should be fixed by the state, and indeed that this should be one of the principal ways in which the central planners would guide the economy. He also says that prices should be flexible. Flexibility is necessary, in his view and in reality, so that the input-purchasing enterprise can persuade its supplier to make the type of goods it needs of the required quality, and reward it for doing so. How can this work in practice without the evasion of central price control and, therefore, the establishment of a sizable free market? Again one must distinguish between types of products in this connection. As we know from Western experience, prices of electricity, steel, cement, can be controlled by the state or by monopolists without undue administrative headaches. But what about textiles? What about the 125,000 items of machinery and equipment? It is not suggested that this, or indeed any other, problems are insoluble, merely that the solution is not indicated by the author of the proposals.

5. Liberman and other Soviet reformers have had much to say about the powers of enterprises. They have been oddly unwilling to distinguish for this purpose between different kinds of activity.

It is clear that an electric generating station, in the Soviet Union as well as in France, receives precise instructions from headquarters when to switch on its generating plant, and the plant management is basically uninfluenced by the greater or lesser profitability of the operations of that particular plant. Many Soviet enterprises, and not only in electricity, are essentially plants within interconnected industrial processes. To many of them precise quantitative instructions apply and ought to apply. This happens in various degrees to productive units within vertically integrated firms in the West. This leads directly to another point. In the West firms become linked with one another by interlocking financial arrangements, are purchased by one another, go bankrupt and out of business. In those branches of the economy in which specialization in large units (either large physically or large units of control) is advantageous, consolidation and specialization takes place in ways which cannot operate in the Soviet system. Or rather, they can only operate in the Soviet system if the central authorities issue appropriate instructions. For example, the First state ball bearing factory of Moscow cannot purchase the Second state ball bearing factory. The dozens of inefficient small furniture factories scattered about the country cannot be driven out of business by the competition of more efficient factories. The effect of all this varies greatly in different sectors of the economy, but it is not out of place to note that Khrushchev, in his speech to the November plenary session of the central committee, spoke at some length on the failure of Soviet industry to specialize and standardize. He contrasted this with the achievements in this direction of Western capitalist countries. He mentioned, for instance, how all office furniture in Italy is made by one firm. No one who has studied Soviet industrial operations can doubt that Khrushchev is perfectly correct. There is ample scope for large scale economies in this direction. However, these are by definition beyond the powers of isolated enterprises to achieve, however perfect the incentive schemes under which they work, without the interference of higher authority.

6. Objections have been taken to some of the detailed content of Liberman's proposals, concerning the retained profits of enterprises, i.e. the incentive fund. Some of these objections relate not to (easily correctable) details but to the essence of the scheme. For example, Liberman advocates a tapering scale of deductions

to the incentive fund, so that, for instance, a doubling of the profit would lead to a proportionately much smaller increase in the fund. At the same time enterprises with larger capital will be entitled to a larger deduction to the fund at a given rate of profit. It would, therefore, sometimes pay enterprises to try and acquire additional capital, even though the percentage rate of profit would fall. (Oddly enough, another critic made the opposite point, that some enterprises would refuse to invest in case it led to a reduction in their profit percentage; but this second critic could not have done his arithmetic correctly.[1]) This sort of manoeuvring may be irrational. However, tapering is essential if high profits are not to be over-rewarded. Liberman claims that undeserved rewards to high profit sectors will be avoided by differentiating the rules under which they can transfer profits to the incentive fund. However, within each sector there is at present a very wide range of profits, and losses, and so one could make a case from making different rules for each enterprise. This, as Zverev duly pointed out, would be appallingly complicated and lead to abuse. Yet not to do so would mean rewarding enterprises who happen to be in a favourable situation or have more than their share of modern machinery. Still another objection concerns Liberman's ingenious idea of persuading enterprises to bid high, by penalizing a low profit plan which is overfulfilled, compared with a high profit plan that is underfulfilled. Since the profits in question are to be part of a general plan covering the entire activity of the enterprise, there is danger here of encouraging a tendency to over-optimism, which can mislead the planners. One has only to study the intelligent criticism put forward by Gatovski to see that there are indeed some cogent objections, of a non-political and non-ideological kind, to be made against some of these ideas.[2]

Several years ago, in a talk on the BBC Third Programme, Professor E. Devons contrasted the macro-order with the micro-confusion of Soviet planning, remarking that in the West we have the contrary: micro-order and macro-confusion. One way of expressing the decentralization problem in a Soviet context is this; how can one have macro-order, directed towards rapid growth and with full employment of resources, without issuing adminis-

[1] Kasitski, *Voprosy ekonomiki*, No. 11, 1962, p. 89.
[2] *Voprosy ekonomiki*, No. 11, 1962, p. 134ff.

trative orders to the enterprises which form the micro world of the Soviet economy? If the plans are to be genuinely built up from below, thus releasing the initiative of management and curing many micro problems, will the result add up to a consistent pattern, and will this pattern conform to the preferences of the central planners? Can the necessary signals be transmitted through price control and similar economic measures? These questions are, I feel sure, genuinely in the minds of many Soviet economists and planners, because these are genuinely difficult problems. Great efforts are being made to devise new planning techniques, and Liberman's ideas are being tested as well as discussed. A search continues for means of identifying, measuring and rewarding 'national-economic effectiveness' — as distinct from quantitative plan fulfilment.

But, meanwhile, no agreed recommendations are reaching the higher political authorities. Immediate troubles call for immediate remedies, and the unexpected rise in military expenditures has added to the strains under which the economy is labouring. Investment resources are acutely scarce, and consumer welfare is below planned levels, as may be seen from the postponement of promised cuts in income tax and the adverse movement in the pay of many collectivized peasants. Faced with administrative weaknesses and scarcity of resources, Khrushchev has reacted by imposing tighter central controls, and by mobilizing the Communist party organizations, turning their 'faces to production', while weakening their purely local links by splitting the local party (this is probably part of the struggle against 'localism'). This by no means excludes a subsequent move towards 'Liberman-type' solutions; certainly the November 1962 reforms are not a solution at all.

There are many other problems which could be discussed in detail; investment criteria, price theory, land rent, and much else besides. However, the scarce factor Time—and the limited patience of the readers—constitutes a powerful and rational reason for stopping at this point.

III. AGRICULTURE

8. *The peasants in Soviet literature since Stalin*

'Writers appeared to compete among themselves: who will most smoothly and artificially show the evolution of a *Kolkhoz* from incomplete happiness to ultimate perfection.' Thus in 1954 F. Abramov[1] castigated the literature about the peasants which appeared in the last years of Stalin's life. There were few exceptions. Nikolaeva's *Zhatva* ('Harvest') did touch on reality,[2] and Valentin Ovechkin's *Rayonnye Budni* ('A working day in the district'), which appeared in *Novyi Mir* in September 1952, was surprisingly hard-hitting. But these exceptions merely proved the rule. There developed a staggering contrast between the deplorable state of agriculture and the sunshine stories insisted upon by the Soviet literary censors, and even more between peasant attitudes as they really were and as they were portrayed in print. Consequently the history of the post-Stalin period is one in which more and more of the disagreeable reality found its way into literature, i.e. there was a closer relationship between literature and the truth. Reality itself was, of course, changing, and on balance the change has been for the better. Few can doubt that the Soviet peasant is, on average, significantly better off in 1963 than in 1953. By contrast, literature has become much more sharply critical, refers in vigorous language to all kinds of abuses. A warning is therefore necessary against treating the increase in critical material as 'proof' that there is also an increase in evils which are criticized. In Soviet conditions there is often a reverse correlation: criticism in print means that action is being taken with a view to correcting the defects complained of. For instance, there was hardly a mention of bad housing conditions in the last

[1] 'The Kolkhoz Peasants in Postwar Prose', *Novyi Mir*, April, 1954.

[2] Nikolaeva later bitterly complained that the censors cut out most of her critical passages.

years of Stalin's life (in fact, the dictator announced, in 1948, that there were no slums in Moscow!). It was after the launching of a major house-building programme that frankness on this issue was permitted. Then, overlaying all such considerations, there have been ups and downs (mostly ups) in the amount of literary freedom allowed to writers and editors in general, and of course this factor has helped those Russian writers who have longed to give expression in their works to real thoughts, grievances, living conditions, of the peasant population.

In analysing literary works on the village, one must distinguish between those who identify themselves with rural officialdom, and those who try to express the peasants' attitudes, who see things from a peasant point of view. Among the first category one finds Valentin Ovechkin, who, while not unmindful of peasant interest, is concerned most of all with the image of the rural party secretary and his method of work. In the course of this he pulls no punches, both in denouncing the bullying ignoramuses who so often carried out the party's policies in the village, and in criticizing the bureaucratic methods of the authorities. Here is an extract from one of his stories which was reprinted in *Pravda* (January 9, 1954), and which says much about '*Kolkhoz* democracy' and the 'election' of chairmen. 'It was usually the case that, at the end of December, before the election meetings in *kolkhozy*, the local party or soviet secretary received a telephone call from the provincial authorities: "In this round of elections you are authorized to replace three *kolkhoz* chairmen." If local officials objected, saying "But what are we to do about the weak chairmen in other *kolkhozy*?" the answer was: "No hurry, friends; remember the sowing and harvest campaigns lie ahead." That is to say, a "reserve" of inefficient chairmen were deliberately left in office; thus there will be a "quota" to dismiss in punishment for the breakdown of the sowing or harvest campaigns or the grain procurement plan.' Later in the same article, the story is told of how the peasants dared to turn down an unsuitable and unpopular party nominee for the chairmanship; the local *prokuror* were thereupon reprimanded for 'his inability to execute the decisions of the party committee . . .'. He also reported in another story on an official who found there was time for only one spring ploughing, since the spring had come very late that year; he was prosecuted for criminal disobedience, since the regulations specified two ploughings. Luckily the local *prokuror* was dilatory, the harvest proved to be excellent and it was found expedient to drop the case.[1] Ovechkin several times returned to the charge, convinced that the peasants as well as the local management were unfairly treated. There have been rumours, of unknown reliability, that he has run into trouble. He has certainly been silent for some years now.

A more 'official' critic of village life is I. Vinnichenko. His vigorous denunciation of certain abuses arising from the far from peaceful coexistence between *Kolkhozy* and Machine Tractor Stations[2] was shortly afterwards followed by the abolition of the latter. It seems reasonable to regard his literary sketches as part of the preparation of the reform. The peasants as such played very little role in his work. But Vinnichenko is rather exceptional. Most other writers, while on occasion reflecting certain official policies, or compelled to keep silent about some sensitive matter, have in no sense been any politician's stalking horses. To their credit and honour, they have spoken up about matters which aroused their genuine indignation, thereby performing that duty of a writer *and* a citizen which is part of the Russian literary tradition.

The first to talk openly about specifically peasant grievances was Pomerantsev, in his essay on 'Sincerity in literature', published in *Novyi Mir* as early as December 1953. While not confining his attention to rural problems, Pomerantsev drew attention to the black spots in village life which urgently required frank discussion. He emphasized the importance of the peasant private plot, the harm done to the peasants (and to output) by Stalin's policy of penal taxation, and the understandable unwillingness of the peasant to work for the collective for little reward. Thus the peasants watched the collective potatoes go under the snow while they took their private vegetables to market. A desperate official mobilized clerks and secretaries to lift the potatoes, with little result. In the end he called the peasants together and said: 'If you get going on these potatoes, for every three sacks you can keep one.' This saved the harvest, but the official was reprimanded for 'pandering to the private-property

[1] *Pravda*, August 15, 1954.
[2] *Oktyabr*, November-December, 1957.

instincts of the peasants'. (The patient reader will discover that such things were still happening nine years later.)

Pomerantsev was attacked by the official press in June 1954, and so was Abramov for (*inter alia*) the sentiments which may be found in the first sentence of the present paper. This induced a temporary caution, and some writers deserved the caustic comment of Gennadi Fish, who collaborated with Ovechkin: 'Sharp conflicts are confined to the period before the party plenum of September 1953, after which we have the blissful silence of paradise.'[1]

The silence did not last. The whole issue of *Novyi Mir* in which Fish's remarks appeared was devoted to village problems and helped to break it. The destalinization of 1956 speeded up the process. A particularly significant milestone was the famous second issue of the almanack, *Literaturnaya Moskva*, which appeared at the end of that year. Several outstanding contributions concerned the real feelings of real inhabitants of the Soviet village. There was a long and thorough examination of the situation of a community in the Yaroslavl province by Efim Dorosh, which pulled no punches in its analysis of what peasants actually think and how the rules and regulations affect their interests (*Derevenskii dnevnik*). Yashin's short story *Rychagi* ('Levers') described the normal, human and strongly critical behaviour of a small group of villagers, who turn out to be the village Communist party group waiting for their meeting to begin; when it does begin they mouth empty slogans and behave like automata, like 'levers', turning human again when the meeting was closed. Finally, Zhdanov (presumably unrelated to the notorious enemy of culture of the same name) wrote a deeply-felt short story about the visit of a Moscow official to his native village. His peasant mother tells him about abuses and neglect, and asks: 'Have we been treated fairly?' So long as he was there, the official was affected by what he heard and saw; but once his car was back on the highway, he forgot, though the small voice of conscience was not altogether silent.

Events in Hungary led to a tightening-up of literary controls in Russia, and, at least to this imperfectly informed author's knowledge, nothing as bold appeared on this theme for some years. An outstanding exception, which must be briefly men-

[1] *Novyi Mir*, August, 1955.

tioned, is Soloukhin's charming *Vladimirskie prosyolki* ('The byways of Vladimir', *Novyi Mir*, Nos. 9 and 10, 1957), which was not about peasants or their problems as such, but which showed a real concern for rural life in general, a love of the village and a feel for its history, so that it would be wrong not to mention it here. It is not suggested that nothing else of interest appeared. In particular, literary journals were used to argue the case for reform (as in the case of Vinnichenko, already mentioned) or to denounce the gross inadequacies of income distribution (e.g. V. Rozhin in *Novyi Mir*, No. 10, 1959). But these two examples concern the non-literary use of literary journals, occasioned by the regrettable timidity of the specialized press on agricultural or peasant problems.

The great move forward began again in 1961. Efim Dorosh, who had done such a fine job in 1956, was again to the fore with *Sukhoe leto* ('A dry summer'), in *Novyi Mir*, No. 7. A few quotations will give something of his flavour. 'The local bosses think only of procurements.' 'Why does the essential work of the village not feed the peasants, so that they have to spend all their free time on cultivating their private holdings, looking after their cows, travelling to town to sell produce?' And the local authorities do their best to obstruct, by compelling tired women to walk miles to the communal pastures to fetch their cows, forbidding cowherds to drive the cows through the little township to their owners. Why should the authorities insist on silage crops instead of the very necessary hay, and then demand deliveries of hay though fodder is very short? Why should peasant labour be wasted on gathering peat and manure which is then thrown out in heaps and not spread at all? (The explanation advanced is that the authorities would include the appropriate tonnage in the statistical report.) And the following passage says much about agricultural statistics. 'Three years ago there was a rule, which may still be in operation, that the rural co-operative shops would only sell certain goods to peasants if those peasants delivered some farm produce to the co-operative. A peasant was seen to buy from the co-operative a barrel of honey which he at once resold to the co-operative, thereby acquiring the right to buy felt boots. On enquiry it proved that the honey came from the only beekeeper of the district. It had served for this purpose for a long time. A customer was glad to lose on the resale of the honey he had bought, since this enabled him to get scarce consumers' goods. The co-operative increased its profits and could claim that it had greatly increased procurements of honey. The story would just be funny, but the mechanism which created it, which turned a pood or so of real honey into 100 or more poods of non-existent honey, also brought about a more serious situation. . . . Once in this province some cattle were supposedly being pastured and fattened on the farms. There is nothing unusual about this, except that these cattle did not actually exist. It could be that some time in the future the collective cows would have calves which would then be sold to the state, but the provincial bosses were impatient to show that these future calves and heifers were already real heavyweights. It was arranged that the collective farms should sell non-existent cattle to the state; on non-existent meadows there were imaginary cows. When the time came, these purely paper cows were slaughtered and the meat was "sold to the local population".' It should be added that, according to Dorosh, part of the non-existent money had to be paid by the collective farms, so that the book-keeping would balance.

Another instalment of Dorosh's account, which appeared at the end of 1962, told how the peasants were (in earlier years) compelled to 'elect' an unpopular chairman, how some peasants were deprived of pasture and hay to compel them to sell their cows, and ends with a comment on the crude and domineering attitude of a local party secretary which was surely intended to have general application: 'He seemed unworried that the peasant, as Lenin warned, might one day say: "If you cannot manage properly, get out!" ' (*esli ty khozyainnichat' ne umeyesh, to poidi von*).[1]

1962 saw further advances. Solzhenitsyn's *Ivan Denisovich* is well known for its picture of concentration camp life, but is also important because it saw this life with the eyes of its peasant hero; and the incidental comments on 'free' village life are very strong. The same author's *Matryonin dvor* ('Matryona's house'), in *Novyi Mir*, No. 1 of 1963, is set in a remote village, to which the man in whose name the story is told (presumably Solzhenitsyn himself) goes to teach after his release from prison or exile. Again there is severe implicit criticism of material conditions of life;

[1] *Novyi Mir*, No. 12, 1962.

particularly memorable is his picture of six women harnessed to a primitive wooden plough (*sokha*) on their household plots (these private holdings can benefit from neither modern equipment nor haulage power). But this is not the essential point. The heroine, Matryona, is a 'just woman' (*pravednitsa*), who worked for others all her life amid the harshest conditions and in the face of much ingratitude. The real point is in the last sentences of the story, and consists of the assertion of moral principle: on such truly moral, 'just' persons there depends the life of the village, of the country, of the entire community. The tale is told with real feeling, underlining the high quality of its author's style and his deep human understanding.

In December 1962 Alexandr Yashin's *Vologodskaya svad'ba* ('A wedding in Vologda province') appeared in *Novyi Mir*. It was full of fascinating details of surviving marriage songs and customs in a primitive north-Russian village, in which there is 'still neither electricity, radio, library or club'. There is abundant evidence given of the contempt in which collective farm work, and the status of *Kolkhoznik*, is held among the people. There are also significant references to the destruction of efficient family farms by forcible collectivization, and to the sympathy felt among the inhabitants for the innocent victims of anti-*kulak* excesses. Yashin, as also did Dorosh, had much to say about the desperate shortage of materials and machines of all kinds, of the need to use various semi-legal and illegal expedients to obtain essential supplies. A story he cites runs as follows: 'A driver smashed up his vehicle and killed a director. He said: "O.K., they'll send us a new director, but where can I get spare parts?" '

The same month, December 1962, saw still another great step forward towards a really sincere picture of peasant life. True, it was concerned with the past, but honesty about what the peasants suffered is essential and greatly overdue. This may be found in the moving and deeply-felt novel by Ivan Stadnyuk, *Lyudi ne angely* ('Men are not angels'),[1] which appeared in the Leningrad periodical *Neva*. This is a tale of a Ukrainian village and its inhabitants, and the second part of it is still unpublished, or perhaps unwritten. Full of tragedy, life and earthy humour, it sees things as the peasants see them. The main characters are

[1] English translation published in 1963 by Mono Press, London. Extracts cited below translated by A.N.

not described as enemies of collectivization; on the contrary. The hero, Platon, is against the *kulaks*, for the collective principle. This makes the condemnation of the brutalities of 1930–33 all the more striking. 'You do not want to enter the *kolkhoz*? Pay a tax in money or in kind. You have paid it? Well, here is another tax. You can't pay? Give up your civic rights and get out of the village!' Alleged *kulaks* were deported, their families made destitute, yet most of them were not *kulaks* at all. 'They ploughed sorrow, sowed disaster.' After the collective was created by such methods, the resentful peasants that remained were subjected to large delivery quotas to the state. The harvest of 1932 was a modest one, and, early in 1933, famine stalks the land. Here, for the first time, is the truth about the Ukrainian famine, described as it hit the village in which the story is set. 'Last year all the grain was transported straight from the threshing floor, from the threshing machine, straight to the storehouses at the station. The representatives of the region conscientiously carried out the orders of the regional leadership. The figures of grain deliveries to the state rose, and the peasants' hopes of receiving anything for their work melted away. They who should have remembered somehow forgot that the peasant too was the state. . . . The incredible happened: the cultivators were left without bread.'

The famine is described in all its horror. Men, women and children died, some went mad. Children were lucky to have a rook's egg to eat. The hero steals a little seed grain, which, he feels, was a deep wrong he had done to Mother Earth. But 'one can't live long on stolen goods'. The family survives because they exchange three Crosses of St George, won in Tsarist wars, for bread-grain. No mention is made of any relief measures of any kind by the authorities. In an affecting scene, a family boil chopped-up pieces of an old and long-empty barrel which once contained pork-fat, and watch desperately as a few precious bubbles of fat rise to the surface. The appalling hunger is painfully described, and if it has taken thirty years for its very existence to be admitted in print, this is hardly Stadnyuk's fault.

Later the hero is arrested on a false charge, is tortured by being compelled to sit without food and sleep for days, sentenced to seven years, and is sent with innumerable others to build the White Sea canal. True to his artistic design, the author presents these events as seen by his characters, and does not discuss national politics. But at several points his hero becomes conscious that he is seeing an infinitesimal part of a vast tragedy. The novel contains a powerful condemnation, from the standpoint of peasant sense of right and wrong, of the essential *immorality* of what had happened. As the weary hero sits endlessly on the bench in the interrogation centre, he imagines Mother Earth speaking to him, and here one finds the one indirect reference to Stalin: 'Hearken unto me, O Platon. In the family of your people trouble is coming. Your ruler saw the sun's rays and imagines that the sun lives already in his soul. Yet a false sun gives a false heat. The soul of the ruler is warmed by the mania of infallibility, fed by the flattery of some, the silence of deadly fear of others. Unable to comprehend the complexity of the people, he who has lost his way, he, unyielding as death, sows sorrow in the land.' But no one individual is really blamed. It is wrong, simply *wrong*, to impose such suffering. 'A bullet once fired is irretrievable; remember: to kill an innocent man is to impoverish the world, to sow human sorrow and to kill a fragment of the Earth.' Nothing is more real or more eternal than a mother's grief. These truths should be 'shouted from the housetops'.

Later in the novel the hero meets a tragic end, during the Purges, never again seeing his native village, and the author repeats his challenging message, adding an even more unmistakable political implication: 'Yes, we do not remember men for ever, but a time will come when people will feel ashamed for those days. Some will feel ashamed and hurt, others will feel fear. No, all will feel fear, when they learn the truth, and if they have memories. And some will pretend that they do not remember. They will be weighed down by fear—for themselves, for their comforts, for what had been done. Maybe done blindly. It can happen, unfortunately, that friend is mistaken for foe. But there is a limit, beyond which such blind men can find no justification, a limit beyond which it becomes clear that their souls are brief as rabbits' tails, their hearts are as empty nutshells, their thoughts tailored, fitted into the steel framework of distrust of humanity. Terrible is their cold blindness!'

It could hardly be said more eloquently, more strongly.

In the same year 1962, F. Abramov, whose 1954 article was

quoted in the first sentence of this paper, published a novel on village themes, *Bezotsovshchina*, which, judging from a sympathetic review, dealt vigorously with the attitudes of peasant youth to collective work and with the causes of these attitudes. (Unfortunately I have not been able to obtain the novel so far.) The same Abramov wrote a particularly hard-hitting sketch of village life in the Leningrad province, which appeared in *Neva*, No. 1, 1963, *Vokrug da okolo* ('Round and about', suggesting perhaps 'Getting no place fast'). This has been translated into English and published in America with a slightly odd title ('One day in the "New Life" '), and in England as 'The Dodgers'.[1]

Abramov's themes are, in the main, the following: stupid bureaucratic orders, inadequate incomes, the importance of the peasants' private plot, and peasant attitudes to collective work. These are all, of course, closely interconnected. The *kolkhoz* chairman is shown to be doing his best in impossible circumstances. With the sun shining, he puts his labour force on to haymaking. He is bombarded with orders to make silage instead —no doubt in line with Khrushchev's insistence on maize as against grass—and finally receives the following 'reward': 'For political underestimation of silage as the fodder basis of collective livestock, the chairman of the New Life *kolkhoz*, the communist Comrade . . . , is severely reprimanded.' (*Political* underestimation! How can agriculture ever be healthy if silage and hay are political issues!) The peasants are sullen, invent medical excuses for not working, go off to pick mushrooms to sell in the free market. Asked to work, they reply as follows: 'I hear such talk for fifteen years now. I worked all summer in the fields, and how much did I earn?' 'I have children, they must go to school soon, and I can't buy clothes or shoes for them.' 'Don't we ourselves have to eat? Here we are, into our second year without a cow.'

Abramov stresses the vital importance of the cow to a peasant family. Yet they are forced to get rid of them, because of lack of fodder. A strict instruction forbids the issue to the peasants of more than 10 per cent of all the hay. (Whose instruction? It is not explained; there is no such published law or regulation.) There is plenty of good grass, which just goes under the snow each winter. The harm done to production, to peasant morale,

[1] Translated by David Floyd. Extracts cited here are translated by A.N.

to their willingness to work, is obvious. Is this understood in *kolkhozy*? Yes, it is understood. And every chairman tries to evade the rule. But then comes the dreaded voice of the procurator: 'Don't you dare! Anti-state practice. Encouragement of the private sector.' Faced with the breakdown of his plan, the unfortunate chairman gets drunk. When he recovers, he finds everyone hard at work, because, so they allege, he has promised them 30 per cent of the hay! He does not recall making any such promise, but realizes that this is the only way out; and the story ends with him preparing to face up to the party secretary.

The observant reader will see a similarity between this story of the hay and Pomerantsev's 1953 story about potatoes. Is it really possible that nine years' experience has taught party officials nothing? Evidently it is possible. Still they nibble and niggle at the private sector, to the detriment of peasant welfare and not at all to the benefit of collective production. The same Abramov story contains a revealing little conversation about peasant status. A peasant complained that he was treated as a second-class citizen because he could not present a passport to a town office as proof of identity, when this was demanded. 'Why have I no passport? Have I no identity, then?' 'Well, you are not the only one. *Kolkhozniki* have no passports.' 'Why not?' 'Because passports are not issued in rural areas.' 'Why aren't they?'

The next major contribution came from V. Ivanov, in *Novyi Mir*, No. 3, 1963, *V rodnykh mestakh* ('In my native area'). The location is the Kalinin province. Here the basic theme is bureaucratic stupidity and its effects, on output, on the management and on the peasants. The situation as described is appalling. On the 12,000 hectares classed as 'pasture' in the district, all but 900 are badly overgrown with alder-trees and shrubs. Yet the management cannot obtain any of the equipment needed to clear the pastures, and is ordered to sow more and more maize, although there was almost complete failure year after year. In 1962, in the production administration area, 16,000 hectares of this crop were sown, only 500 could be harvested. Still it is 'given the best land, all fertilizer', and still there is failure. Meanwhile the party officials reacted to the campaign against *travopolye* (perennial rotation grasses) by issuing orders which appear criminally nonsensical, as the following quotation shows. 'Approaching an unknown village I stopped by a ploughed field. I could see that it had been ploughed in the spring and badly. A little grass was growing on the ridges and here and there one could see some red clover heads. Why was this field ploughed and abandoned? The first old peasant I met in the village said that previously clover grew here, and in the spring "our bosses quarrelled with the clover and sent tractors to plough it up". Altogether about 100 hectares were ploughed up like this and then abandoned. The old man shrugged and turned away from me, presumably suspecting that I was some kind of official. . . . The following is what I discovered about this ploughing. These fields belonged to the *Michurin Kolkhoz*. . . . The Chairman there is new; a former teacher. He was compelled to plough up the clover, although there were no seeds with which to sow these fields. Things sometimes go as far as this! A campaign is declared against the grass rotation system in agriculture, and so with incredible energy it is decided to plough up clover—let the land go to waste provided clover is not allowed to grow.'

In March 1963 came Khrushchev's attack on the liberal intellectuals, and the flow of such stories as these ceased. One may be sure that this is temporary, as were also the other setbacks in the development of literary freedoms since Stalin's death. The novels, stories and sketches cited here contain much critical material, and some readers may suspect the author of cataloguing works hostile to Soviet farming. Such a view of the situation, or of the author's or authors' intention, would be quite false. Since much is wrong with Soviet farming, since peasant attitudes are what they are—and there is little difference of opinion nowadays about these things, however much one may argue concerning the right remedial measures—greater freedom to criticize was bound to give rise to much critical comment. The more so because it had been compulsory for so long to keep silent or to tell lies, about conditions, about what the peasants thought, about how collectivization came about. It therefore follows that the much greater amount of honest expression is a positive phenomenon. Men like Yevtushenko and Viktor Nekrasov appear to see this well enough. The ideologist watchdogs of the Ilyichev type do not. No doubt the watchdogs would prefer to suppress some of these works, and would probably regard the present paper (if they read it) as hostile to the USSR—which it is not. However, it is possible that there are such tensions in the Soviet village that honest presentation in print of critical material presents a real danger. Then, but only then, is there a *rationale* in the Ilyichev attitude. As for Khrushchev, his position has been ambivalent. While he came down in March 1963 on the anti-liberal side, he has in the past shown signs of toleration. It is true that some of the writers criticize the application of certain of his policies (for instance, Ivanov attacks the compulsory sowing of maize and the ploughing up of grasses). But the instances criticized are outrageous examples of official obtuseness, and Khrushchev can no more be expected to defend them than Tsar Nicholas I could defend the officials portrayed in Gogol's *Revizor*. In any case, Ivanov appeared in the same issue of *Novyi Mir* as reprinted Khrushchev's attack on the liberals. It could well be that Khrushchev was under pressure from 'illiberal' colleagues. Anyhow, there is, on past showing, a good chance that he will again take a more tolerant view. (Indeed, since June 1963 he seems to be doing so.) Soviet literature in general would clearly benefit, and literature about peasants will share in the general advance, as it is now sharing in the unfavourable consequences of the counter-offensive of the obscurantists.

*9. Soviet agriculture marks time**

Nine years ago, Khrushchev addressed the first 'agricultural' plenum of the Central Committee since Stalin's death. His frank exposure of the poor state of Soviet agriculture was followed by action along a wide front. Prices paid by the state for farm produce were substantially raised, investments in agriculture increased, peasant incomes showed a much needed and rapid rise from very low levels. Tax and other burdens on the private activities of peasants were eased, to the benefit of all concerned; for example, in five years the number of privately-owned cows increased 25 per cent. In 1958 a major organizational weakness was corrected: Tractors and other machinery formerly owned and operated by the Machine Tractor Stations (MTS) were sold to the collective farms which the MTS had previously 'serviced' (and also supervised). In 1958, too, the Government dropped its complex multiple-price system, under which farms received a low price for a quota of produce and a higher one for deliveries in excess of their quota; this was replaced by a single price for each product, with zonal variations.

The period 1953–58, then, was one of reform, of higher incomes, of large investments, of new methods. It was also one of higher production. The 1958 grain harvest set an all-time record. Sugar beets and cotton also did very well. Milk yields benefited from the improved diet of the cows. According to the official statistics, the *annual* rate of growth of gross agricultural output in the five years 1953–58 was 8.6 per cent. This would be a remarkable achievement, if the statistics were reliable, but there are ample grounds for suspecting some degree of exaggeration. Even so, no serious observer doubts that a substantial advance was recorded in these years.

No doubt inspired by the figures with which they were supplied, Khrushchev and his colleagues projected an even more

* From *Foreign Affairs*, July, 1962.

rapid growth of agricultural output in the Seven Year Plan (1959–65), and onward through 1970. Extremely ambitious plans were envisaged for meat production, in particular, and for other scarce items such as fruit and vegetables. Yet for three consecutive years since 1958 the figures have shown no appreciable change, merely some fluctuations reflecting better or worse weather. Indeed, grain harvests have been below the 1958 record (see table on page 153). How far performance lags behind plan can be seen from the following table (totals are in millions of tons):

	1961 plan	*1961 performance*
Grain	155·2	137·2
Meat	11·8	8·8
Milk	78·4	62·5

Source: Khrushchev, *Pravda*, March 6, 1962.

Allowance for statistical inflation of output would make the shortfall even greater. There is no doubt that Khrushchev is alarmed, because he has admitted as much at great length, and has proposed a number of remedies.

It is the purpose of this article to examine the reasons for the difficulties in which Soviet agriculture finds itself, and to assess the likely efficacy of the measures proposed to set matters right. But before doing so it is important to repeat that there has been a sizable advance since the death of Stalin, and that the crisis in Soviet agriculture is essentially to be seen as a failure to expand, a failure to measure up to very ambitious plans, rather than as a collapse. Various foods are in short supply in many cities at different times of the year, but there is some truth in Khrushchev's assertion that the shortage has been exacerbated by an increase in personal incomes (with retail prices broadly unchanged).

In considering the problems of Soviet agriculture, it is necessary to distinguish several types of difficulty, and, correspondingly, different kinds of policies or remedial measures. There is, first, the complex of problems related to soil utilization, agricultural techniques, equipment and the like, which may be called problems of production. Secondly, there are questions connected with the peasants, with their private interests, incomes, incentives. Finally, there are the many problems of agricultural planning, administration and control. These are all to some extent interconnected, as when, for instance, an administrative measure designed to improve technique affects the peasants' private activities. None the less, it remains true that these various matters are to some extent distinct and can be separately analysed.

PROBLEMS OF PRODUCTION

One of the principal objects—though not the only object—of Soviet farm policy is to increase production. Under any political system, this would involve overcoming serious obstacles, for a large part of Soviet territory is unsuitable for agriculture. Where the soil is fertile there is usually a high risk of drought, and where rainfall is adequate the soil is generally poor. Two of Khrushchev's principal remedies—designed to provide more crops and especially more grain for human and animal consumption—were the virgin-lands and the corn[1] campaigns. The first involved enlarging the area of extensive farming, the second was an attempt to intensify farming. Both have now been running for six years or more, and so some assessment of their effectiveness is possible.

The virgin-lands campaign was a truly formidable undertaking. It added to the farmland of the Soviet Union an area equal to the cultivated land of Canada. Between 1953 and 1956, the total sown area rose from 157 to 194.7 million hectares. So great an expansion in so short a period has no parallel in agricultural history. It was achieved through a major diversion of machinery and with a minimum number of permanent settlers, reinforced at harvest time by migrant labour (volunteers or 'volunteers', probably both). The areas brought under cultivation were in the northern half of Kazakhstan, in parts of west and central Siberia and in the territories east of the lower Volga and the southern Urals. The principal crop was grain, largely spring wheat. The following table gives the official production figures (in millions of metric tons) for the total grain harvest in the years 1953–61, with a breakdown showing that part of the total harvested in the virgin lands, of which Kazakhstan (shown as a further sub-total) is one region.

Clearly, grain production did increase greatly through 1958. In 1954, the first year of the campaign, yields were good but little had yet been ploughed. In 1955, on the other hand, drought

[1] In this chapter, 'corn' is maize.

	1953	*1954*	*1955*	*1956*	*1957*	*1958*	*1959*	*1960*	*1961*
Total grain Harvest ..	82·5	85·6	106·8	127·6	105·0	141·2	125·9	134·3	137·3
Harvested in virgin lands ..	27·1	37·6	28·0	63·6	38·5	58·8	55·3	59·1	n.a.
Harvested in Kazakhstan ..	5·4	7·7	4·8	23·8	10·5	22·0	19·1	18·8	14·8

Sources: For 1953–60, *Narodnoe khozyaistvo SSSR v 1960 godu*, p. 440–1; for 1961, *Pravda*, March 6, 1962.

ruined the crop; in Kazakhstan, for instance, yields in that year averaged a mere 3.8 quintals per hectare, against a nation-wide average of 8.5 quintals in a not very favourable year. In 1956 the harvest was very good—the best to date in the areas with which we are concerned. The 1957 crop was a poor one. Since 1958, a good year, no further progress has been made, and the figures for Kazakhstan, the territory with the highest drought risk, have shown an alarming downward trend.

The difficulties encountered have been of the following kinds:

1. The nature of the campaign itself caused the ploughing up of some land with unsuitable soil, or with excessively sparse rainfall. The causes of such errors will be discussed when we come to analyse administration.

2. A surprisingly high proportion of the machinery is not kept in good repair and cannot be used, owing to lack of spare parts, skilled mechanics and workshops. The situation has been getting steadily worse; thus there were 32,000 combine-harvesters inactive in Kazakhstan in 1959, but 60,000 were in disrepair at the start of the 1961 harvest.[1]

3. The right kind of rapidly ripening seed is seldom available. This, in combination with the shortage of working machinery, delays the harvest, and, in this area of early frosts, heavy losses result.

4. Lack of amenities has driven away some of the permanent labour force, despite repeated criticisms of this state of affairs by Khrushchev and by many lesser officials.

5. The land has been misused. Spring wheat has been sown year after year, although there was no lack of warnings as to the consequences. Weed infestation, soil erosion, reduced natural

[1] These figures are taken from the remarkable speech by the premier of Kazakhstan, Sharipov, in *Kazakhstanskaya Pravda*, December 24, 1961.

fertility are all named as causes of falling yields. No acceptable system of cultivation and crop rotation has yet been agreed upon.

Despite these difficulties, the campaign to date has paid good dividends. It was clear from the start that there would be some bad years, and, whatever discount is made for statistical exaggeration, it is surely true that a substantial contribution has been made to Soviet grain supplies, which could not otherwise have been obtained so quickly. Moreover, poor weather conditions in the Ukraine have often coincided with good ones in Kazakhstan, so that one effect of the campaign has been to spread the risks somewhat.

The future, on the other hand, looks much less satisfactory. It is known that some of the newly opened lands are of good quality, while others appear to have been ploughed up on orders from above and against the better judgment of local experts, but we do not know how much land may be in each category. Nor have we the means of assessing the extent of damage done by prolonged monoculture, or wind erosion, though these factors have certainly contributed to the steady drop in output and yields in Kazakhstan, where the bulk of the least suitable lands happens to be situated. Probably some of the ploughed-up land will have to be abandoned. Remedial measures at present being discussed may well run into administrative difficulties, because of Khrushchev's strong distaste for fallow and grasses, which presumably should be extended in some areas if the land is to be saved. Increased application of fertilizer is unlikely to provide a solution because of lack of moisture. (Very little is used on the somewhat similar Canadian prairies, though rainfall there is slightly higher.) In all the circumstances, it would be sensible to assume that a bigger contribution will be needed from traditional agricultural areas, and that the Soviet Union will be fortunate if means are found to maintain average yields in these marginal lands at the modest levels of the last few years.

Khrushchev was conscious from the first of the need to increase substantially the output of fodder, particularly fodder grains, in the 'old' cultivated areas. This was the primary object of his corn campaign, which was facilitated by the growing of so much wheat in the virgin lands. Corn had been neglected, and its acreage in 1953 was actually somewhat lower than in 1940 and 1950. To enforce a rapid change, Khrushchev had recourse to continuous propaganda and administrative pressures. As a result, the area under corn rose rapidly from 3.5 million hectares in 1953 to 19.7 in 1958 and 28.2 in 1961. With strong pressure to sow corn on good land and to give it a large share of the available fertilizer,[1] yields rose also, as the following table shows:

	1953	*1958*	*1959*	*1961*
Total corn harvest (millions of metric tons)	3·7	16·7	12·0	24·0
Yield (quintals per hectare)	10·6	20·6	13·8	18·2

However, these official averages conceal vast regional variations. Thus in some areas in which corn was sown 'by order', yields were exceedingly low; these include the Volga area and the Urals, where average yields for the period 1957–59 were respectively 5.1 and 4.5 quintals per hectare. This represents utter failure.

None the less, as in the case of the virgin-lands campaign, the underlying idea behind Khrushchev's corn plan was sound, and the substantial increase in silage supplies (from 32 million tons in 1953 to 186 million tons in 1960, largely due to corn) certainly helped in raising milk yields and providing a better diet for an expanded livestock population. The trouble, as in the case of the virgin-lands campaign, has been the 'campaigning' methods themselves, which caused rapid expansion under conditions which were often unsuitable. (Khrushchev has repeatedly claimed that corn can grow even as far north as Archangel.) Orders from the centre demanded that all corn be sown in 'square clusters', although, as several local agronomists sought vainly to point out, it is often more convenient to sow in rows.

Khrushchev has also set unrealistic goals. Thus whole provinces in the Ukraine were expected to achieve a yield of 50 quintals of corn per hectare in 1961, whereas American yields, with more suitable soils and warmer climate, averaged around 32 quintals. Even though the 1961 harvest in the Ukraine was an all-time record, with excellent weather conditions, no province came within 15 quintals of this target. Instead of learning his lesson, Khrushchev has repeated his demand for 50 quintals per hectare

[1] Perhaps this is why potatoes, which 'compete' for scarce fertilizer with the more fashionable corn, have been doing badly of late.

in 1962. One is left wondering which would do more harm: failure (with or without simulation of success), or success bought at the cost of neglecting all other farming needs of the Ukraine; presumably the former. It is this chronic tendency to overdo a good idea, to impose it by decree, which ruins its application and does so much harm to Soviet agriculture. More will be said below about the causes of such practices.

Meanwhile we must turn to consider the latest of Khrushchev's campaigns—to plough up meadows and reduce the area of sown grasses. Its motive, like that of the corn campaign, was the need for fodder, more in quantity and more diversified in type. This called for a further intensification of agriculture, which, as Khrushchev rightly saw, was inconsistent with the previously fashionable *travopolye* (rotational grass) crop system, associated with the name of Vilyams (Williams) and imposed under Stalin on all parts of the Soviet Union, regardless of local conditions. While grass could be a valuable source of fodder in the Baltic States or the northwest, in central and south Russia it grows poorly and provides little hay. Consequently there was much to criticize in these cropping practices. Khrushchev attacked the indiscriminate enforcement of *travopolye* in 1954, but agronomists had been trained in this way of thinking, officials were used to it, and those experts who had opposed it in Stalin's day had been punished or demoted. Consequently, little change actually occurred.

Khrushchev launched an all-out assault on *travopolye* in 1961—in speeches in many parts of the country and at the Twenty-second Party Congress. He pointed to the vast areas of sown grasses, of meadows, of low-yield crops such as oats. He ridiculed those provinces, including Leningrad and Moscow, where 50 per cent or more of all arable land consisted of grasses and fallow. He demanded that such crops as corn, peas, beans and sugar beets be sown instead, in virtually all parts of the country. Only by intensification of agriculture of this kind, he asserted, would it be possible to produce sufficient fodder. Agricultural experts or officials who did not see this would have to be re-educated or removed. Crop rotation, too, must be drastically altered forthwith.

Again, as in the case of the virgin-lands and corn campaigns, Khrushchev appears right in general principle, but the method of enforcing his ideas almost ensures that very serious errors will be made in some parts of the country. The new system will not be understood. New crops will be grown by order in areas where soil conditions or labour shortage or the lack of necessary machinery or fertilizer will make it impossible to apply the directive effectively. For example, in parts of the Baltic States or in the Leningrad province it may well be rational to grow grass, because, although it would certainly be possible to produce more fodder per hectare by planting, say, beans, it would not be worth the extra labour involved. Incredibly enough, Khrushchev hardly mentioned that additional inputs would be necessary; all he declared himself concerned about was the amount of fodder produced. Of course, Khrushchev was careful to warn against excesses; grass was not to be universally banished, fallow might be necessary here and there, and so on. But the general sense of his instructions was such that they are bound to be followed by orders to plough up grass, to ban fallow and sow beans, corn, etc., regardless of circumstances. Thus the Premier of Latvia mentioned that some of his colleagues in the Baltic States were already treating clover as a 'forbidden crop'.[1] Khrushchev must know all this. Yet presumably he can see no other way of breaking up existing irrational farm practices, since his only available weapon is the party machine, and this is the sort of way it works. In his impatience with low yields and general inefficiency, these crude administrative methods must appear to him as irreplaceable.

One cannot envisage a rapid advance of Soviet agriculture by such methods—the more so as the agricultural machinery industry has been undergoing a painful period of readjustment. Production of some vital items has fallen drastically. Khrushchev himself cited with dismay the fact that output of corn silage combines, urgently needed as a result of the expansion of the corn acreage, actually fell from 55,000 in 1957 to 13,000 in 1960.[2] Other sources confirm that the new system of industrial planning has caused much confusion in farm machinery factories.[3] The chronic shortage of spare parts continues, and decrees about expanding

[1] Y. Peive, *Ekonomicheskaya gazeta*, March 5, 1962, p. 5.

[2] *Pravda*, March 6, 1962. Khrushchev there cites other examples.

[3] See in particular the article by the director of the Tula farm machinery factory, *Ekonomicheskaya gazeta*, January 15, 1962, p. 8.

their output and making them available to farms on free purchase (as distinct from administrative allocation) have remained on paper.[1] Finally, fertilizer production and output of other important agricultural chemicals (sprays, weed-killers, etc.) are far behind schedule. Khrushchev contrasted the Seven Year Plan target for mineral fertilizer—an increase from 12 to 35 million tons—with the 'achievement' of an increase of a mere 2.9 million tons in three years. New capacity is being delayed, and the completion plan for the three years is only 44 per cent fulfilled.[2] No wonder the Ukrainian party leader, Podgornyi, complained that fertilizer supplies were inadequate: 'For instance, deliveries to the Ukraine of fertilizer for sugar beet growing, per unit of land, has actually diminished in the past few years.' He also deplored serious difficulties in supplies of timber, vehicles, tyres and metal.[3] These are products of obvious importance to agriculture. The adoption of even the best techniques cannot bring results if the required machines are not available, or if they break down and cannot be repaired, or if, as in some areas, farms do not even have carts or trailers to move into the fields the fertilizer which they do have available.

One purpose of the Party's recent declarations may be to restore a high priority to the industrial sectors which serve agriculture, and surely some improvements are both possible and likely. However, these shortages, which hamper agriculture even with existing cropping arrangements, must greatly hinder the application of the anti-*travopolye* policies, which call for much increased utilization of both machinery and fertilizer. If this call cannot be met, the result is likely to be a large additional expenditure of peasant labour without sufficient return.[4] It should be added that, as a consequence of the ploughing up of grasses, private livestock may be deprived of pasturage, to the further detriment of production and peasant morale. (When the corn campaign was launched, the peasants were promised part of the corn for their animals; but no such promises are being made at present.)

[1] A 1961 decree provides for severe punishment for allowing farm machinery to deteriorate, but often enough the cause of the trouble is lack of spare parts, or of materials with which to build shelter and storage space.

[2] *Pravda*, March 8, 1962.

[3] *Pravda*, March 7, 1962.

[4] The burdens of the labour force which present policies impose were stressed at the Central Committee plenum by P. Abrosimov (*Pravda*, March 8, 1962).

THE PEASANTS

By the end of 1957, many collectivized peasants must have felt considerable grounds for satisfaction. Cash distributions from the farms had risen almost fourfold in five years. They were about to be freed from all delivery obligations to the state from their private holdings, and their private livestock was expanding at a fairly impressive rate. It is true that work discipline was being tightened. But clearly things were improving.

In the past four years, the peasants have been in a much less satisfactory situation. Space precludes anything like a full analysis of the many factors involved. The following is a summary of unfavourable developments:

1. Attempts, sometimes encouraged by the authorities, to pay collective farmers a guaranteed minimum 'wage', instead of in 'workday units' of uncertain value, have broken down in many areas[1] because there is still no financial basis for any regular payment for work done, except on the richer farms. For seven years the press has been publishing articles and letters insisting on the necessity of earmarking a fixed share of farm revenue to pay the peasant members. Yet nothing effective has been done.

2. The 1958 reforms had the unintended consequence of increasing disparities in income between rich and poor farms. This was because, until that year, the more fertile areas were charged a kind of disguised differential rent by having to pay more for work done by the MTS and by being compelled to deliver a bigger quota of produce at low prices. The abolition of the MTS and the unification of delivery prices eliminated these methods. It is true that the unified delivery prices are lower in fertile areas, but the difference is quite small.

3. Peasant income from collective farms appears to have declined since 1957. The evidence for this lies, first, in the fact that there has been statistical silence since 1957, which usually indicates that the figures look bad. Second, two Soviet scholars have used regional and/or sample data to show a fall in distributions to peasants since that date; one of the writers, citing a 15 per cent reduction between 1957 and 1960 in the province of Rostov, lists

[1] See evidence in A. Kraeva, *Voprosy ekonomiki*, No. 8/1961, p. 74.

a number of other areas in which 'the situation is broadly similar'.[1] This happened despite a rise in gross revenues, and appears to have been due to pressure to spend large sums on investment, to exorbitant charges for repairs in state-run workshops, and the need to pay black-market prices to obtain desperately scarce tyres, building materials and spare parts.[2]

4. Restrictions have been imposed on private activities of peasants, and the number of privately-owned cows has declined sharply since the end of 1957. In consequence, and also because of a decline in free-market sales, peasant incomes in cash and produce from their private plots have fallen too. Thus there is evidence of a significant decline in peasant living standards, which must affect incentives.

Several measures have been taken to ease the financial burdens of the collective farms: prices of some items which farms must purchase were reduced in 1961, credit terms were eased, and payments for produce were made in advance. Also, nearly two million collective-farm peasants have been converted to state-farm status since 1957, making them regular wage earners (though the wages are low). However, possibly because of financial stringency, the Government has done little indeed to improve peasant incomes, and must have caused much irritation by its measures against private livestock.

Perhaps the renewed restrictions on private activities of peasants are designed to persuade them to work harder for the collectives. Certainly, it could be shown that millions of man-hours are dissipated on private landholdings and millions more on taking produce to market. The Soviet leaders could well argue that these are not efficient ways of using labour. Yet, in existing circumstances, the private plot and the free market are indispensable, both for the peasants and for urban consumers of foodstuffs. In the first place, the private holdings, though primitively cultivated, are often much more productive, per unit of land, than collective or state farms, due partly to hard work and partly to the concentration of manure on a small area. To take a particu-

[1] *Voprosy ekonomiki*, No. 8/1961, p. 77, and E. Kapustin, *Ekonomicheskaya gazeta*, April 9, 1962, p. 8 (see also p. 188, below).

[2] E.g. see articles in *Ekonomicheskaya gazeta* by M. Semko and A. Severov, respectively March 5 and March 19, 1962.

larly striking example, in 1959 a hectare of potatoes on private holdings yielded 11.6 tons, as against 6.6 on state and collective farms.[1] Second, particularly in small towns and in rural districts, the state distribution network is utterly incapable of coping with food supplies, except for a narrow range of staple items. In this situation a cut in the number of private cows may create serious shortages.

Why, since milk production on state and collective farms has fully offset the decline in private output, does this situation occur? Some would point to exaggerations in the reporting of milk production, asserting that output has in fact fallen. This may well be so. But there is another and simpler reason. To distribute milk in a 'modern' manner is a complex affair. It requires storage, refrigeration, specialized transport, bottles or cartons, and so on. All these are lacking, outside of a few big cities. In these circumstances, even if milk does exist on some farm thirty miles away, it is impracticable to distribute it, and so the local woman and her one private cow are irreplaceable. In villages, except in a very few showplaces, the private plot is almost the sole source of milk and vegetables for peasant families. Given the present structure of Soviet farming and food distribution, measures against the private sector must have unfortunate results, and the quickest way of ensuring an increase in production of many much-needed items is to permit some enlargement of private farming activities. It is extraordinary that Khrushchev, who so strongly criticized the measures taken under Stalin against private plots, should be adopting his present policies—or permitting them, since it is not impossible for the party machine in the villages to take some initiative in these matters. Surely he must know better than anyone that such interference damages not only the supply of food from the private sector but also the morale of the peasants and their work for the collective and state farms. Yet only recently it was proposed that private plots on state farms be done away with and that communal vegetable-growing be substituted.[2] One can imagine the unpopularity of such imposed measures. Here ideology and administrative habit seem to stand directly in the way of increasing production.

[1] Calculated from detailed figures given in the statistical compendium, *Selskoe khozyaistvo SSSR* (Moscow, 1960).

[2] V. Grishin, the 'trade union' chief, *Pravda*, March 10, 1962.

ADMINISTRATION AND PLANNING

The Soviet leaders must surely be fully aware that agriculture does not take kindly to centralized planning, that local initiative is vital. Yet ever since collectivization they have interfered with farming operations. This is to some extent explained by the fact that collectivization itself was imposed by the Party, and it has required constant vigilance to maintain collective farms and to 'protect' them from their peasant members. Party watchdogs must also supervise the party-nominated 'elected' chairmen who were often peasants themselves and therefore liable to give priority to the farm's needs rather than the state's. Low prices, which helped to finance industrialization but offered no financial incentive, made it necessary that the coercive apparatus of Party and state be mobilized annually to enforce deliveries to the state. For many years the principal task of the local party officials in rural areas, and of the political officers within the MTS, was to squeeze out produce for the state from reluctant and potentially backsliding peasants, who had to be restrained from spending their time on their private holdings. Farms could not be allowed to pursue the principle of maximizing revenues, since the price system was (and still is) geared to other objectives. The existence of a free market exercised a particularly distracting influence. Thus collective farms have been accused of marketing vegetables in distant cities at high prices, or growing sunflowers instead of sugar beets because they could sell sunflower seed in the free market at a profit,[1] or even—in the case of a state farm in 1961—growing grass instead of grain because, as a surprisingly honest director told Khrushchev to his face, grass does not need to be delivered to the state and grain does.

Consequently, the habit developed of controlling agriculture from above, and of so organizing farms and planning as to facilitate this control. To some extent the amalgamation of collective farms, which has more than quadrupled their average size since 1950 (and which is still going on), is explained by the greater convenience in exerting control from above, rather than the convenience of management. From the latter standpoint, most state

[1] I. Bodyul, *Ekonomicheskaya gazeta*, March 5, 1962, p. 6. Many similar examples could be cited.

and collective farms are much too big. This tendency to very large size is also explained in part by the traditional Marxist belief that there are substantial economies of scale agriculture.

When, in 1953, the appalling state of Soviet farming called for drastic remedial measures, Khrushchev showed himself very conscious of the harm done by inefficient central planning. The Soviet press printed a long series of articles criticizing the stupidity of inflexible production plans passed down the administrative hierarchy to farms for which they were quite unsuitable. Khrushchev and others declared that this must cease. In 1955, a decree was adopted freeing the collective farms from having production plans determined for them; they were to be given delivery quotas, and were to be free to decide their crop and livestock plans, so long as these were consistent with the quotas. It was repeatedly asserted that farm management and agronomists should be free to decide their own methods in the light of the very varied circumstances which always exist in agriculture.

In practice, since prices of neither output nor inputs reflected either needs or scarcities, direction from above had to continue. The period 1955–61 was one of experiment and frequent change in administrative arrangements. The Ministry of Agriculture was gradually shorn of its powers, part of which were transferred to *Gosplan* (the central planning agency) and part to a new body responsible for supply and utilization of farm machinery and fertilizer (*Sel'khoztekhnika*). A number of changes in purchasing arrangements culminated in the setting up, in 1961, of a Procurements Committee with local organs in close touch with farms, whose production programmes they were supposed to influence. But production planning was also supposed to be the responsibility of the provincial agricultural department, while state farms came under a provincial trust which took its orders from organs of the individual republics.

The result was confusion. Everyone was to some extent responsible, therefore no one was. In practice, the local party organs at provincial (*oblast*) and district (*rayon*) levels exercised the most effective control over collective farms (and to a lesser extent over state farms). They issued orders on a variety of topics, they could and did dismiss the 'elected' chairmen of farms and 'recommend' others. But the responsibilities of the local parties, and the pressures to which they were subjected, gave rise to an administrative disease which is worth analysing more closely.

A rural party secretary has always spent the bulk of his time dealing with agricultural problems. His promotion, or dismissal, depends on his success in coping with them. But how is his success or failure to be determined? The answer in practice has been: by his ability to report the fulfilment of plans to his superiors, if possible ahead of time. These plans tend to be very ambitious, and Khrushchev has systematically encouraged party secretaries to 'compete' with one another by offering to overfulfil them. The plans in question are of many different kinds: they might concern grain procurement, meat deliveries, milk production, the completion of sowing by a certain date, the quadrupling of the corn acreage, the use of some fashionable method of harvesting, and so on. Almost invariably, the plans are either impossible of fulfilment, or (and this is the cause of much trouble) can be fulfilled only if other agricultural activities, which may be important but not at the moment the subject of a campaign, are neglected. Party secretaries are therefore repeatedly placed in an impossible situation. They are, of course, told to administer their areas efficiently, to take into account all the multifarious needs of agriculture. But they simply cannot do this while they are being cajoled to fulfil plans which, in the circumstances, are inconsistent with a healthy agriculture.

By long training, party officials have tended to adapt their behaviour to the need to report success in the current campaign. Therefore cases like these recur repeatedly (all the examples are genuine and could be multiplied): seed grain is delivered to the state to fulfil delivery plans, and later other grain, unsorted and unsuitable, has to be returned for seed; farms are ordered to sow before the ground is fit for it, and/or to harvest by a fashionable but, in the given circumstances, unsuitable method; meat quotas are met at the cost of slaughtering livestock needed in the following year; to fulfil the procurement plan the local party boss orders the state elevators to receive what Khrushchev (in his speech at Novosibirsk) described as 'mud, ice, snow and unthreshed stalks', which damaged the elevator's equipment. Party officials have repeatedly broken up established crop rotations to compel the adoption of whatever was the subject of the current campaign; if they understood the long-term damage which this might do to the soil, they would, in any case, probably be in charge of some other area by then. Other party secretaries inspired or condoned large-scale falsification of plan fulfilment, by such methods as instructing farms to buy butter in retail stores for delivery as their own produce (note that the cost of this operation falls on the peasants), or more simply by 'writing in' non-existent figures (*pripiski*). They did not do these things because they enjoyed cheating or damaging the farms of their area, but as a response to pressures to achieve the impossible.

It is interesting to speculate why agricultural plans are so much less realistic than industrial ones. The uncertainties of the weather constitute one reason, but another is surely the habit of 'campaigning', which is of such long standing, has done so much damage to sound farming and which still continues. A campaign must have clearly defined objectives, priorities and dates on which achievements are to be measured; it must involve strain and effort to achieve success, and must lead, therefore, to neglect of other considerations. But in agriculture this does great harm.

Given these administrative habits, it followed logically that the planning autonomy granted to collective farms in 1955 could never be a reality. It is also easy to understand why all decentralization measures were doomed to failure. Devolution of authority in the existing setting meant in practice devolution to party secretaries, who alone were in a position to enforce decisions, and this led to the systematic neglect of anything for which there was no pressure from the centre. In a genuine effort to encourage local initiative, Khrushchev announced in 1958 that only grain-surplus regions were to be given grain delivery quotas. The idea was to encourage other regions to meet their own needs from their own resources, and in particular to concentrate on fodder grains for their livestock. What happened was that both grain acreage and production fell sharply in the areas freed from delivery quotas. In returning to centralized procurement planning in 1961, Khrushchev himself explained the reason: party secretaries, finding themselves no longer under pressure to deliver grain, instructed 'their' farms to pursue other objectives in which the centre seemed more interested; consequently, the fodder shortage was accentuated.

It is in the light of all this that one must assess Khrushchev's latest administrative reforms. There were two possible ways out: either to grant much more autonomy to farm management, or, on the contrary, to attempt to organize a more streamlined and flexible machine of central control. He chose the latter. Given his own background and the traditions of the Party, he could hardly have done otherwise.

A completely new hierarchical pyramid of control has been created in 1962. A new All-Union Committee on Agriculture is to be headed by a Deputy Premier, and is to include the head of the agricultural department of the Central Committee of the Party, and the heads of other relevant organizations, which retain their identity within, or alongside, the new structure: the Procurements Committee, *Sel'khoztekhnika*, the Ministry of Agriculture (reduced to purely research and advisory functions), plus representatives of the planning agencies. This new committee will apparently not be a policy-making body (Khrushchev would have headed it if it were); it is merely to ensure that party and state directives for agriculture are carried out. But below the all-Union level the situation is different in one all-important respect: the heads of the agricultural committees in republics and provinces are to be the first secretaries of the republican and provincial parties. At provincial level and below, the tasks of procurement as well as production planning, for collective farms and state farms, will be unified under the new committee within a provincial agricultural department. The basic unit of agricultural planning, operating on the instructions of the provincial committee, will now be a new 'territorial state and collective farm administration', which, as a rule, will group together several districts (*rayony*). In each of these territorial administrations there will be a 'party organizer' deputed by the republican or provincial party organization.

This new hierarchy is to have authority to plan production, to issue directives as to methods, crop rotations, procurements, and in general to be in charge of both state farms and collective farm operations. 'Inspector-organizers' employed by the territorial administrations will work within the farms and 'will decide on the spot questions of production and procurement'. The large number of workshops and other minor enterprises carried on jointly by two or more collective farms will be placed directly under the territorial administrations. An end is finally made of the doctrine, so often disregarded in practice, that collective farms are autonomous co-operatives governed by their members.

The reorganization marks a drastic alteration in, and a tightening of, the entire system of administration. Within it, the role of territorial party officials has undergone an important change. Hitherto, however frequently these officials interfered with plans and operations, they were not directly in charge of them. Their job was supposed to be to ensure that the relevant state organs did their job, to act as political commissars and not as army commanders, so to speak. It is true that they did in fact frequently issue commands, but—and this point was made several times—they could and often did dodge responsibility by putting the blame on one or more of the state officials whose formal duty it was to plan this or that aspect of agriculture. Now, the most senior party secretaries at the republic and provincial level have been put in direct command over farming in their areas, have been given full powers to issue orders to ensure that the agricultural plans are fulfilled. The state organs at their level, and beneath them, are at their command. The most powerful man in the new basic territorial controlling organs will be the 'party organizer' whom they will appoint, and even the nominal chiefs of these organs will clearly be party officials for the most part, certainly not professional agricultural managers; both Khrushchev and Voronov warned against appointing farm managers to these posts.[1] One category of party official loses—the district (*rayon*) secretaries—and protests from them were mentioned by Khrushchev. (They will sit on a Council which will be attached to the territorial administrations, but so will farm managers and other lesser lights.) Apparently their behaviour *vis-à-vis* the farms is regarded as having contributed to past distortion, which is true enough. Khrushchev appears to believe that the past failures of party control were due to the fact that it was unsystematic, spasmodic, with many overlaps with various state organs which in turn confused one another and, as he put it, left the farms 'undirected'. Presumably he imagines that, if a party secretary knows he is personally responsible for all agriculture in 'his' province, he will no longer concentrate only on the immediately current

[1] Voronov in *Pravda*, March 28, 1962. The big role played by Voronov in carrying out this reform is surely a significant pointer to his rapidly increasing position of power in the USSR.

campaign, and the many defects of party activities in rural areas will thereby be corrected.

But will they? If our analysis is correct, then the essential weakness arises not from irregularity of their interference but from the overambitious nature of the plans which, willy-nilly, they have to force down the throats of their subordinates, and from the contradiction between these plans and the self-interest of farms and peasants. Party officials will surely continue to try to please their superiors and to organize matters so as to be able to report what these superiors wish to hear. While it is true that a more logical administrative structure has been achieved, it lessens the effective powers of farm managements and farm agronomists. It is on the farms that crops are grown, and it cannot be right to diminish the range of choice open to those who can actually see the crops growing, who bear formal responsibility for farm operations and, in the case of collective farms, for the incomes of the labour force.

CONCLUSION

Soviet agriculture is indeed marking time. The liberal post-Stalin policies did produce quick results, but since 1958 the growth rate has been negligible, for a number of interconnected reasons which I have endeavoured to analyse here. It clearly does not follow that growth cannot be resumed. If more investment funds can be made available for the fertilizer and farm-machinery industries, for instance, then the very low crop yields in the naturally unfertile lands of the centre, north and west of European Russia can be increased. Success in agriculture tends to reinforce itself (higher yields of fodder grains, more livestock, more manure, higher yields, higher productivity, increased incomes, more incentives, therefore still higher productivity, etc., etc.). None of this is impossible, despite the adverse natural conditions under which Soviet agriculture operates. The trouble is that policies toward the peasant and the organizational arrangements of the régime seem inconsistent with the great advance in food production which Khrushchev desires with evident sincerity. And paradoxically, his impatient urgings, and their organizational and 'campaigning' consequences, are among the principal obstacles to soundly based progress. Although we should expect to see some increases in production, there can be no question of fulfilling—or anything like it—the plans for 1965 and 1970, to which so much publicity has been given in the Soviet Union.

Finally, it is only right and fair to emphasize that there is no easy solution to the problems with which the Soviet leadership is wrestling. It is easy to criticize the price system, but it ill behoves us to lecture Khrushchev about the virtues of a free price mechanism when not a single major Western country permits it to operate in the agricultural sector. Difficulties arise in ensuring even modest efficiency in traditional peasant farming in many non-Communist countries, and agricultural plans have a regrettable habit of going awry in places well to the west of the Soviet border. Thus at the moment of writing there is an acute potato shortage in England, due largely to the fact that the Potato Board restricted plantings in the incorrect expectation of favourable growing weather; if there were a 1962 sheep plan in Scotland it would be a failure, since so many sheep have been killed by the severe winter. It is also not to be forgotten that, seen historically, Soviet agriculture has served as a means of financing and sustaining industrialization and has suffered in consequence. This is a disadvantage unknown to farmers in developed Western countries.

Yet it remains true that the huge farms of the Soviet Union have been inefficient in the use of resources and have shown a deplorable lack of flexibility and a failure to mobilize necessary human ingenuity. It is also significant that the only country in the Communist bloc which fulfils its agricultural plans is Poland, where most farms are privately owned and privately run. One reason for this is that Polish plans are reasonable: had Gomulka been so foolish as to promise to treble meat production in five years, he too would have 'failed'. Polish farming has its own weaknesses, and it is surely impossible on practical as well as ideological grounds to apply the 'Polish model' to the Soviet Union. Yet, Polish experience underlines a fact too often overlooked: that with all the familiar inadequacies of small-peasant agriculture, it possesses advantages which Marxist theory has failed to recognize and Soviet practice has yet to find a way of emulating. Khrushchev is making an all-out effort to seek efficiency within the basic institutional and political framework of the Soviet system, and has mobilized the Communist Party machine for this purpose. The next few years will show whether a breakthrough can be achieved under these conditions. Much depends on the outcome—perhaps Khrushchev's political standing, probably also the influence of the Soviet Union on other peasant countries, within and outside the Communist bloc.

* * *

The passage of time since the above article was written has served to provide some striking illustrations of the effects of indiscriminate enforcement of anti-*travopolye* measures. Compulsory destruction of growing clover, even when no seed was available to replace it with any other crop, was reported by V. Ivanov (*Novyi Mir*, No. 3, 1963). Disastrous results followed the forcible introduction of maize in the damp north-west. The adverse effects of various restrictive measures on fodder supplies for private livestock are the subject of vigorous comment by F. Abramov in *Neva*, No. 1, 1963. All this was predictable, and the author claims no special gift of prophecy, only a sense of puzzlement: if we could see that such excesses would follow, why could not Khrushchev himself see this and prevent them, or at least issue his orders in some less obviously harmful ways? After all, he aims to improve Soviet farming!

A drastic decline in the fallow area in 1962 bodes no good either. One must expect trouble in Kazakhstan.

The most important changes have concerned organization. The 'new hierarchical pyramid' described above was altered almost before the ink was dry on the decree. The All-Union Committee on Agriculture, headed by Deputy-Premier Ignatov, seemed never to have met, and Ignatov was dismissed with no successor appointed (or at least no appointment has been announced). Chaos, vividly described by Khrushchev himself,[1] followed from the co-existence of *rayony* (with party officials) and multi-*rayon* production administrations (with their party officials); rivalry and overlapping were rife. The territorial production administration now conforms to the enlarged areas of local government and of the party rural organization. The party secretary at production administration level seems to be in command, playing the role originally designed for the 'party organizer' deputed from above; there has been comment on the

[1] *Pravda*, June 30, 1962.

relatively subordinate role of the chairman of the production administration. There is as yet no evidence that the new organs have made any noticeable difference to the way things are going. The party itself has been split into separate organs for agriculture and industry, and so it is no longer the case that the *first* secretaries in republics and provinces are primarily responsible for agriculture. This very odd change in party structure cannot be analysed here.

Finally, evidence has accumulated that grain harvest statistics have been affected by a change in computation introduced in 1958, which affects our assessment of official claims, and so any figures published since that date require downward amendment.[1] Indeed, the evident signs of grain shortage in the autumn of 1963 would be inexplicable if the 1962 harvest were anywhere near what had been claimed.

And since the above addendum was written, there has been ample evidence of an outstandingly bad harvest in 1963, due largely to poor weather, with very serious trouble in Kazakhstan.

[1] The clearest statement of the evidence is in Gale Johnson's contribution to *Economic Trends in the Soviet Union* (ed. Bergson and Kuznets, Harvard, 1963).

10. Rural taxation in the USSR *

The purpose of this paper is to assess the weight of taxation borne by the *collectivized* sector of the Soviet rural economy. As is known the *kolkhozy* (collective farms) are responsible for the bulk of Soviet agricultural output. No mention will be made of the *sovkhozy* (state farms), or of the few surviving individual peasants (although the latter are heavily taxed). The paper serves as background to the changes announced in the Soviet budget of 1953. A summary of these changes appears at the end of the paper, which perforce had to be completed before the publication of the budget.

Agricultural taxation proper is of two kinds: that falling on the *kolkhoz*, and that paid by the peasant member of the *kolkhoz*. But before considering either, attention must be directed to the system of compulsory deliveries, and to the question of agricultural prices.

Both the *kolkhoz* and its members have as their primary duty the delivery to the state of certain quantities of produce. The quota of compulsory deliveries is related to the amount of arable land cultivated by the *kolkhoz*, and is subject to considerable local variation according to nature of soil, geographical location, etc. The state pays very low prices for these compulsory deliveries; some examples of these will be given later. While it is not the primary purpose of this paper to discuss compulsory deliveries, it is necessary to make some reference to them, because otherwise one would obtain a totally distorted picture of the weight of taxation, since these compulsory deliveries are a form of taxation. Maurice Dobb, certainly not a hostile commentator, observes: 'They represent substantially a tax in kind, which, since it varies in some rough relation to the yield of land, can perhaps be regarded as an instrument for skimming off the differential rent which would otherwise be retained by more

* From Vol. V, No. 2, of *Soviet Studies*, 1953–54.

favourably situated farms.'[1] (The 'differential rent' interpretation is also used by some Soviet commentators,[2] but of course *all kolkhozy*, regardless of favourable situation, have to make compulsory deliveries, so the element of tax in kind remains.) A Soviet commentator, Rabinovich, claims that the effect is 'to hand over to the Government part of the surplus value created in the *kolkhozy*',[3] an interpretation which is certainly consistent with treating these deliveries as a tax in kind.

The *kolkhoz* also has payments to make, generally in kind, to the MTS (Machine Tractor Station) for its services. Unlike the compulsory delivery quota, deliveries to the MTS are related to the size of harvest. It may be that part of this payment-in-kind could legitimately be classified as tax, since the amounts payable may be in excess of the value of services rendered. This is suggested by the fact that *kolkhozy* deprived of the help of the MTS have their compulsory-delivery quota raised by 25 per cent.[4] It is true that the MTS have to be heavily subsidized from the budget, but their 'loss' may be statistical rather than real. The MTS hand over the produce they receive to the state, and are credited with the cash equivalent calculated at the low compulsory-procurement prices, while the fuel used by the MTS carries a heavy tax.

The burden of deliveries to the state and to the MTS cannot be given with any precision, in the absence of any recent statistics. Clearly, the burden is greater in poor harvest years, less in good. Scattered pre-war data suggest that 30 per cent of the gross grain crop, for instance, is a reasonable combined figure.[5]

Before going on to consider taxes proper, a brief survey of the price system is indispensable, especially since some of the tax rates are related to certain categories of prices. The following categories may be distinguished:

1. The compulsory procurement prices, already referred to.
2. *Kontraktatsia*; this applies almost wholly to technical crops

[1] Dobb, *Soviet Economic Development since 1917*, p. 284.
[2] For instance, Alexandrov, *Finansy SSSR*, p. 48.
[3] In the monthly *Sotsialisticheskoye Selskoye Khozyaistvo*, No. 7, 1950.
[4] Kolesnev, *Organizatsia Sotsialisticheskikh Selskokhozyaistvennykh Predpriatii* (Socialist agricultural enterprises), p. 533.
[5] Baykov, *Development of Soviet Economic System*, gives 31 per cent for 1938 (p. 311).

which cannot be sold in the free market. The state buys a given quantity at a modest price, and buys any surplus at considerably higher prices. Some *kontraktatsia* prices are favourable to the producers, certain cotton-growing *kolkhozy* in particular being able to earn high incomes.

3. *Gos-zakupka*—literally 'state purchase'. This is the price paid by the official procurement organizations for deliveries of produce (liable to compulsory deliveries) in excess of the quotas laid down. The price paid is considerably above the 'compulsory', well below the free market price.

4. The free market price. Any *kolkhoz* or peasant member who, having fulfilled other obligations, has any surplus foodstuffs to sell, may sell them in the open market at any price they will fetch. The fact that the prices in the state stores include high turnover taxes enables the peasants to obtain a market price which goes some way towards offsetting their losses from having to supply part of their produce to the state at very low prices.[1]

Finally, there are, of course, the prices charged by the state.

No up-to-date information is available showing the 'spread' between the various categories of prices. However, even rather old figures may give some idea of the orders of magnitude involved. In 1936, in the central areas, rye was bought compulsorily at 7.20 roubles per centner (=100 kilograms); the *gos-zakupka* price was 10.20 roubles; the state's *wholesale* price to the flour-mills was 93 roubles, and the retail price carried an additional tax.[2] According to examples given in a tax inspector's handbook published in 1948, the compulsory price of potatoes was 3.60 roubles per tsentner, and the *gos-zakupka* price was 10 roubles.[3] The market price was very high at this period, but it was still 90 roubles in Moscow in the spring of 1952.[4]

[1] In 1946, consumer co-operatives were allowed to buy from the peasants at market prices, but this concession was, apparently, withdrawn in 1949.

[2] Figures taken from Azarkh, *Oblozheniye Khleboproduktov* (Grain Tax), 1936, and Indenbaum (ed.), *Sbornik po Khlebozakupkam* (Grain purchases), 1936. An extra tax of about 48 roubles per centner on retail sales is cited by Suchkov, *Dokhody Gosbyudzheta* (Budget revenue), 1945 ed., p. 44.

[3] Dankov, *Sbornik Prakticheskikh Uprazhnenii po Nalogam* (Practical tax exercises) 1948 (figures in Exercise No. 207).

[4] This and other current market prices were those observed by visitors to the Moscow Economic Conference. (NB: Detailed information about prices at this period has been published since the above was written.)

It is now possible to consider the so-called 'income tax on *kolkhozy*', i.e. the tax paid in cash by the collective enterprises. This was very small until 1941: 3 per cent on all *kolkhoz* money income, while a similar tax was paid on the value of all produce not sold, the produce being valued at the very low compulsory-procurement prices.

In his 1941 budget speech, the Commissar of Finance, Zverev, stated that it would be necessary to increase the total weight of tax, and that it was proposed to do it in such a way as to encourage the more desirable activities of the *kolkhozy*. Sums received from the state in payment for compulsory deliveries were henceforth exempted from tax, as was produce used for feeding animals, or handed over to the MTS, or used to repay borrowed seed. The following tax rates were established for other categories:

(*a*) On the value, at compulsory-procurement prices, of produce used inside the *kolkhoz* for other productive and communal purposes (e.g. seed grain, products used for communal feeding, or allocated to welfare fund): *4 per cent.*

(*b*) On receipts from other sales to Government (*gos-zakupka* or *kontraktatsia*): *4 per cent.*

(*c*) On the value, assessed at *gos-zakupka* prices, of produce distributed to the *kolkhoz* members (they are paid for their work partly in cash, partly in kind): *8 per cent.*

(*d*) On receipts from free-market sales, and income from other sources (e.g. repair workshop, or provision of transport services): *8 per cent.*

In 1948, these rates were increased. By 1952, they were increased again. The following table shows the magnitude of the increases (for definitions of categories, see above):

RATE OF TAX (PER CENT)

Category	*1941–47*	*1948–51*	*1952*
(*a*)......	4	6	6 (on compulsory-proc. price)
(*b*)......	4	6	9
(*c*)......	8	12	24 (on *gos-zakupka* price)
(*d*)......	8	13	15

Sources: 1941: Zverev budget speech.
1948–51: *Spravochnik Nalogovovo Rabotnika* (1949), pp. 45ff.
1952: Alexandrov: *Finansy SSSR* (1952), p. 317.

The tax on produce distributed to *kolkhoz* members, i.e. (*c*) in the above table, is nominally still 12 per cent, but it is now based on *twice* the *gos-zakupka* price. It is probable that this sharp increase was decided upon in order to discourage those *kolkhozy* which distributed in kind more than the household's needs of the product in question, with the result that the peasant could take the surplus to the nearest market. The increase in the tax on receipts from sales to the state, however, can have no such 'ideological' justification; presumably the motive was simply to secure additional budgetary revenue.

It is important to observe that the cash payments made by the *kolkhozy* to their members come out of the surplus remaining after all other financial commitments have been met (e.g. expenditure on fertilizers, small tools, etc., capital expenditure of various kinds, compulsory insurance payments, cultural fund, welfare fund). The tax rates would not be severe if they related to *profits*; however, tax has to be paid on the bulk of the *kolkhoz*'s gross money income, and tax payments in cash have to be made in respect of a large part of the unsold produce of the *kolkhoz*, including even seed grain. These payments come directly out of the sums remaining for distribution to members.

We now pass to the taxes payable by the *kolkhoz* member.

Every collectivized household is entitled to a plot of land, which generally varies from ¼ to ½ hectare (¼ seems most common); the household may own animals up to certain maxima laid down by law. Some products of this plot are subject to compulsory deliveries at low prices, but the owner is entitled to do as he pleases with the remainder. If he desires to sell produce in the free market, he (or his wife) must face a long journey to the nearest town, carrying in a sack or bundle relatively small quantities at a time, and he must then spend many hours standing around in the market place. This must be a very wasteful system of distribution, but, as visitors to the USSR have observed, a large proportion of the urban food supply is derived from this source. There is evidence[1] that many, if not most, of the collectivized peasantry derived considerably more income from their little 'private enterprise' than from their work for the collective,

[1] For instance, Nesmii's survey of peasant incomes in *Planovoye Khozyaistvo*, No. 9, 1938.

with the inevitable result that the latter suffered. When, in his article published before the 19th Party Congress, Stalin wrote that the *kolkhoz* system in its present form was obstructing the further development of production, this must have been one of the points he had in mind. It is not surprising that he urged his colleagues to consider the gradual cutting down of the free market. Clearly, concentration on the private plot delays the expansion of the large-scale, collectivized sector, and it clashes with the social-political aim of eliminating as far as possible the unplanned market economy and the differences between workers and peasants. These considerations must have deeply influenced tax policy.

Until September 1939, the *kolkhoz* household paid little tax. The amounts varied from 10 to 50 roubles a year, according to region; the variation in the Moscow province was from 39 to 49 roubles.[1] Then a new set of tax regulations was issued, resembling in some respects the type of tax then being paid by the surviving individual peasants. The basis of the new system was this: a given planted area was deemed to produce an income of so many roubles a year, and the tax was levied on this 'rateable value'; animals (but not fowls and rabbits) were similarly assessed.[2] The rate of tax was to be on a sliding scale, beginning with 7 per cent or 50 roubles (the latter was a minimum) and rising to 15 per cent on valuations in excess of 4,000 roubles. As can be seen in the table below, the valuations were quite modest in comparison with later years, and it is not surprising to learn that 52 per cent of *kolkhoz* households in 1940 were 'valued' at under 1,000 roubles.[3]

The 1941 budget included a provision for increasing 'rateable values', in conformity with the rise which had already taken place in market prices.[4] When war broke out, market prices naturally soared still higher, and the valuations were greatly increased in 1943. The following table gives the 'valuations' for

[1] Plotnikov, *Byudzhet Sovetskovo Gosudarstva* (Soviet state budget), p. 191.

[2] Details of 1939 tax rates and valuations are from Ministry of Finance's *Finansovyi i Khozyaistvennyi Byulleten* (Financial and Economic Bulletin), Nos. 25–6 of 1939.

[3] Plotnikov, *op. cit.*, p. 194. He gives tax rates below those quoted here; it seems reasonable to go by those quoted in the more official source.

[4] Zverev: budget speech, *Pravda*, February 26, 1941. He gave no details.

tax purposes of the more important items, introduced in the years 1939, 1943 and 1950:[1]

ROUBLES PER HUNDREDTH OF HECTARE PLANTED

	1939	*1943*	*1950*
Grain	5·40	45	45
Potatoes	12	120	64
Vegetables	25	160	140
Orchards	35	160	160
Natural pastures	3	8	8

ROUBLES PER HEAD OF ANIMALS

	1939	*1943*	*1950*
Cow	600	3500	2540
Sheep or goat	40	350	180
Pig	300	1500	800

The above list, which is not complete, gives *average* valuations for the Russian republic (RSFSR). Regional authorities were given wide powers to vary the rates for particular localities, to the maximum extent of 40 per cent above and below the average set for the given region, provided the regional average is maintained. The variations depend on fertility and, above all, on accessibility of high-price urban markets.

The *rates* of tax were increased several times, as the following table shows:[2]

	1939	*1943*	*1948*	*1950*	*1951*
Minimum rate (%)	7	8	11	11	12
Maximum rate (%) ..	15	30	40	45	48
Amount payable on 5000 r. valuation	—	540	720	750	820

There was a further increase in 1952: a surcharge was introduced amounting to 5–10 per cent on the tax assessed, to cover items which, like fowls, are not separately valued.[3]

Finally, in 1953 peasants were made to pay half their tax in the first half of the year, although previously the tax was collected

[1] The *ukazy* were dated June 13, 1943, and August 16, 1950. It has proved impossible to find details of the upward amendments to valuations announced in the Budget speech of 1941. According to Maryakhin (*Nalogovaya Sistema SSSR*, Moscow, 1952), the first post-war downward amendment occurred in 1946, but details of this are not available to the present writer. Maryakhin's book, which was published at the end of 1952, makes no mention of any changes in valuations later than 1950.

[2] The 1948 and 1951 *ukazy* appeared on July 13th and August 30th respectively.

[3] Alexandrov, *op. cit.*, p. 323.

in the period September-November, i.e. after the year's crop had been sold.[1]

In determining the amounts payable, the tax authorities add to thc above-mentioned 'valuation' the actual sums which the *kolkhoz* members receive from summer lettings, handicrafts and other such earnings 'on the side'. (As we shall see, this provision disappears from the new tax law.)

The peasant pays no tax on his remuneration for work done for the *kolkhoz*, and he pays the normal income tax on his wages for any seasonal work which he may undertake in a town. There are also a number of concessions and exemptions from the private-plot tax affecting some categories: thus, 'rural intelligentsia' and a number of local officials were exempt from tax if the 'rateable value' of their crops and animals is below 3,000 roubles; state employees with allotments below 0.15 hectares and no cow are exempt, as are war invalids, and wives of serving soldiers if with children under eight years of age. Households where the man is over sixty and the woman over fifty-five, with no younger working member, paid at half rates (or in cases of special hardship, were exempted from payment).[2]

The weight of a tax assessed in the above manner naturally increases with every cut in market prices. The *kolkhoz* peasant's 'private' economy was thus under heavy fiscal pressure. Peasants whose holdings are situated far from any urban centre must have found it very hard to pay the tax, and so it was not surprising to read of a *kolkhoz* in the remote Kirov (Vyatka) region where members voluntarily abandoned their private plots altogether.[3]

The *kolkhoz* peasant pays a rural levy, but this cannot exceed the small sum of 20 roubles per annum.[4] The only other direct tax which may affect him is the bachelor and small-families tax. Each adult member of the household of child-bearing or child-begetting age pays a lump sum of 150 roubles if childless, 50 roubles for having only one child, and 25 roubles for two children. Thus the tax handbook cites a family of two forty-year-old peasants with a son of twenty-one and a daughter of seventeen; the two parents pay 25 roubles each for having only two children, the son 150

[1] Article by Kuznetsov in *Finansy i Kredit*, No. 4, 1953.

[2] For these and other details, see Dankov, *Selskokhozyaistvennyi Nalog* (Moscow, 1952).

[3] Tsikoto in *Sovetskaya Agronomia*, No. 11, 1952.

[4] *Spravochnik Nalogovovo Rabotnika* (Moscow, 1950), p. 69.

roubles for having none, and the daughter is below the age-limit. This tax, since 1952, is added to the private-plot tax and collected with it.[1]

As against this, parents of large families receive grants from the state.

Finally, the peasantry is liable to a form of labour-tax; each must provide six days' unpaid work every year to build and maintain roads.

In return for these taxes, the peasants benefit from a constantly developing educational system, and a rural health service which, whatever its shortcomings, is a great advance on the past. However, it remains true that *kolkhoz* peasants derive far less value than do state employees from the taxes they pay, because they are denied any social insurance benefits from state sources. They are deemed to be members of a self-supporting co-operative, and, with few exceptions, it is the *kolkhoz* which looks after the aged, the sick, the orphans, etc., out of its own resources.

It is clear from the above account that the tax policy of the state was deliberately designed to discourage the private plot. Malenkov's speech of August 8, 1953, in the budget debate contained the admission that the number of privately-owned animals and the level of income from the private plot had fallen, and he assigned this to be 'erroneous' tax policy.[2] A drastic change of approach to the private sector has taken place. There is to be a flat-rate tax depending on land area irrespective of the crops or animals upon it, with variations between localities (dependent as before on distance from markets, and on fertility). The intention to encourage 'private enterprise' is exemplified by a provision that *kolkhoz* peasants with no cow have their tax reduced by 50 per cent this year and 30 per cent in 1954, to help them acquire a cow.

The actual tax payable in the Russian republic and the Ukraine is to average 8.50 roubles per 1/100 hectare of the *kolkhoz* member's private land, with local variations from 3 to 14 roubles. The effect, in a full year, will be a 2½-fold reduction in the total sum payable; the latter will be below 4,000 million roubles. Assuming

[1] Gurvich, *Sovetskoye Finansovoye Pravo* (Moscow, 1952), p. 208.

[2] Since that time, there has been abundant evidence in official speeches and elsewhere to show the burdensome nature and discouraging effects of this tax, especially in the period 1949–53.

that something like 90 per cent of the tax is paid by *kolkhoz* members (the rest by state employees and individual peasants), the average tax paid per household will fall from roughly 430 roubles in 1952 to 170 roubles in 1954. Clearly, this is a major concession, viewed against the background of the low money income of the peasantry.

The tax payable per 1/100 hectare is much higher in areas where land is specially valuable, e.g. in irrigated regions and Georgia. It is consistently much lower in all territories annexed in 1939–40. Thus the average for the Baltic states and for the western areas of the Ukraine and Byelorussia is half that of the adjoining 'old' territories.

There is nothing in the new tax law to indicate what tax, if any, is to be paid by peasants on non-agricultural earnings (which were formerly added to 'valued' income for tax purposes).

To protect the *kolkhoz* collective labour supply, the tax is to be increased by 50 per cent if any member of the household fails to work the legal minimum of labour-days. If a resident member of the family of working age is not a *kolkhoz* member and does not work for a state or co-operative organization, the tax is increased 75 per cent. In the case of state employees' land, the latter clause does not operate if the 'unemployed' person is the housewife, but no such exception is made for the peasant. Peasants over sixty (men) or fifty-five (women) who have no younger working person living with them, are now exempt from tax altogether. Certain changes are made in rules governing exemptions of the 'rural intelligentsia'.

There is to be a cut in the level of compulsory deliveries from the private plots.

The tax on the revenue of the *kolkhozy* apparently remains unchanged, though the revenues will clearly go up as a result of an increase in some state procurement prices.

* * *

The above article was written in the summer of 1953, and the concluding paragraphs were added in proof when the Government, then presided over by Malenkov, greatly reduced the peasants' burdens. The efforts made at the time of Malenkov's subsequent resignation to prove that he was not responsible for this measure is at any rate proof of its popularity. The change to per-hectare tax basis encourages effort instead of discouraging it, and the total amount was much reduced. There seem to have been no changes in the rules and tax rates since. Various expedients have been tried, especially since 1958, to discourage peasant private enterprise, but taxation has not been used for this purpose. In 1963, a fierce decree was published in the *Vedomosti verkhovnovo soveta RSFSR* (No. 18, 1963) subjecting to heavy rates of tax any livestock owned by households in excess of prescribed maxima, or any livestock owned by households in which a member failed to work for the *kolkhoz* to the extent prescribed. Tax rates include the following, the amounts being expressed in *old* roubles to ensure comparability with figures cited earlier:

	Roubles
Cow	1500
Sow	550
Sheep or goat	150
Horse	2000
Other working livestock ..	1000

Note that these figures represent actual tax payable, not 'rateable value'.

(The above relates to the Russian republic only, but presumably others have done the same.)

It is possible to interpret this measure as an attempt to impose labour discipline rather than a tax on private activities as such, but we may be sure that it is highly unpopular. It must be seen in relation to another campaign now (September 1963) current, against the purchase of bread, oatmeal, etc., to feed private livestock, with no word about alternative and legal sources of fodder.

The peasant household has benefited, in common with others, from the cut in the bachelor and small-families tax, and also from the elimination of the duty to perform unpaid labour on the roads (see 'Social Welfare in the USSR' in this volume).

The tax on *kolkhozy* has been twice subject to major changes. A decree published in *Vedomosti verkhovnovo soveta* in 1957 (No. 19) abolished the multiple rates of tax, substituting a flat rate of 14 per cent on the total 'income' of the *kolkhoz* in cash and in kind, less a long list of exemptions. The exemptions included virtually all cash expenditures for productive purposes (e.g. on fuel, fodder, repairs and also amortization), as well as receipts from compulsory deliveries of livestock or livestock products. This in practice meant that taxable revenue included sums used for payment of peasants, or transferred to the capital fund (less amortization), or allocated to the cultural fund or for administration, or carried over into the year following. The value of produce used within the *kolkhoz* was to be taxed after deducting amounts used for productive purposes (e.g. seed, fodder, payments to MTS, return of seed loans, and also reserve funds in kind). The taxed produce consisted in the main of that issued in payment for work done and for other human needs, such as communal feeding (the amounts set aside for relief of the aged and infirm were exempted). Produce distributed to peasant members on *trudodni* was valued for tax at compulsory-procurement prices (which had, of course, been substantially increased during 1953–56); other produce liable to tax was valued at *gos-zakupka* prices. The net effect of the change, which took effect in January 1958, was to increase both the range of exemptions and the rate at which tax was charged. But we cannot determine whether, on balance, the tax yield would have risen or fallen. No sooner was this reform promulgated than it became obsolete, since in the spring of 1958 two events transformed *kolkhoz* finances. The first was the absorption by *kolkhozy* of the MTS. This had several effects:

(*a*) It called for immediate expenditure in buying the machinery and equipment.
(*b*) It greatly increased current and capital expenditure on fuel, equipment, repairs, the payment of ex-employees of the MTS, amortization and so on.
(*c*) It also greatly increased cash revenues, in so far as produce formerly handed over in payment for MTS services could now be sold. However, productive and capital expenditure now took a larger *share* of these revenues than before 1958.

The second change was the abolition of the multiple price system. Any product was to be sold at one price, differentiated only by zones, quality or season of the year. With the end of 'compulsory-procurement prices', this form of barely-disguised tax or rent was eliminated.[1]

[1] Some of the prices fixed in 1958 enabled the state to continue to make a sizeable profit (e.g. on grain), while others (e.g. meat, butter) involved state subsidies (see *Vestnik statistiki*, No. 1, 1963).

We are only concerned here with the effects of these measures on *kolkhoz* taxation. Obviously, both cash revenues and cash expenditures rose sharply, and the valuation of produce paid to peasants in kind increased substantially because the new unified prices were far above the former compulsory-procurement prices. A change in the tax law was inevitable, and this was decreed on December 18, 1958, and published in *Vedomosti verkhovnovo soveta*, No. 1 of 1959. The general principles of the tax remained those operative in the previous year, except that receipts from the sales of livestock were only exempt if they were devoted to the capital fund and/or for livestock improvement. The single rate of tax was reduced from 14 per cent to 12½ per cent. This rate can be, and has been, varied within republics in accordance with soil and climate; thus in the RSFSR it varies from *nil* in Kamchatka to 15 per cent in the North Caucasus.[1]

However, the yield of tax increased by 20 per cent from 1958 to 1959.[2] Since there is some evidence that the *net* income of *kolkhozy* (i.e. net of the greatly increased expenditure occasioned by the takeover of the MTS) actually fell, the real burdens of tax rose significantly. This follows from a calculation by another Soviet writer, Buyanov, who estimates that, *as a percentage of net revenues*, the *kolkhoz* tax burden in the RSFSR rose from 12.4 per cent in 1958 to no less than 19 per cent in 1959.[3] One example of increased burdens is that *kolkhozy* now pay tax on cash and produce intended for paying former MTS employees (who are now *kolkhoz* members), whereas previously the amounts paid by *kolkhozy* to the MTS were tax-exempt. All this would help to explain the fall in incomes of peasants which occurred at this time and which is referred to in another paper in the present volume.

The following table shows the rapid increase in the yield of *kolkhoz* tax. It may be thought relevant to include, for purposes of comparison, the total cash revenue of the *kolkhozy*, but this would be misleading, because, for reasons already mentioned, the revenue figure includes a variable (and, since 1958, greatly rising) amount devoted to productive and capital expenditures.

[1] Decree (Postanovlenie) of December 21, 1959.

[2] See table opposite.

[3] P. Buyanov: *Obshchestvennye fondy kolkhozovi raspredelenie kolkhoznykh dokhodov* (M., 1961), p. 87.

It is also worth noting that a proportion of *kolkhozy* have been converted to state farms, so that the figures cited below understate the increased burden on the surviving *kolkhozy*. The figures in the table have been converted into old roubles.

MILLIONS OF (OLD) ROUBLES

	1950	*1955*	*1957*	*1958*	*1959*	*1960*
Kolkhoz tax ..	2540	6252	8486	10314	12376	12073

(*Source: Gosudarstvennyi byudzhet SSSR* (M., 1962), p. 9.)

It remains to be added that a sharp increase in state buying prices for meat and milk in 1962 benefited *kolkhoz* net revenues, and the consequent increase in cash income from sales was not offset by any substantial upward valuation of payments in kind, since only a small proportion of such payments consist of meat or milk.

11. Incentives for peasants and administrators *

It is clear enough that material incentives are required if the peasants are to work, or at least to work with reasonable competence. However, incentives are needed also to stimulate and direct the work of management and, indeed, also of the party and state officials who issue orders to management. Effective decentralization of decision-making requires criteria related to the material advantage of choosing this or that course of action. Some stimuli can be not material but 'moral': the approval of one's superiors, prospects of promotion, the avoidance of demotion. But some criteria there must be. If incentives are confused, misleading, or non-existent, they must be replaced by detailed orders from above, and this is why the whole question is intimately linked with that of administrative organization. One should add that agriculture, with its endless variety of soil, climate and other circumstances, not only requires decentralized decision-making but gets it in practice in some degree, whatever the rules may be. If the pattern of incentives stimulates irrational behaviour or fails to stimulate desired effort, interference from above must try to correct undesirable actions; but it is impossible to envisage a situation in which a set of clear and enforceable central orders cover every contingency.

PEASANT INCENTIVES

Average Incomes

The inadequacy of peasant rewards for work for the collective farms was a major cause of the depressed state of Soviet agriculture in the Stalin period. Most peasants reserved their efforts for their private holdings of land and livestock. In the period down to 1957, however, the situation changed radically, as the following figures show:

* Paper presented at a conference on the Russian economy, Kansas, and published in *Soviet Agricultural and Peasant Affairs* (Univ. of Kansas Press, 1963).

TABLE 1

CASH PAYMENTS

	1952	*1957*
(Old) Roubles per *trudoden*[a]	1·40	4·00
Total paid out (billions old roubles)	12·40	47·90
Total cash revenue, collective farms (billions old roubles)	42·80	95·20

[a] Workday unit. For sources see A. Nove in *Slavonic Review* (London), No. 2, June, 1960, pp. 318–20.

A large part of the income of the peasants from their collective work is in the form of produce, and distributions of produce altered little, so that the sum of peasant incomes in cash and kind rose by much less than appears from the above table. It is not clear how the income in kind has been valued in the table below, but it seems to represent a fair picture of real trends:

TABLE 2

TOTAL VALUE OF CASH AND KIND PAYMENTS

	1952	*1957*
(Old) Roubles per *trudoden*	5·40	7·55
Total paid out (billions old roubles)	47·50	83·80

Sources: As for Table 1.

The total distributed increased faster than the amounts paid per *trudoden*, because peasants worked longer in 1957 than in 1952, owing (in unknown proportions) to more stringent labour discipline and the effects on effort of the higher pay. Thus, in 1957 the peasants' pay could be described as 'not good, but better', certainly much better than in any of the post-war years. Some contrary allegations[1] appear to be totally baseless.

In the years following 1957, however, evidence began to accumulate that the income of peasants has been reduced. Official sources maintained silence about *trudoden* payments after 1957, which was in itself an indication that all was not well. Several Soviet scholars did indeed publish hints of a decline in some areas, and Arcadius Kahan was quickly able to show that there was every likelihood of a fall in peasant incomes from collective sources, coinciding with a reduction in private livestock holdings.[2]

Quite recently, however, conclusive evidence appeared in the

[1] For example, by Ivantsov in *Novyi Zhurnal* (New York), No. 67, 1962, p. 295.

[2] In *Problems of Communism* (US Government Printing Office, November-December, 1961), pp. 54–57.

authoritative *Voprosy Ekonomiki* by V. Khlebnikov.[1] True, he does not cite figures for the USSR as a whole, and he does assert that peasant incomes 'in essence remained at the same level' between 1957 and 1960. However, taking the 1957 level as 100, he gives the following figures for 1960:

Ukraine ..	82	Uzbekistan	83	Moldavia ..	71
Belorussia ..	89	Georgia ..	86		

Since other sources, notably Kapustin, had already given figures suggesting a decline also in several *oblasti* of the Russian republic (RSFSR) and some of the Baltic states,[2] there is a very strong indication indeed of a fall in peasant incomes and, therefore, a positive disincentive to hard work, after 1957. In fact, Khlebnikov himself points out that output must have been adversely affected.

Why did this happen? It is very doubtful that the Soviet leadership intended such a result, which seems to have been due to a combination of the following factors:

(*a*) State purchase prices for farm produce, announced in 1958, were cut, with little or no publicity. According to Venzher[3] grain prices were cut by 15 per cent already in 1958 by reason of the good harvest of that year. True, there was a good harvest in 1958, and it was announced in the price decree of that year that there would be upward and downward variations according to harvest variations. However, the state apparently forgot to raise prices again when less favourable weather led to some fall in production. This may be deduced from the fact, cited by Khlebnikov, that the 1960 average purchase price for grain was 62 roubles per quintal (against 74 roubles in the original 1958 decree). The same may well have happened to several other products, the more so as there was vigorous criticism of alleged high prices in plenary sessions of the Central Committee.

(*b*) The cost to the collective farms of taking over the Machine-Tractor Stations (MTS) seems to have been a burden on their finances. Despite some concessions (e.g. prices of trucks were reduced), farms not only found themselves having to pay for

[1] V. Khlebnikov, *Voprosy Ekonomiki*, No. 7, 1962, pp. 50–53.

[2] E. Kapustin, in *Ekonomicheskaya Gazeta*, April 9, 1962.

[3] V. G. Venzher, *Voprosy Ispol'zovaniya Zakona Stoimosti v Kolkhozakh* (Moscow, 1960), p. 28.

machinery not always desired but also faced a substantial rise in prices of tractors and other equipment,[1] as well as very high charges for repairs and replacements, about which repeated complaints were made in the press. A further burden was the necessity of paying relatively high guaranteed incomes to tractor men and combiners, formerly paid by the MTS. True, the farms' revenues increased substantially as a result of being able to sell the produce which formerly had to be handed over to pay for the services of the MTS. On balance, however, there was probably some loss, though this cannot be demonstrated because of the absence of necessary statistics from Soviet sources.

(*c*) Farms were under pressure to invest more—for instance, in various kinds of cultural investments (school-building, etc.). This was one reason cited by Kapustin for the decline of incomes in some areas.

(*d*) In 1959 and 1960 there were frequent denunciations of collective farms which were alleged to distribute too much to their members. These concerned that small minority of farms prosperous enough to pay peasants better wages than state wage earners receive. It may well be that a number of such farms reduced their pay-outs. But official statements said nothing about increasing pay on those farms which had very little to distribute. Consequently the changes under this head were likely to have adversely affected the overall average.

(*e*) Many of the reported cases of speculation and black-market transactions relate to purchases (at high illegal prices) of such items as building materials and tyres by collective farms, whose desperately-needed supplies could not be obtained from official sources at official prices. These things make a hole in farm budgets and cut into the amount available for distribution to peasants.

(*f*) Finally, pressure to fulfil plans for delivery of produce to the state, at a time when production plans were not fulfilled, reduces the amount available for distribution in kind and/or for sale at high free-market prices.

It seems that all the above reasons contributed in varying degrees to the unfavourable trend in peasant incomes. As there

[1] Evidence kindly provided by Jerzy Karcz. (The rise is in comparison with prices charged to the MTS and to state farms.)

was also some pressure on the private sector, especially affecting the number of privately-owned cows, the peasants evidently had much to complain about. It should not have been beyond the understanding of the Soviet leadership that an actual cut in incomes, especially when the peasants had every right to expect some continued increase, was bound to have ill effects. It is true that Khrushchev, at the time of the 1958 price reform, did say that further price increases were not intended and that future rises in peasant incomes would depend on higher productivity. But, according to evidence cited by Khlebnikov in his article, reductions in incomes occurred despite a sizeable *rise* in productivity per head. One wonders whether officials are so accustomed to squeezing the peasants that it has become a kind of second nature to them.

Proof that these results were not intended may be found in the measures announced during 1962 to put matters right. Increased purchase prices, especially of meat, together with a sharp cut in prices of many items bought by farms, should have the effect, according to Khlebnikov and other authoritative sources, of adding 2.3 billion new roubles to the net revenues of collective farms. Khlebnikov expresses the view that, if the share of peasants in estimated net revenue of the farms were to remain unchanged, this would mean a rise in cash distributions to peasants by some 30 per cent. There should now be an improvement, and we must watch for further evidence.

Variations and Uncertainties of Peasant Income

So far we have confined our attention to averages. However, a major weakness of the incentive system lies in the fact that peasants working for different collective farms receive vastly different rewards for the same work, and, in most cases, have no idea how much they will in fact receive in the next period, since very substantial year-by-year variations in the same collective farm are quite common. This familiar situation arises because farms do not have to pay any predetermined reward for their members' work and because in law the members share out what is left after other needs are met. Examples abound of the effects of this. We have seen that average payment for *trudoden* in 1957 (also in 1956) was close to 7.50 old roubles, if cash and kind are combined. While some farms paid out 4 roubles or less, one farm in Armenia, named after the Paris Commune, paid 62.80 roubles per *trudoden* in 1956, and this despite the fact that 29 per cent of the men and 55 per cent of the women members did not work the established obligatory minimum for the collective![1] (There may be cause and effect here: a backward-sloping supply curve for labour, a strong preference for leisure at the margin.)

The unreasonableness of such variations in payments for *trudoden* is widely recognized, in and out of the USSR. Perhaps it is less well known to students abroad that, owing to big differences in work norms per *trudoden* on different farms, what appears to be similar pay for similar work can in fact conceal substantial inequalities. After comparing norms for similar work in two collective farms in the Vinnitsa Oblast of the Ukraine, the well-known Soviet farm economist Nesmii showed that while they distributed respectively 8.80 and 8.26 (old) roubles per *trudoden*, this in fact represented for one day's average work 22.00 roubles on one farm and 13.05 on the other.[2]

On top of this, there are some income variations within a farm, additional to the skill differentials provided for in the rules (these range, according to the statute, from 0.5 to 2.5 *trudodni* per norm-unit). The liquidation of the MTS involved the collective farms not only in absorbing a number of ex-MTS personnel whose pay rates (in *trudodni*) very greatly exceeded the maximum of 2.5 per norm-unit; it also involved the farms in the obligation of paying these men a guaranteed minimum amount, which in the poorer farms meant a disproportionately still larger sum (compared with the rank-and-file membership). On top of this, the former tractor men were and are entitled as of right to paid vacations and, also, to various social insurance benefits not available to their 'fellow-members'. One can imagine that this leads to some social stresses and strains.

It is true that the range of differences between good and bad farms, and good and bad areas, was even greater before 1953. This, so far as inter-republican variations are concerned, may be illustrated by the following table:

[1] M. Nesmii, *Voprosy Sebestoimosti i Rentabel'nosti v Kolkhozakh* (Moscow, 1959), p. 46. Grapes and cotton were the crops.

[2] *Ibid.*, p. 149.

TABLE 3

CASH DISTRIBUTIONS PER TRUDODEN

	1950=100		*Percentage of all-union average*		
	1955	*1958*	*1950*	*1955*	*1958*
USSR	187·9	316·8	—	—	—
RSFSR	364·5	637·6	39·6	76·8	79·7
Ukraine	249·6	400·0	82·6	109·6	104·2
Belorussia	774·3	851·5	23·5	96·8	63·1
Uzbekistan	84·0	169·4	416·2	186·1	222·5
Georgia	126·4	162·3	332·9	223·9	170·6
Tadzhikistan	75·2	94·3	772·0	303·9	229·9
Lithuania	160·0	451·7	40·3	34·3	57·4

Source: Venzher, *op. cit.*, p. 221.

This table needs to be used with caution, in so far as, for instance, a much larger proportion of the pay of peasants in the RSFSR than in the Central Asian republics consisted of produce, not included in the above table. Nonetheless, the general picture which emerges is broadly correct. In 1950, a few favoured areas in the south, benefiting from relatively good prices for cotton and other semi-tropical products, did far better than Russia proper, Belorussia and the Baltic states, which were depressed by extremely low prices for grains and livestock products, and still suffering from the after-effects of the war. By 1958 there had been some equalization, though it is interesting to note, *inter alia*, that Tadzhik incomes have actually fallen absolutely and that Lithuania is still very far behind the all-union average. But none of this affects or reflects the very wide variations within each republic, according to differences of location and soil fertility, of which more will be said when we discuss costs and rent later on.

Regular and Guaranteed Pay; Incentive Bonuses

Party leaders have gone on record repeatedly in favour of the payment of monthly 'advances' (*avansy*) to collective farm members. Indeed, it is clear that people work better if they receive some cash at frequent intervals, as against a promise to pay an unknown sum many months hence. Yet, owing to an insufficient financial base, only 23 per cent of all collective farms paid their members ten or more times a year; the majority did make several advances through the year, only 4.7 per cent making none.[1] There is still no trend toward greater regularity.

[1] Venzher, *op. cit.*, p. 26. The figures relate to 1958.

Of at least equal importance is the question of a guaranteed share to the peasants of the gross revenues of the farms and/or a guaranteed minimum payment per *trudoden*. Some argue vigorously for the abolition of the *trudoden*, for its replacement by a definite sum in payment for work done, more or less corresponding to a wage. Whichever of these variants is adopted, the effect would be to end the status of peasant members of collective farms as residuary claimants on 'their' farms' income. The need for a change along these lines has been eloquently argued in the Soviet Union for over six years. A whole long catalogue of quotations can readily be assembled from the party and specialized press. In fact, amid approving publicity, some farms went over to guaranteed cash payments, and a small minority still pay their members in this way. However, most farms cannot find a sufficient regular income, or have no adequate financial reserves, to enable them to switch to this kind of payment to peasants. The economist Kraeva cited evidence to show that a number of farms tried guaranteed cash payments and were forced to abandon them and to return to *trudodni*, as they found that they could not honour their promises to their peasants.[1]

Aware of the need for greater incentives, yet unable or unwilling to underwrite guaranteed pay, the Soviet leadership has come out strongly for bonuses related to output. In speeches during 1962 Khrushchev has several times reasserted the need for such bonuses.

On the fact of it, incentive bonuses are self-evidently good for productivity. Yet there must have been a reason for the fact that previously existing bonus systems were, apparently, quietly abandoned in 1956 or 1957. So we are dealing with a revival, not a new departure.

It must be recalled that, in collective farms, the total sum available for payments to peasants is limited, and any additional payments to some automatically reduce the amounts available to other members. In a state enterprise, including state farms, this is not the case. If a worker finds himself entitled to a bonus of 100 roubles, no other employee of his enterprise suffers any reduction in his pay entitlements. The inherent unfairness of collective farm bonuses and also the immense complexity of the incentive schemes seem to have led to their partial or complete

[1] *Voprosy Ekonomiki*, No. 8, 1961, p. 74.

G

abandonment. One may refer to the rules adopted in 1948, which were very fully analysed by Henri Wronski.[1] A peasant's pay came to depend on the amount of work he did, measured in *trudodni*, which were then modified either in relation to achievement of the planned harvest by his brigade or work-squad, or in the proportion which the product bore to the average yield (per hectare, per cow, etc.) in that collective farm, or both. All this was further complicated in and after 1953 by a series of *ad hoc* measures designed to stimulate output of some particular product and promising those engaged in producing it a priority share in receipts from sales or some share in the product itself. By 1956 the situation threatened chaos. In the words of Solyonova in the party's fortnightly *Kommunist* (No. 1, 1956): 'The implementation of supplementary pay and other measures of material incentives is extremely complicated by its variety in relation to various crops and products, by the fixing of definite and occasionally high rates of supplementary pay. This led to substantial and often groundless variations in the payments per *trudoden* within the same collective farm.' She gave some fantastic examples of peasants getting many times more than others according to which crop they were working on.

In 1957, another authoritative party journal took very much the same line: 'It is wrong to issue bonuses or make deductions from pay in relation to harvest plan fulfilment. The peasants would not work when they see the harvest is behind the plan.'[2] The point stressed here is that the harvest so often depends on circumstances beyond the control of the peasants that bonuses would often go to undeserving persons. Others, however, would be discouraged from working harder to save the harvest which is adversely affected by bad weather, since, however hard they work, the planned yield would not be reached, and they in effect would be penalized.

Yet it is this system, or some variant of it, that is now being restored upon orders from the centre. No doubt the intention is to apply these principles while avoiding the excesses and illogicalities of past years, though it may be difficult to do this. In a recent issue of *Ekonomicheskaya Gazeta*,[3] it is suggested that the

[1] *Le Troudoden* (Paris, 1956).
[2] *Partiinaya Zhizn'*, No. 6, 1957.
[3] September 29, 1962, pp. 29, 30.

peasants should be paid a guaranteed basic rate and that the incentive bonus should be a kind of differentiated dividend, payable in cash and in produce, calculated when the final year's results are known. This is similar in principle to the so-called 'accord premium system' which is being applied in state farms. According to another issue of the same journal,[1] the employees of state farms are to be paid their regular wages on the basis of piecework in the normal way, with subsequent upward or downward adjustments when the output of the given product in relation to the plan becomes known. However, as this issue of the journal makes clear, the system is the cause of much confusion in state farms and must be very difficult to apply in practice, if only because of accounting complications. In any event, so far as collective farms are concerned, most of the farms are still unable to pay a guaranteed minimum sum to peasants, and so there will be no sound basis upon which to relate basic pay and incentive bonuses. We may expect a period of experiment.

It is indeed remarkable that so little progress has been made with the obviously necessary task of ensuring a regular income for collective farmers. Its desirability is self-evident on both practical and ideological grounds. Not only will peasants work better if they are assured of some definite pay for their work, but such guaranteed pay is an essential prerequisite to weaning the peasants away from reliance on their private plots. Why, then, has so little been done? One must suppose that the principal reason is shortage of money and resources. Guaranteed minimum rewards would involve the state in paying a subsidy to those collective farms which are unable to pay whatever minimum is prescribed. A possible way out was discussed, when a number of scholars and officials put forward the idea of 'collective farm unions', in which the better-off farms would have their surplus revenues redistributed for the benefit of the weaker brethren. However, this was not in fact done. It would have involved a sharp reduction in peasant incomes on the better-off farms, and perhaps it was also thought undesirable to create new organizations which may act as organized pressure groups on behalf of peasants. The leadership confined itself to partial measures. On the one hand, a number of collective farms were instructed to amalgamate with their weaker neighbours, this being one of the

[1] September 15, 1962, pp. 28ff.

reasons for the continued reduction in the number of farms and the increase in their size. The other solution was to convert the weaker collective farms into state farms. This was done on a considerable scale beginning with 1957, but apparently this process has been halted. Khrushchev has pointed out that many local officials like to create state farms in the place of collective farms, because they then can more easily obtain money from Moscow. Here again, one sees a shortage of resources as a principal obstacle to reform, particularly as, in this instance, a budgetary subsidy would lead directly to higher personal incomes and, therefore, to an increased demand for consumers' goods. Just recently it has been announced in Moscow that the promised abolition of income tax is being suspended, which provides yet another illustration of the difficulties under which the authorities are labouring. It is likely that the recent increases in arms expenditure are partly to blame.

It is of some interest to try to compare the level of incomes of peasants on collective farms and workers on state farms. We have seen that in 1957 payment in cash and kind per *trudoden* amounted to approximately 7.55 old roubles. In the same year, according to an authoritative source, the basic rate for the most unskilled grade of state farm worker was 12.10 roubles a day. Since it takes less than a day to earn a *trudoden*, the source assumed that for this length of time a state-farm worker would earn 8.65 roubles. This is only a little above the average for all collective farmers. But this comparison could lead to a completely misleading conclusion. Not only do earnings normally exceed basic rates, but the average degree of skill of state-farm workers obviously must be well above the lowest grade. Scattered evidence covering many parts of the country for 1957 suggests that actual earnings per worker in state farms averaged roughly 20 roubles a day,[1] or say 14 roubles for the equivalent of a *trudoden*. This is likely to be typical of the country as a whole, since on state farms, not as on collective farms, wage rates are fixed centrally and are guaranteed by the state, so that no very large regional variations should occur.

INCENTIVES FOR OFFICIALS

Incentives for Collective-Farm Chairmen

Under regulations adopted in 1948, the pay of a collective-farm

[1] For the evidence, see *Slavonic Review*, June, 1960, p. 331.

chairman was determined by a very complicated procedure. It depended upon a whole number of factors. He was allocated fixed numbers of *trudodni* per month in respect to the sown area, number of cows, sows, ewes and the like. He also received a cash payment which varied with the gross cash revenues of the farm. For example, if the revenue were 950,000 roubles, he would receive 350 roubles per month. In addition, his income as calculated in all the above ways was increased or diminished by varying percentages according to whether the output of various crops and livestock products was or was not in excess of the plan. In recent years this system has been substantially modified, and on present evidence there seems to be no rule applicable to the country as a whole. It is reported that on some farms his pay is now related to output in physical terms—for instance, 0.4 *trudodni* for each ton of grain. In another district the chairman receives a cash salary which is a fixed percentage of the gross output of the farm, all products being valued at their state purchase price. In some cases there are bonuses for fulfilling certain output or delivery plans. The pay of other officials, such as the chief accountant or the chief agronomist, is often a fixed percentage of the chairman's pay. However, there is no evidence that the chairman's actual behaviour is greatly influenced by these kinds of incentives. Since he depends on party officials for his appointment, and since they can and frequently do dismiss him, it is extremely important for him to ensure that the campaigns and instructions urged upon him from above should take priority. In a choice between obeying an instruction, even a patently foolish instruction, and pursuing the short-term maximization of his own income, a chairman and, with him, other farm officials find themselves under heavy pressure to obey the instruction.

A small example is taken from a report in *Pravda* of July 31, 1962: 'In a field, women peasants are vigorously pulling up weeds. The sugar beet sown in this field had perished and to use labour on cultivation is clearly quite useless. It would be better to use the land for some other purpose. . . . The agronomist replied, "This area is included as under sugar beet. We must fulfil the plan." "But there is no sugar beet here!" "Yes, I told the chief agronomist. And he said that the plan is the plan, it must be fulfilled." '

Much is being said about the need for agricultural efficiency and, therefore, for rewarding agricultural management for the efficient use of the land and resources entrusted to management's care. However, it has been a very difficult task to find a workable definition of efficiency for this purpose. There are many reasons for this state of affairs. For example, the accounts of collective farms still do not show *net* revenues. It is very difficult to compare these, even if they can be calculated, with actual costs. The snag here partly consists in substantial and often irrational variations in prices of material inputs, but above all in the virtual impossibility of finding a satisfactory measure of labour costs. Since, in the majority of collective farms, payment to labour consists of the residual after other charges have been met, profits and losses never appear as such, but are concealed within variation in the 'dividend' paid to the members for their work. It is this which the economist Venzher had in mind when he asserted that '*trudodni* inevitably subvert economic accounting'.[1] Soviet economists have argued for years about whether labour costs should be measured by the value of cash and produce actually paid to the peasant members for their work, or by some standard 'notional' basis, such as the amount they would have received in a state farm. Those who defend the first of the above viewpoints point out that only actual payments represent reality and that in farms where labour is poorly paid costs are none the less high because of low yields and inefficiency. Opponents of this view argue that very substantial variations in the pay of peasants, arising from the residual nature of this pay, can lead to nonsensical conclusions if such variations are taken to represent differences in real cost of labour. For this purpose, so it is argued, state-farm wages do provide a basis for analysis, with the further advantage that a profit or a loss can then emerge. For example, the fact that prices of pork would cover only about 70 per cent of costs, on the assumption that the peasants received state-farm wages, was significant, and analysis in these terms actually did lead to an upward revision of meat price. One difficulty is that widely divergent results can be obtained according to the method by which labour costs are computed.

In the table that follows, a Soviet analyst groups collective

[1] Venzher, *op. cit.*, pp. 160ff.

farms in a given area into four categories, indicated by the Roman figures at the top of the table.

TABLE 4

CALCULATIONS OF COSTS IN COLLECTIVE FARMS

	I	*II*	*III*	*IV*
Harvest of grain (quintals per hectare)	30	22	10	6
Expenses of production in cash and kind per hectare (excluding labour costs) (roubles)	496	384	302	260
Trudodni expended per hectare ..	30	26	22	20
Actual pay per *trudoden* (roubles) ..	29	18	8	4
Payment for labour per hectare (roubles)	870	468	176	80
A. Costs per quintal (roubles) ..	45·53	38·73	47·80	56·66
B. Costs per quintal (roubles) ..	25·50	27·07	49·20	72·16

(Line A, above, takes labour costs as equal to actual payments; Line B assumes payments according to state farm-wage scales.) (All roubles are old roubles.)

Source: Voprosy Sebestoimosti i Rentabel'nosti v Kolkhozakh (Moscow, 1959), pp. 114ff.

It is argued, on the basis of the above table, that line A, if used as a basis for decision-making, would lead to absurd results. We need only note the undoubted fact that the would-be efficient farm official, anxious to respond to any incentives related to efficiency, would have a good deal of trouble in calculating his costs.

Vast variations in pay and in productivity in collective farms are often and rightly attributed by Soviet scholars to a manifestation of differential rent. Some farms are much more favourably situated than others, by reference to soil conditions, distance from consuming centres, and closeness to railways or hard-surface roads. In particular, accessibility to a free market in which scarce perishables can be sold at a high price brings great advantages to a collective farm. The same farm will generally also benefit from the services of the consumer co-operatives which sell in the market on commission and from some other authorized urban buyers who can offer a good price. As abundant reports show, the remoter farms face great difficulties in finding anyone willing to handle their perishable products, despite the shortage of these in most Soviet cities.[1] In other words, poor communications and the deplorable inadequacies in the organization of trade greatly enhance the unavoidable differences between

[1] For instance, see articles in *Sel'skaya Zhizn'* on July 28 and August 7, 1962.

farms. These operate cumulatively, since the disproportionate effect on the (residual) peasant rewards of these advantages and disadvantages stimulates or discourages hard work, which naturally makes matters worse ('To him that hath shall be given').

The Soviet planners are well aware of all this. One of the objects of the 1958 price reform was to help the weaker farms by abolishing the two-tier buying price system, since the less productive farms frequently found themselves with only enough produce to sell at the low 'quota' price, while their better-off neighbours could obtain higher prices by selling additional quantities over and above the quota. The 1958 reform also provided for some price differentiation between low-cost and high-cost areas (though this existed also before the reform). However, it is the unanimous view of Soviet scholars that these price differences are far smaller than the differences in costs, however costs are computed. In any case, the price zones are far too big. As one critic, Seryakov, pointed out, one grain-price zone, Zone VI, 'includes 26 *oblasti* whose total territory is five times greater than that of France'.[1] Within so large an area, there is, of course, need to take into account very substantial variations in natural advantages. It is also the case that the 1958 reforms had the effect of eliminating two ways by which a rough-and-ready 'rent in disguise' was in fact levied. One such way, while the MTS existed, was by charging the more fertile areas higher payments in kind for the work of MTS machines; this was eliminated when the MTS were abolished. The other was through levying higher quotas of low-price deliveries on the better-off farms; this too ceased, when the two-tier price system was ended. The trouble is that no rent *as such* is charged, the farms being considered rent-free occupiers of nationalized land. Several of the economists we have quoted here, including Venzher, have urged that the already existing tax on collective farms be greatly enlarged and differentiated to even out relative advantages; this would be a land rent in all but name and would represent a step forward in a necessary and overdue redistribution of income.

Irrational Output Prices

However, the incentives available to farm management suffer also from the irrationality of output prices in relation to one

[1] *Ekonomicheskaya gazeta*, January 8, 1962.

another and also to inputs. Irrationality is here not defined as some abstract concept related to consumer sovereignty, but is defined simply in relation to the achievement of the planners' own objectives. Quite clearly, it would not be practicable to instruct farm managements to seek to maximize gross revenues, even though, as we have seen, their own salaries are frequently calculated on the basis of gross output. The totals so arrived at include double-counting and cash obtained from selling in free markets at higher prices. In any event, the state's own purchase prices were a poor guide to the desired pattern of production:

TABLE 5A

UKRAINE PRICES IN 1958 AS PERCENTAGE OF COSTS

Grain (except corn) ..	198
Corn	224
Sunflower seed	632
Sugar beets	200
Milk	90
Beef	70
Pork	75

Source: Venzher, *op. cit.*, p. 46, with labour cost valued at actual pay.

TABLE 5B

USSR, 1960, PRICES AS PERCENTAGE OF COSTS

Grain, excluding corn ..	155
Potatoes	147
Sugar beets	164
Milk	86
Beef	65
Pork	67
Mutton and lamb ..	98
Wool	143
Eggs	65

Source: Khlebnikov, *op. cit.*, p. 53, with labour cost valued at state-farm wages.

The price increases for meat and some other livestock products, decreed in 1962, are clearly explained by the above figures and will help to put matters right, but only to a limited extent. There will remain large local variations in profitability, contradicting production and procurement plans laid down for the given area or the given farm. Left to themselves, farms or peasants must frequently do the wrong thing if they try to maximize revenue.

Indeed, peasants are still finding it very profitable to buy bread to feed to livestock[1] despite legal prohibitions.

It is logical, therefore, that economic incentives to management are largely replaced by administrative decision and guidance. It remains for us to examine the incentives which affect the behaviour of those who decide and guide.

The Position of the Local Party Official

It is beyond dispute that the secretaries of the *obkoms* and *raikoms* of the Communist Party have played a dominant role in the control of collective farms. At earlier periods they shared their powers in varying degrees with the political officer (or deputy-director, political) of the MTS. They shared some authority also with local officials belonging to one or other of several state hierarchies operating in the agricultural sector. Their powers have been substantially altered by the 1962 reforms, which have greatly reduced the role of the *raikom* and established in a very strong position the 'party organizer' (*partorg*) operating within the new territorial administration.[2] However, we are not concerned here with the intricate and frequent changes in administrative responsibility. The point was, is, and remains, that instructions to farms originate very largely with the local officials of the party. State officials in rural areas are either wholly subordinate (*de facto*) to the party, as is the case with the *oblast* or *raion* Soviets and is surely to be the case with the new territorial administrations, or they are concerned only with a single function, like buying grain or repairing machinery. One should, therefore, ask: Why do party officials issue particular orders, and to what incentives do they respond?

It is clear that the incentives are not monetary, even though Khrushchev did once raise the question of relating officials' salaries to the output of 'their' areas. The chief object of a local party official's activities is to be able to report success to his superiors, especially to Moscow. Of course, it could be argued that, if one assumes that Moscow wishes to hear about an all-round rise in agricultural production and efficiency, this necessity to report success to one's superiors would merely act as a

[1] For the latest report see A. Michurin, *Ekonomicheskaya gazeta*, September 29, 1962, p. 37.

[2] See p. 170, above.

stimulant to various desirable acts. Alas, this is not how it has ever worked out. As we have already had occasion to note, it has never been possible to define for practical purposes what is meant by maximizing output or efficiency. The success indicators of officials have in fact always been related to campaigns. These might be regular annual campaigns, such as sowing, harvesting, and deliveries to the state. Or the campaigns may reflect central policy decisions of the moment in relation to agriculture. A wide range of examples include the virgin-lands and corn campaigns, the replacement of grasses by 'higher-yielding' crops,[1] limitations on private ownership of cows, the sowing of this or that crop 'on the square', and so on. All these campaigns, regular and 'irregular', are tied in with extremely ambitious output and delivery targets for particular crops or livestock products. The local official, unable as a rule to achieve an 'advance on all fronts', must concentrate on those campaigns to which his superiors devote greatest attention at the given moment. If he is able to report success at these vital points, approval and promotion await him. For example, one of the most powerful men in the USSR today, Voronov, was promoted very rapidly after 'his' province, Orenburg, had fulfilled some key plans in agriculture. If, on the contrary, the principal campaigns fail, dismissal is the common fate of the party secretary, as very numerous examples in recent years show all too clearly. Success in a 'secondary' sector will not help. Thus, if there are campaigns to produce and deliver some vast tonnage of meat and wheat, the fact that the potato crop was a good one will hardly be taken into consideration, since, at least for the present, potatoes are not the subject of a campaign.

All this compels the harassed party official to consider only the immediate campaign. Short-term goals are predominant in his mind; he cannot be concerned with the long-term health of agriculture. Nor are officials likely to give much thought or priority to the revenues of collective farms or the incomes of the peasant. One has only to read the reports of the last four plenary sessions of the Central Committee, which every winter discusses agriculture, to see how little attention is paid to the finances of farms or the welfare of their members. By contrast, output of 'fashionable' crops and, above all, deliveries to the state, are at the centre of attention. Local party officials are encouraged to

[1] See N. Jasny's paper, in *Soviet Agricultural and Peasant Affairs.*

promise to overfulfil ambitious plans and are urged to 'challenge' other localities to 'competitions'. This is still going on. For example, the party's newspaper, *Sel'skaya Zhizn'*, reported competitive obligations to deliver extra quantities of grain, adopted for Rostov on July 19, 1962, Bashkiria and Tambov on July 25, and others in subsequent issues.

The unhealthy consequences of such a system on the behaviour of officials and on agriculture are all too familiar. The Soviet press and literary magazines have been reporting them for years. Officials urge the adoption of sowing or harvesting methods, or dates of starting or completion, which look good in the report rather than the most suitable in the given circumstances. To fulfil high delivery targets, farms are ordered to deliver seed grain, or produce required for its own animals and its own peasants. They are told to overslaughter if big meat-delivery plans are required by the centre, or they are forbidden to slaughter aged and unproductive cows if the centre, alarmed by overslaughtering, has urged the build-up of herds. Crop rotations are repeatedly broken up, corn is ordered to be sown in unsuitable areas, and fallow must be reduced even if (as in parts of Kazakhstan) it is essential to have more fallow. Obedience to the expressed or implied wishes of the party headquarters, and not efficient farm operations, becomes the dominant determinant of official behaviour. One can hardly blame the individuals concerned. Faced with the same pressures, most of us would be compelled to do the same.

Therefore, 'decentralization to officials', devolution of decision-making powers to party secretaries in the localities, cannot succeed. The local party secretaries have no rational basis for their activities except superior orders. This helps to explain why the freeing of many areas from centrally imposed deliveries of grain in 1958 led to a sharp and unintended drop in grain output in these areas. As Khrushchev himself told the Central Committee, local officials considered that Moscow was not interested in grain in these areas and ordered a shift of resources into other crops, which could please Moscow more. So, in 1961, there was a forced return to centralized planning of deliveries.

The administrative reform of 1962 enhances the role of the party official in agriculture. But it leaves untouched the basic weakness analysed above. The dominant incentive for officials will still be the short-term campaign to fulfil the 'fashionable' plans of the moment, and, indeed, campaigns are the success indicators for officials. Incentives for farm management or for peasants are unaffected, save possibly that the management will now have a smaller range of choice. The basic problems remain to be solved.

CONCLUSION: WHAT COULD BE DONE?

It would be foolish for us to pretend that the answer to the problem of incentives could be provided simply by a free price mechanism. It is surely not a coincidence that free farm prices do not exist in any major country in the world, West or East. However, *operational autonomy*, on farms of manageable size, seems to be a vital precondition of efficiency, and this in turn calls for more intelligent and flexible use of price stimuli as incentives to management. This requires a form of accounts in which profits and losses can be identified and, for this reason and also to provide incentives to the peasants, the share of labour in farm income must be guaranteed with some set minimum. The balance between collective and private activities presents many difficulties within collective farms, but it is clear that only an assured and regular income can ensure active and willing participation in collective work. It is interesting to note that Venzher, in his already cited book, stressed the usefulness of the *trudoden* as a way of underpaying peasants during the early stages of Soviet industrialization, but he now expects its replacement by regular cash payments.[1] In fact this has been urged by many influential experts for many years now. Perhaps the much-needed move away from centralized control toward local initiative, linked with adequate incentives, is delayed by the long-ingrained habits of party leaders, habits derived from the time when agriculture was primarily regarded as a supplier of cheap resources for industrial growth. These same habits have bred in the peasants an understandable suspicion of official intentions. Surely there is an urgent need of a new approach.

[1] Venzher, *op. cit.*, pp. 24, 124, 160.

IV. LABOUR PRODUCTIVITY, WELFARE

*12. A study of Soviet wages**

Soviet work on Soviet wages has suffered from several deficiencies. There was no lack of official handbooks giving basic wage rates for various occupations, the skills required to qualify for particular grades, the regulations governing piecework, social insurance entitlements, overtime rates and so on. From these handbooks much could indeed be reconstructed concerning the various rules under which the Soviet workers earned their daily bread, and the (relatively generous) incomes which they received if sickness, incapacity or old age deprived them of earning power. However, since the war there has been silence on the actual wages earned. This contrasts with the situation before 1937, when large statistical compendia provided detailed information about wage payments in each industry. Clearly, lists of basic rates are no substitute for wage statistics, since, in Russia as elsewhere, there is a substantial (and variable) gap between basic rates and actual earnings. When, in 1956, the reviewer discussed this regrettable statistical lacuna with some Soviet economists, he was assured that wage data would be published again before long. So far, this has not happened. Indeed, even so 'elementary' a figure as the average wage has not been published as such in any official statistical source. We have had to make do with some scattered percentages which were occasionally linked with a 1940 base and which did indeed permit the average to be calculated with some precision. For example, the economics textbook *Politicheskaya ekonomiya* gave the average wage in 1953 as 203 per cent of 1940. Since it is known from other sources that the 1940 average was

* From the *British Journal of Industrial Relations*, 1962, No. 1.

about 4,060 (old) roubles per annum, one can arrive at the 1953 figure fairly simply. However, none of this appears in a Soviet source in actual roubles and kopeks.

One of Figurnov's[1] many merits is to go as far as he can in deploring the unsatisfactory statistical situation. For example, on the very last page of the book he notes the disappearance from statistical digests issued since 1956 of even an index of real wages, and expresses the hope that 'the cessation of publication of this index is temporary and that it will reappear on a sounder basis'.

The 'sounder basis' to which he refers concerns, firstly, the distinction between nominal wages and paid-out wages, and his discussion of this point is an interesting aspect of his book. In the USSR the difference between the two consists of taxes (income tax and bachelor tax) and the virtually compulsory deductions made from wages for the purchase of premium bonds, a practice which ceased in 1958. The difference for particular years can be significant. For example, according to Figurnov, the average nominal wage in 1955 rose by 1.7 per cent, but paid-out wages fell by 1.8 per cent (p. 192). This was because of a sharp increase in premium bond purchases decreed in that year. Commenting on the 1955 situation (on p. 54) the author points out that in 1953–54 wage increases and price reductions had led to an unreal rise in 'real wages', which did not correspond to the availability of goods; hence 'a compulsory halt in growth of real wages' in 1955. By contrast, in 1957 nominal wages rose by 3.9 per cent and real wages by 7.8 per cent, as a result of some tax reliefs and a reduction in bond sales.

Figurnov also criticizes official methodology in several other respects. Thus (on p. 193) he attacks the planning organs for including premium bond winnings in real wage statistics. He goes on to criticize with considerable skill and ingenuity the official cost of living figures which form the basis of such real wage data as have been released by the Central Statistical Office. The point he makes is interesting enough to be worth setting out in some detail.

[1] S. P. Figurnov: *Real'naya zarabotnaya plata i podyom material'novo blagosostayania trudyashchikhsya v SSSR.* (Real wages and the raising of material welfare of the working people in the USSR.) Social-economic editors, Moscow, 1960. 199 pp.

Figurnov points out that the officially-published figures contain a contradiction: real wages in 1953 were alleged to be 165 (1940=100), official retail prices stood at 146, and the price index for all goods and services was 122. But, since 80 per cent of personal expenditure was at official retail prices, it follows that the gap between the two price indices cited above is far too big. The gap is excessive, writes Figurnov, because of a failure to take proper account of the change of the share of free market sales in total purchases. This is a complicated matter for several reasons: there can be a change in the relative weight of free market purchases in total purchases, changes in the commodity composition of free market sales, and also changes in relative prices at which these commodities are sold in official and in free markets. Figurnov shows in some detail that these complexities are inadequately dealt with, and that the official methodology results in an understatement of the rise in living costs in the period 1940–53, i.e. real wages rose by less than 65 per cent. This is because, on his calculation, a proper assessment of the relative share of free market purchases (at higher prices) shows them to have been higher in 1953 than in 1940. By contrast, because of a relative fall in free market sales after 1953, the official methodology understates the increase in real wages since that date. The detailed discussion raises some nice points of statistical procedure, and shows that Soviet scholars no longer have to take officially-blessed indices, even of real wages, as compulsory gospel truth.

In the process of discussing these topics, Figurnov provides us with a series of index numbers of money wages and real wages which have never appeared together before in a Soviet publication. It is not clear whether this represents the use of unpublished material or is a gathering together of data from many different but published sources. The following figures are either given as such by Figurnov or can be easily calculated from those he does give:

AVERAGE WAGES
(1940=100)

	1950	*1951*	*1952*	*1953*	*1954*	*1955*
Nominal wage ..	191·1	195·5	199·4	205·5	210·3	213·9
Paid-out wage ..	180·8	180·8	183·2	197·9	203·4	199·7
'Real wage'* ..	106	—	—	143	—	149

* Related to paid-out wage and calculated in relation to retail price index and other data by Figurnov himself.

The 1953–54 leap forward in disposable incomes, made worse by unwise price cuts, shines forth clearly and suggests that Stalin's death was followed, under Malenkov, by a somewhat unsound bid for popular support by large concessions to the people which went far beyond any real means of satisfying their needs. In these circumstances, the term 'real wages' should be used with caution. Prices can be, and were, cut at a time when the relative scarcity of consumers' goods would justify a price increase. The resulting rise in 'real wages' was somewhat unreal, in so far as many goods could not be purchased at the lower price. This certainly happened with, for instance, potatoes and vegetables in the 'Malenkov years'. In the period 1955–58, according to Figurnov, the paid-out wages rose by 17 per cent, the cost of living by 1 per cent, real wages therefore by 16 per cent.

The table opposite gives a figure for 1953 nominal money wages which is slightly higher than the one cited earlier from the economics textbook. This could be due to rounding (the Figurnov index is given in terms of increases per annum, which are here aggregated), or could be a genuinely different figure. The difference is not very big.

Figurnov gives many other figures and calculations, unfortunately without any explanation as to their origin. One must suppose that he has had some access to unpublished information, which he supplemented with cost-of-living calculations of his own—and there is no lack of price data for a scholar willing to use them. Thus he gives the following figures, which are valuable for any student of Soviet wages in the post-war period:

(*a*) In 1945 average money wages were 30 per cent above 1940 (39 per cent for industrial workers).

(*b*) In 1947 money wages were 72 per cent above, real wages 50 per cent below, the 1940 level. For industrial workers money wages were 86 per cent above 1940 at this date.

(*c*) In the period 1947–54, average money wages rose by 21.9 per cent, but real wages increased much more rapidly due to successive price cuts. The author notes that part of the increase in average money wages at this period occurred through an increase in the relative weight of high-paid employment, as distinct from increases in actual rates. There was also a tendency towards increased overfulfilment of work norms by pieceworkers which led to some rise in earnings. Figurnov also notes an important upward shift in wages of 'non-priority' occupations, which had lagged far behind. These increases occurred after 1953, and must have been part of the Malenkov policy and contributed to the sharp rise in average wages in these years. Thus in 1951–55 average wages in metallurgy rose by only 4 per cent, but fishermen received increases of 36 per cent, lumbermen 29 per cent, employees of the dairy industry 26 per cent, and so on.

(*d*) There are useful figures about the price-level in the free market, in which peasants sell their surpluses. The level of these prices is an indication of the scarcity of foodstuffs at official prices in state stores. In 1940, under the impact of stockpiling on the eve of the war, prices in the free market were already far above official levels (a figure given but not documented by Figurnov suggests they were roughly 75 per cent above in that year). The author states that by 1943 free market prices had reached a peak: almost thirteen times above 1940. At the end of the war they had fallen to roughly five times the 1940 level, and by 1947 the index (1940=100) was 372. By 1953 it had fallen to the 1940 level, but was still above state-shop prices for the same goods. In 1954–55 free market prices were 10 per cent above 1953 levels, despite a cut in state prices of foodstuffs, reflecting higher personal incomes (and the unwise official price reductions), though food production did increase. Since then, however, free market prices have fallen by some 13 per cent. Yet, though Figurnov does not give this figure, they still averaged some 36 per cent above state prices in 1960.[1] It is an observable fact that the quantity and quality of food in state shops are often inadequate.

Looking at the pattern of wage and price changes in the post-war period, one is struck by the relative stability of the Soviet scene, relatively, that is, to the wage and price inflations in Western countries. Wages have undoubtedly been rising in the USSR, and faster than plans and wage schedules had envisaged. Yet, at any rate from 1947, things never got out of hand. The excess of purchasing power could not directly influence prices in

[1] According to price indices given in the official compendium, *Narodnoe Khozyaistvo SSSR v 1960*, p. 719.

the shops, so there were queues and shortages, which were also reflected in free-market prices. However, increases in money wages were generally not such as to cause increases in costs, save in some highly labour-intensive industries such as coal and timber. Factory transfer prices, and wholesale prices excluding tax, were indeed greatly raised in 1949, but this was because the wartime rise in costs (and fall in labour productivity) had been largely offset by subsidies until that date. Since 1949, industrial prices and costs tended downward, again with a few exceptions. This does not entitle us to assert that inflation is unknown in the USSR. Many inflationary symptoms lie concealed beneath the surface of stable prices: for example, there appears to be a lively black market in certain kinds of building materials, and supply shortages of many kinds bedevil Soviet industry. The introduction of the death penalty for bribery and embezzlement is another symptom of strain. Yet the relationship between the rise in labour costs and of productivity appears to be genuinely healthier in the USSR than in any Western economy. This may well be partially explicable by the inactivity of Soviet trade unions, as well as by the tight central control over wage schedules and the 'wages funds' of state enterprises. It is true that these controls are frequently evaded: 'easy' piece-rates, unjustified up-grading, bonuses of many kinds, tend to lead to some overspending of the wages fund. But the Soviet planners have been successful in keeping the excess to manageable dimensions.

This was certainly not the case in the pre-war years. In the period 1928–40, according to Figurnov, the total wages fund increased twenty-fold in money terms, three-fold in unchanged prices, while the labour force also trebled. He argues that the conclusion that there was no increase in real wages at this period is confusing and inaccurate. This is because the increase in the labour force was due largely to the transfer to urban employment of many millions of unskilled peasants, whose incomes rose by comparison to their lot in their villages, that the real wages of established workers rose at this period, and that the average was misleadingly affected by a relatively heavier weight of unskilled workers in the total. All this is no doubt true, but there are grounds for supposing that the 1940 real wage has been overstated by Figurnov; this is because it was a year of acute 'eve-of-war' shortages, whereas in 1928 the goods which formed part of the price index calculation were freely available at established prices. It would also be interesting to know more about the weights used in calculating the rise in the cost of living in 1928–40, since a much less favourable result may be obtained by using 1928 weights (one must suppose that Figurnov stuck to the much more 'convenient' Paasche formula, convenient in this instance to the Soviet scholar who wishes to avoid embarrassing results, such as having to show a sharp fall in living standards). But Figurnov's great omission, due quite possibly to his editor or the censor, consists in not discussing at all the spectacular drop in living standards which occurred in 1929–34. This would contradict the formula, compulsory for Soviet writers on this theme, about a continuous (*neuklonnyi*) rise in wages under socialism. True, he admits to a sharp drop during and just after the war, but this was obviously due to the appalling human and material losses which followed the German invasion and every reader knows it. The 1929–34 story is one of disasters—such as the collapse of agriculture under the strain of forced collectivization—for which the Soviet Communist leadership was itself responsible. It seems clear, from all the evidence, that 1933–34 were years of terrible hardship, that recovery was rapid in 1935–39, and that this was followed by a withdrawal of resources from the citizen as war drew nearer.

Meanwhile, wage rates multiplied, regardless of plans and financial controls, though the confusion was greater in some years than others. It would be valuable for a Soviet scholar to explain the mechanics of these semi-spontaneous increases in money wages, and also to discuss why the same pressures were much more successfully resisted in the post-war years. Certainly those who drafted the first five-year plan (1928–32) were aiming to avoid wage or any other kind of inflation. Figurnov quotes from the first five-year plan document the following passage: 'With regard to the relationship between changes in money wages and changes in labour productivity, it is necessary to ensure that labour productivity should grow faster than wages; but the difference between their growth rates should be smaller the greater is the role of intensification of labour in the rise of productivity, and, conversely, the difference should be larger the greater is the relative importance of technical improvements' (p. 130). This was written in 1929. It would seem that these considerations were utterly inapplicable in the confused circumstances of the 'Soviet great leap forward'. Figurnov adds: 'The relationship noted above is included also in the planning methodology elaborated by *Gosplan* for the present seven-year plan.'

In discussing the pre-war wage pattern, Figurnov refers to the wage reform of 1931–33, which, in the middle of the most confused years of the first five-year plan, was designed to increase wage differentials. For example, the 'spread' between unskilled and most skilled in the iron and steel industry was increased from 1 : 2.8 to 1 : 3.7. The average wage in iron and steel was 27 per cent higher than in textiles in 1928, and 53 per cent higher when the period ended. The effect of this on labour recruitment and on actual wage payments should be the subject of careful research, and it is a pity that Figurnov does not take the matter further. For example, the 'spread' of 1 : 3.7 was already of largely nominal significance by 1935, because, as pre-war handbooks on labour statistics demonstrate, the lowest grades of unskilled labour had virtually no one working in them, i.e. it was impossible in practice to recruit anyone at the unskilled rates of pay. Even raw peasants evidently were graded semi-skilled. On the other hand, the 'thirties and also the post-war period down to 1956 were years in which special incentive bonuses of many kinds (especially so-called 'progressive piecework') made for very much greater differentiation in actual earnings between individuals, rather than categories of individuals, than was provided for in the regulations. For example, for several years coal miners received treble rates for any coal dug in excess of the norm. Since 1956 these excesses have been eliminated and the nominal wage differentials reduced to 1 : 2. Unfortunately, it is not clear how far this represents a real diminution of differentials, because it is possible that the lowest grades of skill will now be paid as such, instead of as semi-skilled. Perhaps the biggest gainers from the wage reforms of recent years were the appallingly-paid auxiliaries (cleaners, janitors, railway porters, etc.), who benefited most from the introduction of, and increases in, the minimum wage after 1956.

The wage reforms which were begun in 1956 and which had been continued since are worth serious study. The situation on the wages front in 1956 was highly confused. For a great many years there had been no systematic review of the wages structure as a whole. In many industries the wage schedules were still those of pre-war years, modified by the general increase which had been granted in 1946 in preparation for the abolition of rationing. As has already been shown, wage increases had been granted in particular industries since that date, but this apparently took the form of *ad hoc* adjustments. The gap between wage tariffs and actual earnings had grown very substantially. There was abundant evidence of both confusion and unfairness. Persons doing identical work in different industries received widely differing ranges of pay. Industrial ministries differed from one another in the zoning and wage scales and in the various incentive bonuses which they adopted. In some branches of activity piece workers found norms hard to fulfil, because flat-rate increases in norms, ordered from above, were unrelated to any change in their conditions of work. According to evidence cited at the time, this particularly affected some sections of the building industry. In some branches, on the other hand, workers found themselves overfulfilling norms by 50, 70 or even 100 per cent. Workers on time work and some categories of salaried personnel found themselves left far behind. As can well be imagined, the task of eliminating such a large number of anomalies was an extraordinarily complex one. It is hardly surprising that the process took many years to complete. It is only in 1960 that new wage scales were operative for all employees in manufacturing and extractive industry and building. According to the intentions of the authorities, new wage scales should be in operation in all branches of the national economy by the end of 1962.

Under these reforms basic wage rates have been substantially increased, with a simultaneous increase in work norms and reduction in various bonuses. Actual earnings are now much closer to the nominal tariff wage. Similar jobs in different industries are now similarly graded. The total number of grades and tariff rates have been very greatly reduced and much simplification achieved. In fact, according to Figurnov, before the reform there were no less than 1,300 different tariff schedules, within which the number of grades varied from five to fifteen. These have now been standardized on a basis of a maximum of six grades.

Figurnov claims that the net effect of the reform on productivity and also on earnings has been favourable. He cites a number of figures which do indeed show exceptional increases in money wages. Thus 'in the period 1957–59 its level rose by 26 per cent in the coal industry, by 14 per cent in the ferrous metal industry, by 21 per cent in the non-ferrous metal industry, by 13 per cent in the chemical industry. By the end of 1960 the average wage of workers in light industry will be increasing by 13.5 per cent, in the food industry by 20.7 per cent, in construction by 12.3 per cent.' Presumably all these figures relate to a comparison with the pre-reform year, 1956. It is not surprising to learn that a reform of this kind involves quite substantial increases in earnings. Faced with numerous anomalies, the Soviet authorities were doubtless reluctant to reduce the wages of any large category of workers, and this compelled them to level up. The carrying out of this reform particularly benefited the lowest paid categories of workers. Figurnov's book discusses these reforms and cites a number of facts concerning them, but one would wish that he devoted much more space to a discussion of the numerous problems which are known to have arisen. Yet we can hardly complain if Figurnov does not discuss all these points, since his book primarily concerns real wages.

One point which he mentions in passing does raise some conceptually difficult problems. He frankly points out that housing has been, and remains, despite an enlarged building programme, a source of great discomfort and hardship. In 1957, so he tells us, living space per head in towns amounted to just six square metres. In fact the available statistics show that it was less than this. (Living space must be differentiated from 'total space'; the latter including the area of corridors, bathrooms, etc.) Even six square metres per head imply that every reasonable-sized room had about four persons in it, and in fact one family per room, with shared kitchens, was almost the rule in many cities and is still very common. Housing is strictly rationed, and the state provides living space at a very low price per square metre, the rentals covering only a fraction of the cost of maintenance and repairs. The free market price of accommodation may be judged by the very much higher rents which private individuals charge for letting a room or even on occasion a part of a room. Apart from some private lettings, it is also relevant to note that many urban (and almost all rural) residents live in private houses which they may have bought and which they have to keep in order at their own expense; even in 1960 almost 40 per cent of all urban housing space was privately owned. This raises two questions. One concerns the extent to which cost of living indices, official or Figurnov's own, take into account costs incurred on private housing (owned or rented); this is very far from clear, and official sources seem to evade the issue by referring to the very low rents charged by state organs. The second is the more general question of assessing real wages and comparing them over time (or with other countries) when a vital element in living standards—housing—is so restricted in quantity and is administratively allocated (outside the private sector) at a very low price, and when the vast majority of citizens would be delighted to pay more if they could only obtain a few extra square metres and greater privacy.

It is a familiar theme of Soviet pronouncements on labour and wages that in the USSR a particularly large role is played by the 'social wage', i.e. by benefits of many kinds additional to the individually-distributed wage. This is indeed the case, but some official claims suffer greatly from vagueness about what is supposed to be included in this category. Figurnov himself complains that some authoritative writers are apt to include in the social wage the whole of government expenditure on social-cultural objectives (including, for instance, state investments in housing and schools). He would reject this. It may be of interest to reproduce here his table which analyses the make-up of the additional incomes earned by Soviet working people. These he expresses as a percentage of the paid-out money wage (i.e. wages less taxes, etc.). Presumably, in view of the criticism which was cited above, he includes here only the current expenditure on the provision of various social services. The actual figures he describes as 'a sample calculation', but they appear to be based on real statistics.

The list contains some items which give rise to legitimate queries. Thus Figurnov, like all his colleagues, includes holiday pay as additional income. Since, according to available evidence, holiday pay comes out of the general wages fund and is paid by the enterprise and not out of social insurance, this would seem to be double-counting. One would also like to know more about the content of 'culture and enlightenment'. If it represents a subsidy to the Bolshoi theatre, then well and good, but it may well include expenditure on propaganda, which some of the recipients may prefer not to treat as 'income' in any sense. Finally the figure for the maintenance of houses must logically represent the *loss* on housing, i.e. the amount by which the low rents fail to cover current expenditure, though Figurnov does not make this clear. One wonders what the British equivalent figures would be, calculated on the same basis. Yet when all is said and done, there is no doubt that social wages, howsoever defined, are relatively more important in the USSR than elsewhere. Pensions (since 1956), sick pay, the duration of paid holidays, all compare favourably with the situation in Great Britain, and it is only right and proper to emphasize this.

ADDITIONAL INCOMES OF WORKERS AND EMPLOYEES

(Per Cent of Paid-out Wage)

Individually paid-out incomes	*20·4*
of which: Pensions	9·4
Paid holidays	5·5
Relief payments	4·5
Scholarships	1·1
Incomes in the form of social consumption	*26·6*
of which: Kindergartens, nurseries	2·1
General education	6·3
Higher, specialized and technical education	4·2
Medical care	8·1
Rest homes, spa treatment	0·6
Culture and enlightenment, PT, sport	1·3
Maintenance of houses, services and urban amenities	3·9
Old people's homes	0·1
Total additional incomes	47·0

On a more critical note, one must observe sadly that Figurnov (or his editor) thought it necessary to start the book with a chapter entitled 'The tendency towards reduction in real wages in conditions of contemporary capitalism'. This is a rehash of vulgar-Marxism and carefully selected 'illustrative' statistics designed to support the thesis of 'relative and absolute impoverishment' of the working class. Rejecting as totally mistaken, or as 'bourgeois apologetics', the contrary argument of Galbraith, Cole, Strachey and others, Figurnov insists that real wages tend to fall. He produces (on p. 13) figures showing the rise in profits on a 1938 base (i.e. a recession year) without any correction for price changes, which leads him to the conclusion that profits in America rose more than fourteen-fold in the period 1938–56. Not very surprisingly, he then argues that wages show a much less favourable development. Indeed, his real wage index (on p. 23) is a remarkable piece of statistical special pleading. For the United States he takes as his base the year 1944, and for Great Britain the year 1946. Both were years of shortages and rationing. It is simply laughable to pretend, as he does, that real wages in both countries in 1955 were lower than in 1944 and 1946 respectively. Does Figurnov really not know that there is a relationship between real wages and the volume of goods and services available? Or does he suppose that the much greater volume of consumption in 1955 was wholly absorbed by the capitalists out of their greatly increased profits? It is surely time that Soviet analysts stopped producing such crudities as these. It is true that Figurnov admits that the habitual level of consumption can rise over time, that there does occur a change in diet ('more meat, butter, fruit') and in living habits ('gas, electricity, domestic appliances, a bicycle, sometimes a motor-cycle or even a private car'). These new consumption patterns he treats as 'necessary for the normal functioning of the labour force', i.e. basic needs change. He suggests that the means of satisfying the growing minimum needs become increasingly inadequate. This is indeed a possible version of the theory of absolute impoverishment, but one which is open to some rather obvious criticisms. A worker acquires a car and a TV set, which his father could not aspire to, and finds it difficult to keep up his payments. This may indeed be a cause of dissatisfaction, which may have political and economic significance. However, statistically this must show itself in a rise in real wages, as these are conventionally defined in East and West alike. Yet nowhere will Figurnov admit any figures which show any appreciable rise over any long period. In fact, on page 35 he quotes figures which purport to show that in the period 1900–50 American real wages rose by 3 per cent, but that in this same period expenditure on food and clothing both declined by 20 per cent, apparently so as to make room for the new consumer durables which became a necessary part of an American worker's life. . . . He insists that 'all-round analysis wholly destroys reformist assertions about the cessation of the absolute worsening of the material conditions of the proletariat in conditions of contemporary capitalism' (p. 37). When will these questions receive serious analysis in the USSR, without the author being driven (by the editor or publisher?) to the prearranged ideological conclusion? Perhaps it is not Figurnov's fault.

Yet the book here discussed is a useful, serious work, so long as it is concerned with the USSR. It deals reasonably realistically with a variety of problems, and in it one can find many figures and a good deal of valuable analysis of statistical material. Several other matters are dealt with in detail by the author: the level of taxation, the fluctuations in premium bond sales and of the repayments and lottery winnings received by the population in various years. This is one of a growing number of Soviet monographs on wages and labour problems, and there are also several specialized periodicals wholly in this field. Thus anyone capable of reading Russian now has at his disposal a growing volume of material. Some serious gaps do indeed remain, especially in wage statistics, but there is ample scope for research. The present review article is in fact primarily designed to draw the reader's attention to the kind of material (and the kind of opinions) which can be found and used. There is an encouraging tendency in the USSR to discuss more freely, to cite more facts. May it continue.

*13. Social welfare in the USSR**

As some critics see it, the Soviet state is exclusively an organ of oppression. The motivations of its leaders, they believe, are to be found solely in the pursuit of world revolution, of national aggrandisement, of personal power—or of all these at once. The attitude of the Soviet leaders toward their own people is often represented as if it were mainly inspired by the objective of keeping the mass of Soviet citizens on the lowest possible living standard consistent with the necessity of providing minimum work incentives.

Hence such critics are inclined to view all Soviet measures which seem to increase public welfare as 'concessions' wrung from a reluctant régime by irresistible force of circumstance or popular pressure. It is but a short step from this view to the conclusion that such measures are, in themselves, proof of the régime's weakness or instability. If more was done to improve welfare in the first years after Stalin's death, these critics might argue, it was only because the struggle for power among Stalin's successors was undecided, and because the police apparatus had lost much of its capacity to intimidate. Conversely, now that Khrushchev has become unquestioned boss, they should logically expect a return to the old ways.

The purpose of the present article is to inquire into the validity of such interpretations of the 'welfare' aspect of Soviet rule. But it is necessary first of all to define the area of discussion. To take a negative approach, the author does not propose to discuss such matters as wage rates and consumer goods production. It is acknowledged fact that real wages in the Soviet Union have been rising slowly but steadily, that peasant incomes and retail trade turnover have gone up, and that the present Soviet leadership has declared its intention to continue this process through the period of the Seven-Year Plan (1958–65). It is also true that the

* From *Problems of Communism*, Vol. IX, No. 1, January-February, 1960.

upward trend in these areas is highly relevant to welfare in the general sense and should be duly noted. In the present paper, however, attention will be concentrated rather on activities of a more direct 'public welfare' nature, i.e. on the various social services (health, education, etc.), on housing and such other state measures as affect the everyday life of Soviet citizens.

A LOOK AT THE RECORD

Before inquiring into the question of motivation, it is also necessary to set forth a few facts showing what actually *has* been done, or is being done, by the Soviet Union in the area of welfare. Such a survey of the record may best begin with a look at budget allocations for social and cultural expenditures during the 1950–59 period, presented in the table overleaf. Keeping the general trend toward increased outlays in mind, the individual categories of welfare listed are reviewed below with particular attention as to whether or not there has been any recent change of policy.

Health

There is no evidence that Soviet policy in this field has undergone any basic change in recent years. Vigorous efforts to expand medical and health services were already a feature of Stalin's reign, and the progress that was achieved is clearly indicated by the fact that the Soviet Union, as the following figures attest, has since 1951 boasted a larger number of doctors per thousand inhabitants than most Western countries:

USSR (1951)	13·9
USSR (1957)	16·9
United States (1954) ..	12·7
United Kingdom (1951)	8·8
West Germany (1955) ..	13·5

(*Source: Dostizheniia sovetskoi vlasti za 40 let* [The achievements of the Soviet Government in 40 years], Moscow, 1957, p. 348.)

Thus, while the 1957 and 1959 budget figures show relatively sharp increases in health expenditures, it is clear that these are not a new departure in Soviet policy, but rather a continuation of past trends.

It is true that the equipment of many Soviet hospitals is antiquated, that drugs are often scarce, and that the general

USSR SOCIAL-CULTURAL BUDGET: 1950–59

(in billions of roubles)

	1950	*1953*	*1957*	*1959*
Total Health	21·4	24·2	38·3	44·0
(of which)				
Hospitals and clinics, urban ..	10·3	12·3	18·6	—
Hospitals and clinics, rural ..	2·6	3·1	4·6	—
Total Education	56·9	61·1	80·7	94·3
(of which)				
General schooling (*a*)	30·4	32·2	37·6	—
Higher and technical	18·3	19·3	24·2	—
Science and research (*b*)	5·4	6·2	13·6	23·1(*c*)
Total Social Security	22·0	22·8	52·8	88·2
Total Social Insurance	12·7	16·2	23·5	—
Total Maternity Assistance	1·2	4·5	5·2	5·5
Total, Social-Cultural ..	116·7	128·8	200·5	232·0

Source: Raskhody na sotsialno-kulturnye meropriiatia po gosudarstvennomu byudzhetu SSSR (Expenditures for Social-Cultural Measures in the State Budget of the USSR), Moscow, 1958; also Finance Minister Zverev's speech, reported in *Pravda*, December 23, 1958.

Notes: (*a*) Includes kindergarten and adult education. (*b*) As most all-Union expenditures for science and research are kept secret, no complete breakdown of this item is given in the budget, but nuclear research is doubtless a major element. The item as a whole has practically no relevance for 'welfare' in any sense. (*c*) Part of the big increase in 1959 is accounted for by a change in definition hinted at in Zverev's budget speech.

level of health facilities is not up to the best Western standards. Nevertheless, a great deal has certainly been done to spread hygiene, combat epidemics, and reduce infant mortality. The services of state doctors and hospitals are free, although most medicines have to be bought by the patient.

Education

Here again, recent Soviet policy has not basically altered Stalin's approach in so far as the latter aimed at a large-scale expansion of the educational system, but there have been important changes in emphasis and direction. Thus, the decision of the 20th CPSU Congress (February 1956) to extend full-time secondary education to all has since been modified in favour of part-time education after the age of fifteen, and Khrushchev's reform of higher education also seems likely to result in a reduction of the number of *full-time* university students. It is not, of course, within the scope of the present article to discuss the detailed causes and consequences of Khrushchev's reforms of Soviet education. Regardless of the effect they may have on academic standards, however, it can be stated that these reforms are unlikely to result in any modification of the upward trend in Soviet educational expenditures (except for a possible large saving in student stipends).

One notable reason for this assumption is the evident rise in the school building programme, partly as a result of an overdue effort to remedy the overcrowding which at present necessitates a two-shift, and sometimes even three-shift, system of attendance, and partly to set up the new-type boarding schools in which Khrushchev plans to train the 'new Soviet man'. It is only fair to add that, in contrast to the continuing shortage of physical facilities, the situation of Soviet schools with regard to the ratio of teachers to pupils compares very favourably with that in many other countries including the United States, as evidenced by the following figures:

	Pupils	*Teachers*	*Pupils per Teacher*
	(in thousands)		
USSR (1956–57)	30,127	1,811	16·6
United States (1955)	30,531	1,135	26·9
United Kingdom (1956) ..	7,981	309	25·8

(*Sources:* For the USSR *Dostizheniia* . . . p. 274; for the US and UK, *United Nations Statistical Yearbook*, 1958.)

Mention should also be made of the Khrushchev leadership's action in 1956 to abolish all fees in schools and universities, which reversed one of Stalin's counter-reforms. It will be recalled that free education had been a feature of the Soviet régime from the beginning and was explicitly guaranteed by the 1936 Stalin constitution. Despite the constitutional guarantee, however, educational charges were imposed in the top three grades of secondary schools and in universities by a simple decree of the Council of Ministers in 1940. Although the action did not have such a serious effect on university students because of the fact that the large majority were receiving stipends from which the fees simply were deducted, its impact on children of poor families enrolled in secondary schools, where stipends were not payable, was much more severe. Without doubt the restoration of free education was a highly popular act.

Social Insurance, Social Security, and Pensions

Sick-pay benefits in the Soviet Union have long been on a relatively generous scale, and there have been no significant changes in rates of payment in recent years, although overall expenditures for this purpose have increased as a result of the upward trend in total numbers of employed and in the average wage. As part of the campaign launched in the 1930's to reduce the high rate of labour turnover, full rates of sick pay were made conditional upon a minimum period of work in the same enterprise or office, except in cases where workers had transferred under official orders. These rules remain in force, although with some modifications in favour of the worker.

Provided he is a trade union member, a worker who falls ill is paid the following proportions of his actual earnings (non-members receive one-half these rates, subject to the minima referred to below):

Years of service	*% of Earnings*
Less than 3	50
3–5	60
5–8	70
8–12	80
More than 12	90

Present regulations provide for minimum monthly payments of 300 roubles in towns and 270 roubles in rural areas, and a maximum payment of 100 roubles per day.[1] Those who are injured at work or suffer from diseases caused by their work are entitled to sickness benefits at the rate of 100 per cent of their earnings regardless of length of service. Where a worker leaves his job of his own volition, he is not entitled to sickness pay for ordinary illness until a period of six months has elapsed, but the limitation does not apply (since February 1957) to cases of accident or

[1] To give the reader some idea of the purchasing power of the rouble, here are the official Soviet prices (in roubles) of a few representative commodities (per kilogram in the case of food, unless otherwise stated): chicken, 16·5; beef (stewing), 12; pork, 19·5; average fish, 11; butter, 28; milk, 2·2 per litre; eggs (10), 7·5; rye bread, 1·24; potatoes, 1; cabbage, 1·5–2; coffee, 40; wool-mixture blanket, 100+; cotton print dress, 200; wool dress, 475; man's overcoat, 720; man's all-wool suit, 2,000; shoes (adequate), 200; bicycle, 450–600; motorcycle, 4,200; radio, 400; washing machine, 2,250; family divan, 1,300; toilet soap (bar), 2·2; lipstick, 4·5–6. *Source:* Lynn Turgeon, 'Levels of Living, Wages and Prices in the Soviet and United States Economies', *Comparisons of the United States and Soviet Economies*, Joint Economic Committee of the US Congress, US Government Printing Office, Washington, 1959, pp. 335–6.

disease caused by a person's work.[1] Of course, the social insurance rates described here apply only to disability for a limited period of time, permanent disablement being dealt with under pension regulations.

The maternity benefit rate itself also has not been changed in recent years, but in 1956 the period of paid maternity leave was lengthened to 112 days.[2] This was, in effect, a return to the regulation which had been in force up until 1938, when the period of maternity leave was reduced from 112 to 70 days.

The biggest improvements in this general area recently have been in the field of old-age and permanent disability pensions. Their effect, according to Finance Minister Zverev, was to raise the average rate of all pensions by 81 per cent,[3] but certain groups of workers who had fared relatively worse under the pre-1956 pension regulations secured much bigger gains than this, for the following reasons: The previous regulations nominally entitled a worker qualifying for an old-age pension by length of service to receive payments at the rate of two-thirds of his final wage. This looked extremely generous until one noticed the proviso, often omitted from propaganda statements, that the two-thirds was to be calculated on the basis of a *maximum* 'reckonable' wage of 300 roubles per month, meaning an effective maximum pension of 200 roubles per month. This figure, when originally fixed some twenty-five years earlier, was quite legitimate, but wages and prices subsequently multiplied without any upward revision of the allowable maximum. The result was considerable hardship for ordinary workers, while on the other hand exceptional treatment was granted to certain categories including not only the professional and official classes but also workers in some priority occupations. For example, coal miners, steel workers, and those engaged in electricity generation were allotted a much higher reckonable maximum. Similar discriminatory rules applied also to pension benefits for surviving dependents and victims of industrial accidents and the like.

The reform of 1956, while reducing certain very high pensions,

[1] These details are taken from S. A. Mitin (ed.), *Spravochnik po trudu i zarabotnoi platy v stroitelstve* (Reference Book on Labour and Earnings in Construction), Moscow, 1957, pp. 438–41.

[2] G. A. Prudenski (ed.), *Voprosy Truda v SSSR* (Problems of Labour in the USSR), Moscow, 1958, p. 66.

[3] In *Finansy SSSR* (Finances of the USSR), No. 10, 1957, p. 17.

established an all-round minimum old-age pension of 300 roubles per month for those qualified by length of service, an advance of great importance. In addition, it put into effect a new scale of payments benefiting lower-paid workers, so that those earning up to 350 roubles per month now receive pensions amounting to 100 per cent of earnings, with progressively smaller percentages for those with higher earnings, and with a maximum overall ceiling of 1,200 roubles per month. An average worker earning, say, 750 roubles per month qualifies for a pension of 487 roubles under the new rules, as against probably only 200 under the old.[1] One offsetting feature of the reform is that working pensioners are no longer permitted to receive full pensions on top of their wages.[2] (This provision, together with the better pension rates, has very probably encouraged many old people to retire.) On balance, however, the net gain to Soviet pensioners can readily be measured by the increase in pension expenditures shown in the following table (in billions of roubles):

	1950	*1956*	*1957 (prelim.)*	*1958 (plan)*
Total pensions	30·1	36·5	59·9	66·0
(of which)				
Non-working pensioners	8·8	12·6	27·6	34·2
Working pensioners	4·7	5·1	5·3	5·8
Ex-military and families	15·6	17·5	23·5	23·4

(*Source:* A. Zverev, in *Planovoe Khoziaistvo*, No. 12, 1957, p. 24.)

The improvement in old-age pension benefits was accompanied by substantial increases in pensions for those suffering permanent disability of varying degrees and for dependents, the increases reportedly amounting to 50–65 per cent.[3] Further sizeable increases in minimum pension rates have been also promised under the Seven-Year Plan, along with a raising of minimum wages. No doubt exists regarding the general popularity of these measures.

[1] Prudenski, *op. cit.*, p. 357.

[2] The normal payment to working pensioners is now only 150 rubles per month.

[3] See *Vedomosti Verkhovnovo Soveta* (Supreme Soviet Gazette), July 28, 1956.

There has also been a good deal of talk about extending social insurance and pension rights to collective farmers, who have thus far never enjoyed them. Some farms are reported to have adopted a system of paying fixed amounts of money and produce to their sick and aged members, which represents a step forward from the normal collective farm practice of extending relief to such members out of a small fund set aside for this purpose. Cases where fixed payments have been instituted are still the exception since the vast majority of collective farms do not yet have sufficient revenues for this purpose, but it is a fact that the number of such exceptions is steadily growing, and the extensive publicity given to them in the Soviet press indicates that the new system is officially regarded as a desirable development. It must be noted that, at present, all such payments are made out of the resources of each farm, and that the state has no responsibility, financial or otherwise. However, as the régime's policy toward the peasants is, in principle, to reward regular collective work with regular pay, and to bring the status of the peasant gradually closer to that of the industrial worker, it seems to follow that the state eventually will have to accept some responsibility for at least ensuring that the collective farms are financially capable of providing social-insurance benefits. This is all the more necessary because the collective farms have now absorbed the workers of the disbanded Machine Tractor Stations, who were promised the continuation of the benefits they formerly enjoyed as state employed workers. It is too soon, however, to say how the problem will be tackled.

OTHER WELFARE BENEFITS

Holidays

Turning to other kinds of social welfare benefits for state-employed persons, there appears to have been no appreciable change in the rules governing paid holidays, which already were on a fairly generous scale under Stalin. These regulations compare favourably with those of some Western countries, especially for workers in what are deemed to be arduous or unhealthy occupations. For example, miners, steel workers and bus drivers are allowed up to four weeks of paid vacation per year. Overall statistics showing the distribution of the total working force according to numbers of paid (working-day) holidays per year are as follows:

Days of vacation	*% of Total Workers*
12	43
15	12
18	11
21	3
24	19
Over 24	12
	100%

(*Source: Vestnik Statistiki*, No. 10, 1958, Statistical Supplement.)

A less desirable feature of the Soviet holiday system is the practice of spreading vacations over the whole year, so that many are on vacation when the weather is unfavourable. There is also a grave shortage of holiday accommodations: despite the existence of much-publicized trade union rest homes charging low prices, these can accommodate only a small fraction of the workers.

Working Time

There has been significant improvement in respect of hours of labour, although here again the reform effected by the present leadership so far represents, in large part, a return to the more liberal regulations which prevailed prior to Stalin's oppressive labour legislation of 1938–40. A 1940 decree lengthened the standard workday from seven to eight hours, increasing total hours for the six-day work week to forty-eight. This remained unchanged until 1956 when the Khrushchev leadership, implementing its promise at the 20th Party Congress to reduce working hours, took an initial step to cut down Saturday work to six hours, leaving most of the afternoon free and thus creating the beginnings of a Soviet 'week-end'.

During 1957–58 further reductions of working hours were made effective in certain industries, notably mining and metallurgy.[1] These were followed by still greater promises at the 21st Party Congress in January 1959, when the leadership explicitly pledged a standard forty-hour week (and a thirty-five-hour week in unhealthy occupations) by no later than 1962, with further

[1] See *Pravda*, January 27, 1958, and November 4, 1958.

reductions to follow later in the decade. There was even talk of achieving 'the shortest working week in the world' by 1967. The promises have been so definite and attended by such great publicity that it will be hard indeed for the leadership to go back on its word, except in the event of dire emergency. Reduced hours are in fact already being put into effect in several key industries. A statement jointly issued by the CPSU Central Committee, the Council of Ministers, and the central trade union organization, and published in the Soviet press on September 20, 1959, announced a detailed time schedule for the gradual extension of the seven-hour day to 'all workers and employees in the national economy'. (With six-hour Saturdays, this will reduce the standard working week to forty-one hours.) The process began on October 1, 1959, and is to be completed in the fourth quarter of 1960.

Some Western critics, pointing to the fact that planned productivity increases are greater than would be necessary to compensate for the reduction of working hours, conclude from this that the reform is in some way not genuine since there will have to be greater intensity of effort in the shortened work period.[1] Such a view hardly seems justifiable. It is obvious, in the first place, that a shorter working week requires greater work intensity and higher productivity not only in Russia but in the United States or any other country. If output per hour remained the same while hours were reduced by 15 per cent, then—other things being equal—total output would go down by 15 per cent and everyone would be correspondingly poorer, a situation which no one could possibly want. Nor is it true that the Soviet Union intends to increase productivity solely, or even mainly, by imposing heavier physical burdens on labour. This is quite evident from the great attention being paid to the mechanization of labour-intensive processes, especially in auxiliary occupations (loading, moving of materials, etc.).

The charge that weekly wages are being cut as part of the reduction in working hours is equally untenable. The fact that a major reform of the Soviet wage system has coincided with the reduction of the working week makes it difficult to determine the

[1] This was argued, for instance, by Dr E. Kux, writing in the *Neue Zürcher Zeitung* (December 16, 1958), in tones suggesting that the reform was practically a fraud.

precise effect of either change, but average wages appear in any event to be displaying their usual tendency to rise slowly. Thus, the cut in the working week is as genuine as these things can be in an imperfect world. Those who assert the contrary are guilty of using against the Soviet Union the very same—quite unfounded—arguments by which Soviet propagandists seek to explain away the reduction of the working week in the United States.

Other Employment Reforms

Brief mention should also be made of recent steps extending the special privileges of juvenile workers. Since May 1956 workers between the ages of sixteen and eighteen have enjoyed a working day shortened to six hours, with extra piecework pay to make up any loss in earnings. In addition they are allowed a full month's vacation each year and special facilities for study.[1] These privileges have, indeed, caused many managers to try to avoid employing juveniles—a tendency which has aroused official criticism and contributed to the difficulties experienced by high school graduates in seeking employment.[2] The compulsory drafting of young people into labour reserve schools, introduced in October 1940, had already been terminated by a decree of March 18, 1955, and has been replaced by voluntary recruitment.

The worker's right to change his occupation, while not explicitly recognized, has been made more real by the present régime's abolition, in 1957, of criminal penalties for leaving one's job without permission. These penalties, as well as others for worker absenteeism and unpunctuality, had been instituted by decree in 1940. Although the decree gradually became a dead letter under Stalin's successors and was no longer mentioned in Soviet legal textbooks from 1954 on, it apparently survived on the statute books until 1957.

In still another reversal of Stalinist policy, the 1936 decree which required the rural population to give six days' unpaid labour per year for working on roads was repealed by the present leadership in November 1958. Instead, responsibility for building and repairing local roads has been placed on the 'collective

[1] A. I. Denisov (ed.), *Trudovoe Pravo* (Labour Law), Moscow, 1959, p. 441.

[2] A decree to combat this was issued by the party Central Committee and the government on September 12, 1957.

farms, state farms, industrial, transport, building and other enterprises and organizations'. Of course, the job still has to be done, but presumably the individual is now entitled to be paid for doing it.

Wage Questions

Although wages as such are outside the province of this discussion, it may be useful to refer briefly to changes in this field in so far as they are indicative of political attitudes. The practice of the Stalin period was to maximize wage differentials, which indeed reached record dimensions; on the contrary, the trend in recent years has been in the opposite direction. In 1956, a minimum wage law was adopted, fixing a floor of 300–350 roubles per month in urban areas and 270 roubles in the country. The measure particularly benefited the appallingly underpaid groups of auxiliary personnel (janitors, cleaners, messengers, etc.) and the lowest grades of shop assistants, railroad workers, and others. This process of raising the level of the lowest-paid workers is to continue. The decree on the Seven-Year Plan provides for increasing the minimum wage to 400–450 roubles monthly during 1959–62, and to 500–600 roubles during 1963–65, as well as for a consequential (but smaller) upward revision of the pay of middle-grade workers. Since the average increase in all money wages is to be only 26 per cent, it is evident that the spread between top and bottom will be sharply reduced.

This policy is reflected in other aspects of wage reform now in progress. Apart from introducing smaller differentials in basic rates, the reforms are tending to eliminate the more exaggerated forms of progressive piecework bonuses, which will cut down disparities in actual earnings. The gap between skilled and unskilled workers' pay on collective farms is also being significantly reduced.[1] There have apparently been cuts in very high salaries, such as those of government ministers and university professors. (Though no statement to this effect seems to have appeared in print, the cuts are apparently a matter of general knowledge in the Soviet Union and have been confirmed to the writer several times.) The relative position of the lowest-paid has also been im-

[1] Some farms are adopting a pay ratio for unskilled as against skilled labour of 1:3 instead of the previously 'recommended' 1:5. See *Voprosy Ekonomiki*, No. 2, 1959, p. 114.

proved as a result of a decree of March 23, 1957, reducing direct taxation on incomes below 450 roubles per month. All this certainly does not indicate that the Soviets are embracing hitherto-condemned 'petty-bourgeois egalitarianism', but it does show that the *excessive* inequalities of the Stalin era are being corrected.

Housing

Something must also be said about housing, since the fact that rents in the Soviet Union are far too low to bear any relation to housing costs justifies treating it as a social service rather than as a species of commercial transaction. At 1.32 roubles per square metre per month (somewhat higher for new apartments in some cities), rents are generally insufficient even to cover bare maintenance, which may explain why this is so often neglected.[1] At the same time, the miseries caused by the shortage of housing and consequent overcrowding are too well known to require comment here. Khrushchev has declared that his aim is eventually to provide a separate apartment for every Soviet family instead of the single room which is the usual situation today. It is evident from the housing provisions of the Seven-Year Plan, however, that the separate apartments will be very small by Western standards: the plan calls for the construction of fifteen million apartment units with a total floor space (including corridors, bathroom and kitchen) of 650–60 million square metres —or, at most, 44 square metres (430 square feet) per apartment. A British working-class family would be shocked at having to live in so little space. Still, no one can doubt that Soviet citizens will be much happier if and when each family can have its own front door and no longer have to share the kitchen with several neighbours.

There is no question about the sharp acceleration of housing construction under the post-Stalin leadership. This is fully evident from the following figures showing housing space (excluding private rural housing) completed in four different years from 1950 to 1958, and the Seven-Year Plan goals:

[1] In Moscow, for example, the average revenue from tenants for rent and 'other items' is 1·75 roubles per square metre, while running costs, inclusive of capital repairs, average 4·31 roubles per square metre. See *Novyi Mir*, No. 10, 1959, p. 211.

Year	*Total*	*State*	*Urban Private*
	(*in million sq. metres of total space*)		
1950	24·2	17·8	6·4
1953	30·8	23·2	7·6
1957	52·0	38·5	13·5(*a*)
1958	70·1	45·6	24·5(*a*)
1959 (plan).. ..	80·0	—	—
1960 (plan).. ..	101·0	—	—
1959–65 plan, total	650–60·0	—	—
do., annual average	93·0	—	—

(*Source: Vestnik Statistiki*, No. 5, 1959, p. 94.) (*a*) These figures include private house-building by state-employed persons engaged in agriculture and forestry.

Despite the sharply-increased effort since Stalin's death, it is clear that there is still a very long way to go before tolerable housing conditions will be achieved, since a large part of new construction is necessary merely to keep pace with urban population growth. It has been pointed out that the Soviet *per capita* rate of house-building, even allowing generously for peasant construction, remains below that of the (West) German Federal Republic.[1] Nonetheless, the facts reveal considerable progress in the USSR. The ambitious plans for rebuilding villages in connection with Khrushchev's contemplated revival of the *agrogorod* necessarily call for a still greater expansion of housing construction in rural areas, although the financial burden involved is to be shouldered by the collective farms.

Services

Finally, brief mention must be made of improvements in badly needed consumer services—restaurants, cafes, shops, repair facilities and the like. This is a very backward sector of Soviet life. To cite just one example, an article in *Pravda* (March 14, 1959) estimated the total capacity of shoe-repair establishments in the Russian republic (RSFSR) at fifteen million pairs annually, although 100 million pairs of new shoes are sold each year and may be presumed to require repair at least once annually. A recent decree embodied plans for increasing the turnover of service and repair shops of all kinds to 10.3 billion roubles in 1961, as against 6.2 million roubles in 1958.[2] There have also been measures to increase the number of shops and restaurants.

[1] S. Wolk, in *Bulletin* (of the Munich Institute for the Study of the USSR), No. 5, 1959 (in square metres, not numbers of dwelling units).

[2] *Pravda*, March 13, 1959.

MOTIVATIONS OF RECENT POLICY

This, then, is the actual Soviet record in social welfare. It suggests, first of all, that even under Stalin's rule much attention was paid to the expansion and improvement of health services and education, and fairly generous rules adopted in regard to such things as sickness benefits and paid vacations. In the late 1930's, however, some steps backward were taken, particularly affecting hours of labour, maternity leave, and the worker's right to change his occupation, and it was only after Stalin's death that moves got under way to restore the conditions which had prevailed until the mid-1930's. In the last few years, the record shows, much more has been or is being done to improve old-age pensions and disability pay, to reduce working hours, to build more housing, and to provide more consumer services, even though the Soviet citizen certainly still has—and probably will continue to have—much to complain about.

Only the wilfully blind will refuse to take all this seriously. But more than *what* has been done, the vital question is *why* has it been done, and what significance, if any, do these developments have from the standpoint of assessing the nature of the Soviet system? No single, definitive answer is possible of course, but here, for what they may be worth, are a few thoughts on the subject.

While it is arguable that the Soviet rulers do as little as possible for the citizen in order to devote the largest possible share of national resources to heavy industry and weapons, such a formulation begs the question. One could reverse it and say that they devote as much as possible to improving the citizen's lot, subject to the necessary investment in heavy industry and weapons —which would sound better from the Soviet point of view, but mean equally little. Is the glass half-full or half-empty? In any case, neither formulation explains why more is being done for the Soviet citizen today than in the past.

One relevant factor may simply be that the USSR is now powerful enough economically to permit the diversion of an increasing amount of resources to the satisfaction of the needs of its citizens, without curtailing ambitious plans for the expansion of heavy industry. To carry out the first Five-Year Plan

(1928–32), Stalin found it necessary to reduce living standards drastically, but it would be foolish to take this to be what lawyers term 'evidence of system'. It is obviously no part of communist ideology to make people poorer; on the contrary, communism lays great stress on abundance. The 'abundance' of communism may well be—in the author's opinion it definitely is—a meaningless, even nonsensical concept, but it surely was the intention of all Soviet leaders, including even Stalin, to raise living standards at some future date, once the painful sacrifices of 'primitive accumulation' were no longer necessary. The Soviet citizen was, and still is, denied adequate housing, but it would be a mistake to conclude that the leadership believes in bad housing in the same sense that it believes in the undesirability of private peasant enterprise. Soviet leaders have been willing to sacrifice a generation, to neglect urgent needs for years, but it would be patently foolish to represent them as favouring poverty and hardship as such. They surely would concede, and even advocate, improvements in popular welfare if doing so would not interfere with the pursuit of their basic aims.

Before leaving the subject of ideology, two other points are worth making. One is the enormous attention which communists always pay to education: however they may twist its content to suit their purposes, they have invariably lavished resources on its development, whether under Stalin or under his successors. It is true that this effort is due, in part, to the urgent need of developing technical skills, but this is far from the whole explanation. Indeed, the promise made at the 20th Congress to extend full-time secondary education to all went far beyond practical necessities, and its implementation even tended to aggravate social tensions, which was one reason for Khrushchev's subsequent counter reforms.

The second point is the great importance, from the standpoint of communist ideology, of appearing to be doing something to improve the lot of the working masses. Even when nothing or little is actually being done, the party leaders must of necessity claim to be acting in that direction. Too great a contrast between words and deeds, however, can lead to general cynicism, as in fact it did under Stalin. Khrushchev is now engaged in an evident effort to revive the fervour of the party and to replace passive bureaucratism with initiative. It is reasonable to suppose, therefore, that with this aim in view he wants to show that the party is genuinely doing something to carry out its promises to the people.

One example of this ideological influence is the régime's insistence, for political reasons, on cheap bread and low rents even when these are economically irrational and administratively inconvenient. Thus, Khrushchev recently reasserted the *political impossibility* of raising bread prices despite the fact that, at these prices, it pays to feed bread rather than regular cattle feed to private livestock. In short, cheap bread is essential to the party's outward picture of itself.[1]

THE ROLE OF INCENTIVES

Other factors, too, have a bearing on the régime's attitude in regard to welfare. For a number of reasons too complex to be analysed here, the functioning of the Soviet economy is coming to depend more on incentives and less on compulsion. Prisoners can be kept working even when forced to live in overcrowded barracks on a minimum diet, but unless there is some emergency to spur them free men work better when they can expect to live better by greater effort. To achieve the leadership's ambitious plans, better work, more efficient organization, more initiative at the grass roots are all objective necessities. To some extent, of course, this was also true under Stalin and was acted upon, as evidenced by the lavish rewards given to Stakhanovites. But few analysts question that there has been a shift toward much *greater* reliance on incentives in recent years, paralleled by a scaling down of the number and powers of the police. To give but one of many examples of how this works in practice, the author, during a tour of the Soviet Union, was shown a new apartment block in Kiev, which he was told was being erected by the building industry for its own workers because, now that they could change employment without incurring criminal penalties, they would not remain in the industry 'unless we replaced the barracks and hostels with decent housing'.

[1] This picture has been obscured in the West by denunciations of an allegedly huge Soviet turnover tax on bread. Although it is true that the tax was for years the major constituent of the price of bread, the reason for this was that the tax was calculated on the basis of a ridiculously low procurement price for grain. The real economic incidence of the tax was not on consumers, but on the producers—the peasants.

Of course, people's attitudes and expectations are relevant to the efficacy of incentives as well as to political stability. The more the Soviet Union boasts of its great technical progress, of its Sputniks and moon rockets, of its equality with or superiority over the United States in weapons, the more impatient its citizens become with their backward living conditions, and the less reasonable it seems to them that nothing drastic is done to improve them. Confronted by such a popular state of mind, an intelligent leadership is likely to see the wisdom of taking some action to satisfy it.

The increasing range of contacts between Soviet citizens and foreigners plays a dual role in this process. Many more Soviet citizens are now learning at first or second hand how the other side lives, and this affects their own expectations. Then, too, with the increasing flow of foreign visitors to Russia, it must certainly appear politically advantageous to the leadership to impress them with higher standards of living. This is much more than a matter of impressing unsophisticated tourists from the West, who can if necessary be fobbed off with Potemkin villages. Much more important are the thousands of students and others from underdeveloped countries, as well as from the Soviet Union's own allies, who actually spend some time living among the Russians and cannot help learning the truth. Khrushchev is well aware that relative living standards will play an important role in the world impact of the two opposed systems.

SOME POINTS OF LOGIC

For all its simplicity, one should not overlook still another point: Khrushchev wants to be popular. He may genuinely care to reduce poverty, or he may be acting on the basis of cold political calculation—it does not matter which. He may even aspire to go down in history as the man who brought prosperity to the Soviet people—on the foundations laid by his grim predecessor. There are some Western observers who seem to shy away from even considering such motives possible, as if to do so would label them as pro-Soviet. This is clearly an illogical attitude. What is primarily objectionable about the Soviet system is its totalitarian character, its lack of intellectual and political freedom; and this character is not directly affected by the shortening of working hours or the provision of a separate apartment for every family.

It is indeed true that certain features of the Soviet economy are inconsistent with the proper satisfaction of consumer demand. It may also be true that the ultimate logic of a better-educated and materially more satisfied citizenry is incompatible with the totalitarian one-party state. Let us hope that it will prove so. But that is no reason for closing one's eyes to the realities: much is being done on the Soviet 'welfare' front, and there is no sign that Khrushchev's consolidation of his political power will cause any change in this respect, especially since the policies being followed must, in his judgment, appear rational, right and necessary.

V. STATISTICS

*14. The purchasing power of the Soviet rouble**

The object of this paper is to calculate the purchasing power of the Soviet 'consumer rouble' in terms of sterling. The author is by no means the first to utilize Soviet retail price quotations for comparisons with prices outside Russia, or with Russian prices at earlier dates. However, hitherto there has been no up-to-date information on product weights, nor has there been an adequate basis for making allowances for free-market prices. The publication in 1956 of a statistical compendium, *Sovetskaya Torgovlya* (Soviet Trade), makes it possible to fill these gaps, at least approximately, and this is the justification for the present exercise—together with the fact that the author has been able to observe prices and qualities on the spot.

There is still no official information from Soviet sources on a worker's budget. Therefore, the first step must be to use the trade statistics to reconstruct the probable pattern of spending. This reconstruction should be confined to *urban* areas, since the Russian peasant still obtains only a relatively small proportion of his wants by purchases from the shops, so that the rural trade pattern can be of little value as a guide to what is actually consumed. Fortunately, the institutional arrangements of Soviet trade enable one to distinguish, albeit somewhat roughly, between trade in urban and rural areas.

Weighting Procedure

Before explaining how the pattern of urban spending was cal-

* From the *Bulletin* of the Oxford University Institute of Statistics, 1958. The author gratefully acknowledges the practical help and advice of Mr J. A. Newth.

culated, it is necessary to describe briefly the organization of Soviet retail trade, which naturally affects the way in which the Soviet statistics are presented.

(*a*) *State trade* covers sales by retail outlets owned and operated by state agencies. These are generally under the Ministry of Trade (more rarely under some specialized ministry — e.g. medicines may be sold by the Ministry of Health), but there are also appreciable sales by the so-called 'workers' supply departments' of state enterprises.

(*b*) *Co-operative trade* is of three kinds:

(i) 'Consumer-co-operatives', under an agency known as *Centrosoyuz*, are responsible for the bulk of retail outlets in rural areas.

(ii) Also under *Centrosoyuz* are *co-operative commission sales* of farm produce, on behalf of collective farms or peasants. These sales occur at prices which are commonly well above official level and almost entirely in towns.

(iii) Other co-operative sales consist mainly of the disposals by producers' co-operatives of products of their manufacture.

(*c*) *Free market* sales are made by individuals selling their own produce, or by collective farms disposing of their surpluses. Only sales in urban markets are included in the Soviet statistics. Prices are uncontrolled. Almost all such sales consist of farm produce.

Urban transactions, then, will consist more or less[1] of the sum of (*a*), (*b*) (ii) and (iii) and (*c*). One must also separate out the turnover of restaurants and canteens, since, as we shall see, they tend to be relatively cheaper than the retail prices of the foodstuffs consumed in them. The nature of the available statistics makes the following steps necessary:

Firstly, in column 1 of Table 1 we have the total value of *state and co-operative trade including restaurants.* Column 2 shows the sales of commodities in restaurants of all kinds. Column 3 gives us all *Centrosoyuz co-operative sales*, including those in that organization's restaurants. This column also includes *co-opera-*

[1] Note quite. The Trade handbook, p. 21, shows total sales in rural areas, including restaurants, as 133,200 million roubles, whereas total *Centrosoyuz* co-operative sales, excluding commission trading, were worth 139,900 millions.

tive commission sales, and these are given separately in column 4. Finally, free-market sales are given in column 5, but only as rough approximations, because the detailed product breakdown is only available for seventy-one large towns, which may not be typical of the whole (the weighting applicable to these towns has been applied, *faute de mieux*, to the total urban free-market turnover).

Secondly, column 3 is deducted from column 1, to arrive at urban turnover. Then the estimated urban restaurant sales are also deducted (i.e. the larger part of column 2, since *Centrosoyuz* restaurants had a total turnover of 12.9 million roubles, out of a total of 58.8, and the figures in the table clearly imply that much of it is drink).[1]

Thirdly, columns 4 and 5 are added, since they are part of urban turnover. Transactions recorded in these columns take place at prices well above those in state shops (more of this below).

Fourthly, in arriving at the estimated total of urban sales (excluding restaurants), which appears in column 6, it is desirable to adjust downwards for so-called institutional purchases, i.e. for sales to offices, hospitals, schools, etc., in the retail network, including the free market. Fortunately, the biggest sales of this kind are made by the *Centrosoyuz* network (to collective farms) and so are in any case excluded from our calculations. In all but three cases it is thought to be sufficient merely to 'round down' to the nearest convenient number in hundreds of millions of roubles. This is not strictly sufficient, but it should not upset the weighting unduly. However, in three cases, there are good reasons for a sizeable deduction; these are 'Paper and office materials', 'Building materials' and 'Other, non-food'. In each case institutional purchases are thought to be more than usually important ('Other' includes petrol, which collective-farm lorries are thought to buy in cities on occasion: it has also been noticed that some building materials are bought by representatives of farms in

[1] For example, total sales of meat and sausages in *all* restaurants came to 6,779 million roubles. Total turnover of co-operative restaurants was about a quarter of those of the state, but the proportion is likely to have been smaller in the case of meat, if only because the share of drink in rural turnover is relatively larger. The total value of drinks bought in restaurants is arrived at by taking the difference between two tables, one showing turnover with and the other without restaurants. The difference comes to 17,400 million roubles.

TABLE 1

THE VALUE OF A CONSUMERS' GOODS ROUBLE

Turnover figures in millions of roubles (1955)

Commodity	*1* *State and Co-op trade including restaur-ants*	*2* *Restaur-ants*	*3* *Co-op (Tsentro-(soyuz) including restaurants*	*4* *Co-op com-mission sales*[1]	*5* *Free market*	*6* *Estimated urban sales*	*7* *Weights (%)*	*8* *Rouble value (pence)*	*9* *Sterling value (Col. 6 x Col. 8) (£ mill)*	*10* *Weights in UK prices (%)*
Meat	23,138	6,779	3,079	1,322	13,800	29,400	7·29	5	612	5·78
Fish	9,512	1,143	1,871	19	500[2]	7,300	1·81	5	152	1·44
Canned goods	6,405	1,116	986	0	0	4,200	1·04	4½	79	0·75
Butter	9,110	1,208	521	100	750	8,100	2·01	2½	84	0·79
Vegetable oils	5,412	607	1,590	254	750	4,100	1·02	3	51	0·48
Other fats	5,301	849	638	53	200[2]	4,000	0·98	2	33	0·31
Milk, milk products, cheese	7,984	1,888	587	202	2,900	8,400	2·08	5	175	1·65
Eggs	1,733	518	155	54	1,300	2,400	0·59	4	40	0·38
Sugar	20,893	1,384	3,814	0	0	15,900	3·94	1¾	116	1·10
Confectionery and pastries	21,107	3,882	6,196	0	0	11,500	2·85	2	96	0·91
Tea	2,471	141	1,244	0	0	1,100	0·27	5	23	0·22
Salt	783	35	466	0	0	300	0·07	17	21	0·20
Bread and rolls	41,184	4,565	8,239	0	0	29,000	7·19	11	1,329	12·56
Flour	10,726	1,261	5,570	798	2,400	11,500	2·85	6	288	2·72
Grain and pulses	5,655	669	1,082							
Macaroni products	3,793	476	595	0	0	2,800	0·69	8½	99	0·94
Potatoes	2,204	541	553	319	5,700	7,200	1·78	4	120	1·13
Vegetables	3,455	729	623	326	8,400	11,000	2·73	3	137	1·29
Fruit and melons	5,084	820	1,271	802	11,000	14,900	3·69	2½	155	1·47
Drinks	72,606	17,447	25,000[4]	152	400[2]	36,000	8·92	9½	1,425	13·47
Other food	9,316	2,425	2,017[4]	502	800[2]	6,600	1·64	4	110	1·04
Restaurant food sales	(7,462)[5]	(7,462)[5]	(1,399)[5]	0	0	43,400	10·76	8	1,447	13·68
Total Food and Drink	275,334	55,945	67,496	4,903	48,900	259,500	64·31	6 (6·09)	6,592	62·30

Cotton fabrics	25,427	—	12,151	—	—	13,200	3·27	7	385	3·64
Wool fabrics	7,443	—	1,950	—	—	5,500	1·36	2	46	0·43
Silk and rayon fabrics	11,614	—	3,498	—	—	8,100	2·01	2	67	0·63
Linen fabrics	1,172	—	398	—	—	750	0·19	12	37	0·35
Clothing	39,382	—	9,507	—	—	29,800	7·39	3	373	3·53
Furs	2,110	—	543	—	—	1,500	0·37	4	25	0·24
Headwear	1,982	—	678	—	—	1,300	0·32	5	27	0·25
Knitwear and stockings	13,900	—	3,664	—	—	10,200	2·53	4½	191	1·81
Leather footwear	15,265	—	4,222	—	—	11,000	2·73	3½	160	1·51
Other footwear	8,830	—	3,407	—	—	5,400	1·34	10	225	2·13
Soap and cosmetics	6,357	—	2,398	—	—	3,900	0·97	4½	73	0·69
Haberdashery, leather goods, thread	10,384	—	3,132	—	—	7,200	1·78	4	120	1·13
Tobacco and products	11,999	2,856	3,921	—	—	8,000	1·98	20	667	6·30
Matches	953	—	499	—	—	400	0·09	10	17	0·16
Paraffin	1,536	—	916	—	—	600	0·15	8	20	0·19
Furniture	6,350	—	1,815	—	—	5,000	1·24	6	125	1·18
Cooking utensils	5,182	—	2,754	—	—	2,400	0·59	12	120	1·13
China and glassware	1,888	—	809	—	—	1,000	0·25	5	21	0·20
Paper and office materials	2,751	—	775	—	—	1,500[6]	0·37	9	56	0·53
Newspapers and books	4,929	—	391	—	—	4,000[3]	0·99	14	233	2·20
Bicycles and motor-cycles ..	2,496	—	1,325	—	—	1,150	0·29	5½	26	0·25
Sports goods, toys, 'other cultural goods'	4,255	—	1,108	—	—	3,100	0·77	10	129	1·22
Radio and TV	2,785	—	808	—	—	1,900	0·47	10	79	0·75
Musical goods	1,210	—	388	—	—	800	0·20	30	100	0·95
Building materials incl. glass ..	9,051	—	6,180	—	—	2,000[6]	0·50	9	75	0·71
Other, non-food	26,878	—	10,066	—	—	14,200[6]	3·52	10	592	5·60
Total, Non-Food	226,603	2,856	77,307	—	—	144,000	35·69	6½ (6·65)	3,989	37·70
Total, All Goods	501,937	58,801	144,799	4,903	48,900	403,500	100·00	6¼ (6·29)	10,581	100·00

[1] Also included in column 3.
[2] Estimates, as these items were not separately specified.
[3] Allowance made for rural purchases in towns, e.g. large-scale postal subscriptions for newspapers and periodicals.
[4] Source gives 'drink' and 'other food' together.
[5] These figures represent the running costs and profits of restaurants.
[6] Downward allowance made for institutional purchases.

towns, while most stationers' shops sport a notice drawing attention to the fact that they supply offices). An arbitrary amount has also been allowed for villagers' subscriptions to newspapers, etc., which would inevitably be included with urban statistics.

Certain minor adjustments are rendered necessary by a few omissions in the Soviet tables. For example, the co-operative turnover statistics give 'drink' and 'other food' together, while market sales include no separate heading for fish, though fish appears quite commonly in markets. Rough estimates are made in these cases. It must be noted that sales in urban areas cannot be assumed to be identical with sales to the *urban population.* The many peasants who journey to urban markets buy goods to take back to their villages. Naturally, such purchases cannot be separately distinguished. Apart from bread, which peasants do often buy in towns, the bulk of peasant buying must consist of manufactured goods. Consequently, to this extent our table may somewhat overweight manufacturers *vis-à-vis* foodstuffs. Also, many urban consumers own allotments, and therefore the recorded purchases must somewhat understate their consumption of foodstuffs.[1] No claim to any absolute 'correctness' can be, or is, made, but it is thought that these weights are still a useful approximation. The purist may object to the use of 1955 trade statistics with 1956 price observations, but this would still seem better than 1937 weights; at the latter date, the share of bread in total state and co-operative sales was 17.7 per cent, against 8.3 per cent in 1955, a difference which must influence the result of any calculations. While some of the adjustments may seem arbitrary, the large items are reasonably firm, and the margin of error likely to have resulted from such adjustments should be reasonably small.

Price Quotations

In order to arrive at a sterling value for Soviet consumers' goods, it is necessary to find comparable values in British and in Soviet prices, to devise a sterling-rouble ratio for each product. Soviet price quotations are derived largely from observation in the USSR and from scattered price lists encountered in publications.

[1] According to *Sovetskaya Torgovlya*, No. 6/1956, p. 11, the urban populations obtained from its own private allotments the following amounts *per capita* in 1954: 44 kilograms of potatoes, 11 kilograms of vegetables, 27 litres of milk, 5 kilograms of meat and lard, etc.

In the case of foodstuffs, the official prices are generally prominently advertised in stores, the products are not too difficult to define and identify, and the disparity between official and free-market prices can be deduced from official statistics, as well as observed on the spot. The official statistics in question take the form of indices by quarters, for the years 1954 and 1955, based on sample surveys in 102 towns. These indices show considerable seasonal variation. To avoid unnecessary complication, seasonal prices of July will be used. The excess of co-operative-commission and free-market prices over official levels in the third quarter of 1955 are shown in Table 2.

TABLE 2

CO-OPERATIVE COMMISSION AND FREE MARKET PRICES

Product	*(State price=100)*	
	Co-operative Commission	*Market*
All goods	138	170
Flour, coarse	130	137
Flour, fine	154	183
Pulses	150	176
Potatoes	175	246
Vegetables	164	216
Fresh apples	203	274
Beef	149	177
Mutton	162	205
Pork	114	130
Milk	114	146
Butter	163	170
Vegetable oil	116	153
Eggs	137	176

Source: Trade handbook, pp. 133–4.

The disparity between official and free prices reached a peak in 1955, because, in previous years, there were repeated reductions in state retail prices at a time when farm output was not appreciably expanding. By 1956, some market prices had fallen, the aggregate fall being officially put at 9 per cent. This is allowed for in the price calculations made in this paper, which relate to 1956. Official prices changed hardly at all between 1955 and 1956.

So far as manufactures are concerned, the element of purely subjective judgment is, unavoidably, rather substantial. This arises inevitably from the nature of many of the commodities. The precise English equivalent of a Russian radio, TV set, bicycle, dress, stockings, can hardly be defined in any very scientific manner, and is certainly not immediately apparent to any inexpert observer. The author being an inexpert observer, all he can do is to give as honestly as possible what seem to be equivalent prices. Errors there must be, but there is no conscious bias.

Since Soviet weights are used, it is thought right to adopt as a basis of comparison those commodities actually consumed in Russia even though no UK equivalent of the given type or quality may exist. Thus, the 'black bread' of central Russia is taken to be comparable with the standard white loaf in England. Cheap Russian suits are assumed to be equal to the cheapest products of an English multiple tailor, though nothing quite like a cheap Russian suit is obtainable anywhere in this country. In general, Soviet quality is often inferior, and the Soviet consumer suffers from delays in service and from the non-availability of the product or type preferred at established prices. However, degrees of consumer dissatisfaction, impatience or annoyance are not susceptible of statistical measurement. We can only assert that there is evidence to show that these things are more common in Russia than in Great Britain. A formal expression of this tendency is the limitation on sales of most foodstuffs to any one consumer in state shops. A notice limits purchases to half a kilo of sugar, five eggs, etc., per purchaser, thus compelling frequent visits to the crowded shops.

Detailed price comparisons are discussed in Appendix I. Only the bare results, in terms of the rouble value in pence for each product, appear in the principal table. It will be seen that the value of a consumers' goods rouble works out at a little over 6¼d.

Some Thoughts on the Price Pattern

One is struck by the immense 'spread' of rouble values. In part this is due to fiscal policies of both Russia and Britain. Thus, 'basic' bread is relatively cheap in Russia, and this stands out in the table, in that the 'exchange value' of the bread rouble is much higher than that of any other foodstuff. This also explains why Russian peasants find it profitable to buy bread and feed it to animals, since the prices of animal produce make such activity pay handsomely, to the embarrassment of the authorities.[1] On the other hand, drink and tobacco are so heavily taxed in Great Britain that this causes a price ratio favourable to the Russians.

[1] In July 1956, the Soviet Government announced measures to forbid the purchase of bread for feeding livestock.

In the case of drink, it must be added that the vodka-whisky ratio is very different to that of beer, and an 'English' weight for beer would produce a lower rouble value than the one here adopted. Russians certainly prefer vodka to beer, which, taking into account the quality of their beer, is most understandable.

It is often thought that the Russian pattern of retail prices differs from ours primarily through the operation of turnover tax, which is said to 'tax necessities' particularly heavily. The table does indeed show how very expensive necessities are in Russia. All basic foods except bread are dear, as are clothes and furniture. By contrast, many other manufactures, especially those made of metal and/or by the light engineering industry, are relatively very much cheaper. However, it would perhaps be wiser to see these price differentials as reflecting supply and demand conditions. Looked at from the angle of supply, the cause of the high prices of many necessities is failure to take effective steps to increase production. This is (or was) obvious in the case of farm produce, and in textiles the 'blame' can be shared between inadequate investment in the industry and inadequate production or imports of the raw materials. Given the supplies available, tax policy becomes a consequence, and not a cause, of the present price ratios. Indeed, it may be argued that the Soviet authorities are not ruthless enough in carrying out a logical price-and-tax policy. For example, let us take three of the relatively most expensive items: sugar, butter and fruit. These were in fact very hard to obtain in many parts of the country, and on pure supply-and-demand, queue-elimination grounds, there were grounds for a price *increase*. A cut in turnover tax on these articles would merely have lengthened existing queus. By contrast, some items with the lowest rouble-penny ratios—e.g. cooking utensils, metal toys, non-leather footwear, electric lamps—are readily available at existing prices, and bear a relatively low rate of turnover tax. Such facts as these may provide a sound basis for criticizing the Government's investment policy, or import restrictions, but hardly supports the view that the high price of necessities is 'due' to turnover tax.

Some Possible Conclusions about the Purchasing Power of the Rouble

So far, the entire discussion has concerned the purchase of goods.

What about services? Unfortunately, data on these are inadequate. One of the biggest problems is that of rent. Controls have made the position in Great Britain chaotic enough, while in the USSR the relatively low rents payable must somehow be adjusted for the woefully inadequate quantity and (often) quality of the available space. Other services show a great variety of price-ratios. For example, a rouble devoted to making a local telephone call is worth about 2s, but on the railways its value is nearer 7d. This lower figure would apply also to cinema seats and internal postage rates, while a 'haircut rouble' is worth a great deal more—though visiting women have expressed themselves very critically about Russian permanent waves and styling. Repairs, dry-cleaning and similar services are apt to be expensive. Without any reliable information on relative weights, it is hard to put this and other information together. It is therefore proposed to take a drastic short cut, and assume that the services rouble averages out at around 1s. The weight of services in total urban expenditure must be somewhere about 10 per cent.

Allowing any reasonable margin of error, inherent in the short cut which has just been taken, it would seem that the purchasing power of the rouble is about 6¾d, giving an exchange rate of around 35 roubles to the pound. This relates, of course, to the roubles found in the pockets of citizens. It is not suggested that it is proper valuation for roubles of other kinds; for instance, the exchange rate for machinery would certainly be far lower, perhaps 15–20 to the pound or even less.

What does this tell us about real wage rates? It appears from reliable Soviet sources that the all-round average of wage and salaries in the USSR in 1956 must have been roughly 8,500 roubles per annum.[1] This includes managers and top bureaucrats, but also several million low-paid labourers in rural areas. It seems likely that a moderately-skilled worker in an average factory, and many a white-collar worker of the accountant or higher clerical officer type, would earn somewhere about this average, say 750 roubles per month. Very roughly, it would seem that a similar type of person might be earning £42–£44 per month in Great Britain. Like all such generalizations, this one is wide

[1] In 1954, the average was 206 per cent of 1940 (according to the textbook *Politicheskaya ekonomiya*). In 1940 it was 4,060 roubles per annum. The tendency since 1954 has been upwards, by roughly 2 to 3 per cent each year.

open to criticism, since anyone familiar with wage rates in the two countries will think of numerous exceptions. For example, while wages are higher than this in engineering and coal mining in both countries, a Soviet railway engine driver is relatively much better off, unskilled auxiliary labourers very much worse off, than might be suggested by the above comparisons. Be this as it may, 750 roubles a month at 6¾d per rouble is the equivalent of only about £20 15s, or shall we say £21. A comparable British wage-earner is likely to be receiving twice as much at least, probably more. This comparison gives the USSR the benefit of every major doubt, and is, of course, based on Soviet weights. Taking quality and availability into account, the disparity is doubtless greater still.

Before concluding that the Soviet standard of living is under half the British, two other factors must be taken into account.

The first of these concerns the number of earners per family. A considerably larger proportion of married women work in Russia. Then, owing to the housing shortage, more grown-up members of families stay with their parents when going out to work. For the same reason, pensioners often live with the younger generation, and indeed grandma commonly acts as baby-minder, thereby permitting the mother to go out to work. Such facts as these can be given no statistical precision.[1] None the less, they are bound to narrow the gap between the purchasing power of Russian and British families.

The second factor concerns taxes and receipts from the state budget. So far as taxes are concerned, if we assume a family with two children, the advantage is distinctly with the British. Income tax on 750 roubles a month is about 50 roubles, whereas such a British family earning £42 per month will pay hardly any tax. (A childless couple would be liable to more tax in England, but would be paying a 6 per cent 'childlessness tax' in Russia.) The family with two children would be receiving 7s 6d allowance in Great Britain, but would have a small extra tax (0.5 per cent of income) to pay in Russia for having only two of them. This alone would balance the fact the Russian worker pays no social insur-

[1] *Vestnik Statistiki*, No. 1 of 1957 has published the composition of 'sample-survey' workers' families. 48·1 per cent of the total were working, 5·4 per cent received pensions or stipends, and only 46·5 per cent were dependents. The 'sample' was 14,800 families, and one wonders how typical this can be.

ance contribution. The Russians seem to be the more generously treated in respect of sick pay and disability benefit, and the period of paid leave in occupations classed as unhealthy is longer than is generally the case here. Those who are fortunate enough to be given one of the limited number of places in rest homes and sanatoria also do fairly well. On the other hand, medical drugs are fairly expensive in Russia and have to be paid for (except by in-patients in hospitals). On balance, taking taxes and the 'social wage' together, there would seem to be no appreciable absolute advantage to either. However, since the money wage payments are so much smaller in Russia, the 'social wage' is relatively more important there.

Any more precise conclusion on living standards would seem to be rendered impossible by lack of necessary information, especially about the make-up of Russian family budgets. Fortunately, the present statistical 'thaw' in the USSR gives ground for hope that more material will be forthcoming.

Addendum (*in 1958*)

Since this was written, the following changes have occurred:

(*a*) Couples with children no longer pay small families tax.

(*b*) Prices of a few articles have been cut, including pork, TV sets and poultry.

(*c*) Prices of vodka, wines, cars, motor cycles and carpets have been appreciably raised.

On balance, early in 1958, state retail prices are slightly higher than in 1956, but free market prices, especially for meat and dairy produce, are distinctly lower. For these products the share of sales at official prices has risen.

APPENDIX I

PRICE QUOTATIONS AND EQUIVALENTS

Notes. As far as possible, both Russian and British prices relate to July 1956. Where not otherwise indicated, the Russian price is official. Market prices are indicated by the letter (M). All food prices are per kilogram, except where otherwise specified.

FOOD

Meat

Beef 12.00; 21.00 (M), for poorish stewing variety, UK 7s 0d. Mutton 13.00; 22.00 (M), quality very moderate, UK 7s 0d. Pork 19.50; 23.00 (M), quality sometimes fair, UK 8s 0d. Good meat dearer, e.g. steak in Moscow 30.00 (M). Frankfurter-type sausage 16.50 (UK pork sausage 7s 0d). Salami-type sausage about 35.00 (UK 15s). Ham and bacon dear and scarce. Estimated average weighted price 17.00, for fresh meat. Relative scarcity of meat in state shops compels abnormally large purchases of sausage (45 per cent of state sales). 1 *rouble*=*5d.*

Fish

Types bought very different from UK. Herrings (above 40 per cent of the total) sell at a variety of prices between 9.50 and 20.00, according to quality and origin. A coarse salt fish (salaka) costs only 4.00. A popular fresh-water fish (sudak) is sometimes obtainable at 9.50–10.00. Miscellaneous local fish on sale in many markets, widely differing prices. Average fish price likely to be around 11.00 or more, UK 4s 6d (cod). 1 *rouble*=*5d.*

Canned and Preserved Goods

Assortment available far smaller in USSR. Small tins of cheaper fish (e.g. carp in sauce) cost about 5.80 (UK brisling, say 1s 9d). Large tin of 'shproty' (sardine-like) cost 12.10; compare two tins of sardines in UK, 3s. Soups are sold in jars with metal tops for about 4.00, may compare with UK cans at 1s 6d. 1 *rouble*=*4½d.*

Butter
28.00; 40.00 (M), UK 6s 6d. 1 *rouble*=2½*d.*

Vegetable Oils and Fats
Margarine, 14.00 and up, UK 4s 3d. Sunflower and cottonseed oil sold for cooking at prices varying from 14.00 to 21.00 (highest is M). UK (cooking fat) 4s 3d. 1 *rouble*=3*d.*

Other Fats
Lard costs 23.00; also up to 33.00 (M), UK 4s–4s 6d. 1 *rouble*=2*d.*

Milk
Generally 2.20; 2.50 (M), UK 1s 2d. 1 *rouble*=6*d.*

Cheese
Prices varied from 22.00 to 39.00. Cream cheese (M) 20.00–25.00, UK Cheddar about 5s 6d. 1 *rouble*=2½*d.*

Eggs (prices for ten)
7.50; 12.00 (M). Small sizes, UK 3s. 1 *rouble*=4*d.*

Sugar
Averages 10.00. Scarce. UK 1s 6d. 1 *rouble*=1¾*d.*

Confectionery and Pastries
Chocolate extremely dear (a UK 1s bar would cost about 14.00). Moderate toffee is 3.00 per 100 grammes. UK equivalent at most 8d. Pastries also dear and of moderate quality. Ice cream is good and widely available (large cone costs 1.90, UK perhaps 8d). *Say* 1 *rouble*=2*d.*

Tea
70.00 and up. UK 13s 6d. But Russians drink tea much weaker, from choice. As we consume tea, not tea leaves, Soviet price is arbitrarily divided by two for purposes of comparison, so 1 *rouble*=5*d.*

Salt
Cooking salt about 0.60, UK 10d. 1 *rouble*=1*s* 5*d.*

Bread

Cheapest bread is about 1.24–1.30 (rye). Grey and almost-white bread available at around 1.40 in the south, but white bread in Moscow is very dear, cheapest seen being 2.35; Vienna-type loaf is about 5.00. Big relative weight of cheapest bread consumed. UK white loaf about 1s 5d. Difficult to adjust for Russian purchases of dearer bread. Rough estimate. 1 *rouble*=11*d.*

Flour, Pulses, etc.

Flour in USSR bears extra tax to make it relatively dearer than bread. Wheat flour priced at 4.00; also 5.00 (M), UK 1s 6d. Grain (wheat and rye) may often be bought at 2.00–3.00 (M). Semolina 5.50, UK 2s 4d. Macaroni 3.70, UK 2s 7d. Rice 7.90, 10–13.00 (M), UK 2s 3d. Pearl barley 2.60; 3.00 (M), UK 2s 3d. Dried peas 3.00; 5.00 (M), UK (lentils) 2s. Rough average: Grain and Pulses, 1 *rouble* = 7½*d.* Flour, 1 *rouble* = 4½*d.* Macaroni and similar, 1 *rouble*=8½*d.*

Potatoes

1.00; 2.00–2.50 (M), UK 6d. 1 *rouble*=4*d.*

Vegetables

Highly seasonal prices in Russia, due to poor storage, worse transport arrangements, dreadful marketing. For same reasons, big geographic divergencies in availability. Late July quoted: Cabbage 1.50–2.00 (mostly M), UK 4½d. Carrots 3.50 (M), UK 8½d. Onions 3.00–4.00 (M), UK 1s. Beetroot 0.90; 1.20 (M). Quality and availability patchy. *Say* 1 *rouble*=3*d.*

Fruit, Melons, Cucumbers

Fruit almost unobtainable in July at any price, apart from berries: Lemons 3.50 each, UK 3d. Strawberries ('flush' price) 15.00, UK 6s. Apples when available 20.00 (M), UK about 2s 6d. Prunes 17.90, UK 4s. Small cucumbers 3.00 each (M), UK about 8d. 1 *rouble*=*about* 2½*d.*

Drink

Size for size, vodka costs about as many roubles as whisky costs shillings. Very heavy weight of vodka in Russian drink purchases can be observed everywhere: Beer, small bottle, 3.00–3.50, UK equivalent 1s 2d. Adequate Georgian wine 20.00, UK (Burgundy) 6s 6d. Minerals relatively cheaper. 1 *rouble=about 9½d.*

Other Food

This includes coffee (40.00, UK 15s 6d), jam (6.00 and more per jar, UK 1s 9d), mushrooms, condiments, honey, etc. On a rough count. 1 *rouble=4d.*

Restaurants and Canteens

This must be regarded as a separate item owing to relative cheapness of meals compared to cost of ingredients. Quality of cooking will be passed over in silence.

Typical 'dining room' (*stolovaya*) makes possible adequate three-course meal for 6.00, UK equivalent about 3s 6d.

Factory canteens cheaper in both countries.

Trade statistics show that of the total turnover of all public feeding establishments, 30 per cent consists of drink; from observation this includes a fair amount of vodka. Allowing for this 1 *rouble=8d.*

NON-FOOD

Cotton Cloth

Cheapest cotton prints are around 6.50 per metre, of very poor quality. UK (better) equivalent is about 4s. Better cloths proportionately dearer in both countries. 1 *rouble=7d, at most.*

Wool Fabrics

Wool is scarce and dear, all-wool cloths command luxury prices. A modest wool-mixture blanket is apt to cost over 100.00 (UK 20s). Mixture-cloth cheap suiting costs about 120.00 (UK say 25s). Cheapest wool cloth of reasonable quality was 200.00, fairly good gaberdine is 306.00, UK 50s, while good imported worsted ranges up to 500.00 per metre, UK 45s–65s. 1 *rouble=at most 2d.*

Silk and Rayon Fabrics

Good-quality silk dress fabrics cost 110.00–125.00, UK say 17s 6d. So-called 'rayon crepe-georgette' was 57.00–62.00 per metre, UK 7s. 1 *rouble=at most 2d.*

Linen Fabrics

Linen still widely used. Single bed sheet was about 70.00, UK 70s. 1 *rouble*=1*s*.

Clothing

This is a very large class, and the very different exchange-rates for various materials make it hard to make any estimate without more information about weights of various items. The following sample prices illustrate the wide range:

		UK £	*s.*	*d.*
Cotton print dress, moderate quality*	200·00	3	0	0
Rayon dress, more or less adequate	280·00	2	10	0
Crepe de chine dress, good	480·00	10	0	0
Cotton housecoat	337·00	2	10	0
Wool (mixture) frock	475·00	2	17	6
Woman's winter overcoat, fur trimming, best quality	3500·00	20	0	0
Cheap shabby-looking winter overcoat.. ..	750·00	6	10	0
Man's autumn-weight overcoat	720·00	6	10	0
Man's suit, wool mixture, poor	700·00	8	0	0
Man's suit, all wool, fair	2000·00	20	0	0
Man's suit, summer-weight, linen	650·00	10	0	0
Poplin-type shirts, adequate	50·00	1	5	6

Underwear is relatively expensive and poor quality. Children's clothes are relatively cheaper in all types.

* The Russian equivalent of our cheap chain-store dress was never seen on sale. Apparently Russian women buy cheap cloth and make it up themselves, or take it to a private dressmaker.

Reasonable average 1 *rouble*=3*d.*

Furs

Soviet furs are surprisingly expensive and moderate in quality, in home market. Roughly 1 *rouble*=4*d.*

Headwear

Man's felt hat costs 69.00, UK 25s. Straw hats at about 40.00, popular in summer. Fur caps (63.00 to 300.00) widely worn in winter. No equivalent. Women's hats very dear, but most women wear headscarves. Reasonable average 1 *rouble*=5*d.*

Knitwear

Wool knitted articles scarce and very dear, e.g. cardigan at about 125.00, UK 30s.

Wool socks of adequate quality are about 11.00, same quality UK 4s. Women's 'capron' stockings range from 14.00 to 30.00. Nylons at 6s 11d may perhaps compare with capron at 19.00. Capron petticoats about 100.00 (UK nylon say 28s). 1 *rouble*= $4\frac{1}{2}$*d.*

Leather Footwear

Leather is dear. Adequate shoes (men's or women's) cost 200.00, UK 50s.

Allowance must be made for policy of cheaper shoes for children; thus boy's leather shoes at 85.00 (UK 27s). 1 *rouble*= $3\frac{1}{2}$*d.*

Other Footwear

By contrast, non-leather footwear is much cheaper.

Poor galoshes can be bought for 18.00, canvas shoes on rubber soles for 27.00. Felt boots are much used in winter, cost about 140.00, and have no UK equivalent. On balance 1 *rouble*=10*d.*

Soap and Cosmetics

Cake of household soap costs 1.85, UK about 6d. Toilet soap, moderate quality, about 2.20, UK about 7d. Detergents still feebly developed. Lipstick costs about 4.50–6.00, UK (cheap) equivalent 2s to 2s 6d. 1 *rouble=about* $4\frac{1}{2}$*d.*

Haberdashery and Thread (including travel goods and handbags)

Cotton reel 0.95, UK 6d (thread is about a sixth of sales under this head). Pocket comb 3.20 to 6.10, UK 6d to 9d. Clothes brush 7.80, UK 3s. Fibre suitcase 90.00, UK about 30s. Woman's handbag, imitation leather, 37.00, UK 15s. Woman's handbag (real leather) 140.00, UK 45s. 1 *rouble=perhaps* 4*d.*

Tobacco and Products

Most popular Soviet brand, Belomorkanal, cost 2.20 for 25. UK tipped cigarettes cost 3s 3d for 20, but even these have more tobacco. Allowing this, roughly 1 *rouble=about* 1*s* 8*d.*

Matches

0.20, UK 2d. 1 *rouble*=10*d.*

Paraffin
Still much used for urban cooking and rural lighting. 0.65 per litre, UK 2s 3d per gallon. 1 *rouble=8d.*

Furniture
Soviet quality generally very poor. Prices vary, as some sold by co-operative workshops at uncontrolled prices. Rough unpainted wardrobes seen at 600.00–900.00, UK £12–£18. Well finished wardrobe might be as much as 1,700.00–3,000.00.[1] Metal bedstead, no mattress, can cost from 120.00 to 220.00, UK £2. Soft furnishings tend to be dear. Roughly, 1 *rouble=6d.*

Cooking Utensils
These appear to be good, cheap and abundant. Thus aluminium frying pan, quite large, costs 7.50–8.50, UK could be 7s 6d–8s 6d. 1 *rouble=1s.*

China and Glass
Big variety of types and prices in both countries. Very roughly, 1 *rouble—5d.*

Paper and Office Materials
Writing paper, fifty sheets, lined, 1.80 (UK say 1s 3d). School exercise books, about twenty pages, 0.40, UK 5d. Pencil 0.20; adequate fountain pen 17.50, say UK 12s. Box of ten coloured pencils 9.00 (UK 3s 6d). Ink is of such bad quality that comparison is pointless. 1 *rouble=9d.*

Newspapers and Books
Newspapers, four big pages, 0.20; six-page issues 0.30, UK 2d. New books *much* cheaper in USSR, 8.00 against 12s 6d. Technical books even more so. However, our paper-backed reprints at around 3s compare favourably with their equivalents. 1 *rouble= perhaps 1s 2d.*

Bicycles and Motor Cycles
Cheapest bicycle at around 450.00 is of very low quality. Adequate machine, corresponding to our £15 model, costs at least

[1] Cheaper wardrobes, and other furnishings, sometimes appear on official price lists, but are very hard to find in the shops.

650.00. Motor-cycles 350 c.c. 4,200.00 (UK £150). 1 *rouble*=5½*d.*

Sports Goods, Toys, 'Other Cultural Goods'
Big variety, relatively cheap, e.g. a football for 35.00, similar to an imported Pakistan one at 28s. Elaborate mechanical toys often surprisingly cheap. Soft toys less good and dearer. Cameras and photographic equipment quite good and cheap. Quite good FED costs 500.00 (UK about £15). Adequate roll film 5.80 (UK 3s 6d). 1 *rouble*=10*d.*

Radio and Television
Quite good radio for 400.00, UK about £20. Cheaper varieties available. TV, approximately 14-in. screen, 2,400.00, UK £60. Record players (pick-ups) 250.00–350.00, UK £10–£13. 1 *rouble*= 10*d.*

Musical Goods
Folk instruments cheap, e.g. balalaika from 40.00, accordions 300.00 to 1,000.00. LP records very cheap, 12-in. classical costs 7.90, light music dearer (UK LP about 39s); 10-in. ordinary popular record is about 3.00, UK 5s 6d. 1 *rouble*=*around* 2*s* 6*d.*

Building Materials and Window Glass
Big variety, availability very patchy. Tend to be fairly cheap when obtainable. Only roughest estimate can be made. 1 *rouble*= 9*d.*

Other Non-food
This group includes various electrical domestic articles, which tend to be relatively cheap. Thus 60-watt bulb 1.30, UK 1s 3d. Fairly good washing machine 2,250.00, UK £90. Good refrigerator 2,000.00; UK equivalent about £80. (Cheaper varieties available in both countries.) Cheapest vacuum cleaner 425.00, UK £25. Electric iron 35.00, UK 45s. Electric kettle 76.50, UK 48s. One-kW. electric fire, small, 120.00, UK 30s.

Watches (if they belong here, and are not 'other cultural goods') are relatively dearer. Thus an alarm clock would be about 30.00–50.00, UK 20s–25s, but cheapest pocket watch 180.00, UK 27s. Popular cheap wrist watch about 500.00, say UK £8.

Private cars sell moderately (in 1955 there were 46,000 cars sold retail in towns, according to the Trade Handbook). Pobeda sells at 16,000 roubles, equal to say the Austin A50, £820. Long queue at this price.

Private petrol averages about 0.60 per litre, say 3.00 per gallon. A rough balance of such items suggests 1 *rouble*=10*d.*

* * *

Little has happened since 1956 to invalidate the general conclusions of the above article. The following are a few relevant points worth noting:

(*a*) All the figures cited above are in old roubles. In most cases present prices in new roubles may be arrived at simply by shifting the decimal point with some rounding up or down. Thus the cheapest black bread in Moscow, which costs 1.24 roubles, now sells at 12 kopeks, while a wage of 800 roubles a month is now 80 roubles.

(*b*) Soviet prices of meat and butter were sharply increased in the spring of 1962, but, compared with 1956, the official retail price index shows a rise of under 2 per cent. Owing to shortages, free market prices have tended to rise on average. At the same time money wages have been increasing and it seems reasonable to assume that Soviet real wages in 1962 were perhaps 15 per cent above 1956 levels, despite the meat and butter increases. The absence of an official wage index and the variations in availability at established prices make precision impossible at this stage.

(*c*) British retail prices have, of course, risen considerably in the last few years, so that the rouble-penny ratio in 1962 would be somewhat more favourable to the rouble. On the other hand British money wages have increased much faster than Soviet money wages. On balance there could not have been much difference in the rates of increase in real wages in the two countries.

(*d*) The Soviets announced the abolition of income tax by easy stages. After some reductions in the tax liability of low income groups, the process of abolishing income tax was suspended in 1962. However, the net effect of changes since 1956 has been relatively to improve the tax position of the Soviet family.

15. Occupational patterns in the USSR and Great Britain

Some Comparisons and Contrasts *

What differences in the utilization of manpower can be expected to flow from differences in social systems? The question seems to be of real interest and not have been seriously explored in recent years. The publication during 1960–61 of many figures taken from the USSR census of population provides a basis for such comparison which was previously lacking. Indeed, the results of the previous Soviet census (1939) remained largely unpublished, and in the years since the war and until 1959 very little indeed was published in the USSR about the labour force and the population. It is true that statistics did appear giving the division of the *state-employed* labour force between principal branches of activity (industry,[1] building, agriculture, transport, trade, and so on) and between main categories (workers, auxiliaries, engineer-technical staffs, office staffs). However, there were a number of omissions which made serious analysis difficult. Thus data on non-state employment were quite inadequate. In the USSR the major part of agriculture is not in the state sector, but is undertaken by collective farms and by families working on their own small plots of land. Until 1960, there was silence about the numbers so engaged; we only had figures on 'households', with no information about how many were in each household. There were also some other individuals or groups omitted from the published figures. There was nothing on the numbers in the Armed Forces, for instance. There was also silence on the age and sex composition of the population.[2] The motive was, no doubt, security. It is surely no coincidence that the first publica-

* First published (without addendum) by The Manchester Statistical Society, 1962.

[1] The word 'industry', whenever used in connection with Soviet statistics, ncludes manufacturing and mining, the electricity and gas industries, fishing, lumbering, the slaughter and processing of livestock. It excludes construction and installation work.

[2] Indeed, the size of the total population remained a secret from the war until 1956; most Western analysts overestimated it, i.e. underestimated war losses.

tion of the age and sex data, the number of working peasants and the numbers in the Armed Forces came almost simultaneously. No doubt the authorities feared calculation by remainder, and indeed some Western analysts did try to deduce the size of the Armed Forces (and also the number of forced labourers) by such methods. Fortunately, such excessive nervousness on statistical security is a thing of the past, though, as we shall see, plenty of irritating gaps still remain in the published information.

However, any comparison with British data is fraught with grave perils, and the author of this paper is acutely aware of them. There is, as always in international comparisons, the problem of comparability, made worse in this instance by the almost total lack of explanatory matter on the Soviet side. It has been possible to obtain some verbal explanations from some personally helpful Soviet economists, but much remains unclear. We will have repeated occasion to cast doubt on the validity of this or that comparison for that reason.

Another difficulty arises from the existence in the USSR of a large number of peasants. Peasants are always hard to fit into labour statistics. How, for example, should one treat a peasant woman? For part of the year she may work hard on the land, but she may spend half of the year looking after her babies, or on domestic handicrafts. Her husband may have no farm work to do in winter, and may or may not go off on seasonal work elsewhere. For all these reasons, one expects a very considerable difference between the number of man-years worked in agriculture and the number of persons recorded as peasants. In the USSR there is a further complication due to the importance of part-time work on private plots and allotments, to which further reference will have to be made. There are many Soviet collective farmers who are engaged for much of the year in non-agricultural pursuits within the collective farms (e.g. building work, small-scale manufacturing, or providing minor personal services such as hairdressing, etc.), and who only join the strictly farm labour force at peak periods.

Finally, there is the category of comparison problems which relates more directly to the difference in economic system. There is no obvious Soviet equivalent for the British 'employer', especially for the quite numerous 'self-employed' farmers and shopkeepers. Nor can one easily discover an English equivalent of 'chairmen and deputy-chairmen of collective farms'. The resultant snags can never be very satisfactorily overcome.

As in Great Britain so in the USSR, the census figures are very hard indeed to reconcile with statistics of employment, which are compiled in this country by the Ministry of Labour and in the USSR by the Central Statistical Office. This is inevitable, but causes problems when one wishes to use non-census data to fill gaps.

The Problem of the Soviet Total

The population of the USSR in January 1959 was 208,827,000. This was divided as follows (thousands):

A. All occupied persons (excluding members of families of collective farmers, workers and employees engaged in private subsidiary agriculture)	99,130
of which	
Workers and employees of state, co-operative and social organizations and also persons hired by groups of citizens, carpenters, stovemen and other workpeople engaged in individual construction and repair work.	
(*a*) Counted in the Census	62,961
(*b*) Annual average	58,900
Collective farmers engaged in the socialized economy.	
(*a*) Counted in the Census	32,280
(*b*) Annual average	24,500
Individual peasants and individual craftsmen	266
Armed Forces	3,623
B. Members of families of collective farmers, workers and employees engaged in private subsidiary agriculture	9,865
C. Dependants of individuals (children, old people, and able-bodied persons engaged only in the home and in bringing up children)	85,422
D. Pensioners (living principally on their pension)	12,423
E. Scholarship holders	1,718
F. Persons having other sources of income, or not indicating source	269

(*Source: Vestnik statistiki,* No. 12/1960, p. 49; this will henceforth be referred to as *VS*12.)

Even the lower total given for 'workers and employees' in the above table (58,900,000) is much higher than the normally-published figure of 'workers and employees' for that date (54,300,000).[1] The difference is partly accounted for by those

[1] *Narodnoe khozyaistvo SSSR v 1959 godu* (hereinafter referred to as *NK*59), p. 585, gives this figure for 'the end of 1958', presumably December. The total at the census date, January, 1959, could hardly be appreciably higher.

engaged in co-operatives or 'hired by groups of citizens', etc., but it could include prisoners, whose numbers remain a state secret and who do not fit easily into any of the above classifications, and/or domestic servants or communist party officials, or policemen. The last two categories may be thought properly to belong to the 'workers and employees' group, but there is some evidence, confirmed by verbal answers to questions, that neither of these normally figures in labour statistics under that head. As will be shown in subsequent analysis, it is impossible to identify their presence in any of the sub-groups into which the census total is broken down.[1]

Let us return to the question of the total which should be used in any analysis of occupation and for comparison with the British figures. It should be clear that precision is quite out of the question. Orders of magnitude are all we will get.

The total number of occupied persons which could be derived from the above table includes many part-timers: pensioners who work a part of the year, housewives who spasmodically cultivate cabbages, and so on. While it is true that British statistics do not make adequate downward allowance for part-timers, this factor is far less important in the British than in the Soviet economy. This is most obvious in agriculture. Thus according to the same census report (*VS*12, pp. 5 and 6), while 31.7 million collective farmers (out of 32.3) plus 6.6 million state-employed persons and 0.1 million individual peasants were engaged in agriculture, on an annual basis this represented a total not of 38.4 but of 26.8 million persons. The addition (on an annual basis) of private subsidiary agriculture brings the total to 'about 33 million', according to the same source. If this is so, then, still on an annual basis, this private sector occupies 6.2 million persons, and these persons include some collective farmers, since most of them devote a part of the year to cultivating their private plots. This is a far smaller total than could be deduced from the gross figures. It might be added that the use of the higher figure for labour productivity comparisons by some Western analysts leads them to exaggerate the undoubtedly very great superiority of the United States in this respect.

But this does not solve our problem. The least harmful way of proceeding seems, in my view, to be this. *For purposes of occupa-*

[1] It has since become possible; see addendum.

tional analysis, we will have to use the total of 99.1 million, because the detailed figures cited by the Soviet source all relate to this total. The exaggeration in the number of peasants which follows from the use of this total is roughly offset by the omission from it of the 'private subsidiary agriculture'. However, in analysing *labour utilization by sectors of the economy* (Table 3) we will have to use a different and lower total for the USSR, if we are to avoid an undue degree of non-comparability. This is neither entirely logical nor particularly accurate, but critics are asked to suggest a workable alternative.

'Workers by Hand and Workers by Brain'

Both the Soviet and the British census statistics distinguish between those engaged principally in physical and in mental labour ('manual' and 'non-manual'). Neither do this particularly logically, but the British classification seems the least logical, since, for example, actors and musicians are classified with 'manual labour' (Group 10, skilled operatives), while charwomen mysteriously appear with barbers and hall-porters in Group 8, which is deemed to be non-manual. In any event, comparability can best be achieved by recasting one set of figures, and it seems logical to alter the British ones to suit the Soviet classification (though with one exception to be noted). The principal changes for this purpose require a shift of the following British groups into the 'workers by brain' category.

Musicians, actors and similar.
Foremen and similar (from Group 9 in the British classification).
Laboratory assistants and technicians.
Farm managers and farm bailiffs.
Some categories in the British Group 8 (servants, etc.) have been shifted into the 'manual' class.

Soviet 'brigadiers' and those 'in charge of livestock departments' on farms, which for some reason are in the 'workers by hand' category, must be deemed to be predominantly using their brains. This is not only in fact usually the case, but is essential if they are to form part of a comparison with British farmers, most of whom are in command of a far fewer number of people than the above-named Soviet farm 'foremen'. Since the comparison is in any case bound to be distorted by the inclusion of many very small farmers on the British side, it is necessary, to avoid completely misleading conclusions, to make this adjustment, which involves the 'transfer' from the 'physical' side of 740,000 Soviet farmers.

Subject to some unavoidable margin of error, the figures now look as follows:

	USSR, 1959 (thousands)	*per cent*	*GB, 1951 (thousands)*	*per cent*
Physical labour ..	77,895	78·6	14,921	66·1
Mental labour ..	21,235	21·4	7,657	33·9

Sources: For USSR, *VS*12, p. 7, adjusted as explained above.
For GB, Census of 1951, 1 per cent sample, as shown in Table 1 below.

A relatively far larger number is clearly engaged in mental labour in Great Britain. Why? Who are they? Of course, we can surmise that the much larger number of Soviet farm labourers is one explanation. But there are others, which may emerge from a more detailed examination of the statistics on 'workers by brain'.

'Workers by Brain': A Closer Analysis

Table 1 represents an attempt to compare the various sub-groups of those engaged on 'mental' labour. A sizeable margin of error is possible, but the general picture is still likely to be correct even if the detail is not. The British figures are taken from the 1 per cent sample of the 1951 census. The use of this sample made it possible to complete the tables in time. It would no doubt be practicable, with much more work, to amend them in the light of the final census returns, but the advantages of such precision would scarcely be significant in an exercise such as this.

In using the table, one should pay particular attention to the percentages rather than to absolute figures, for the obvious reason that the Soviet population is about four times higher and the occupied population higher still.

There are two kinds of comments called for. One concerns questions of comparability. The other relates to differences between the proportions in the two countries and the significance to be attached to them.

There are some obvious non-comparabilities, which follow

from the different designation of certain activities: thus, for instance, there is no Soviet equivalent to 'clerks of works, building', and one is at a loss to find a precise British equivalent (or indeed a clear definition) of the Soviet term 'agents and dispatchers' (*agenty i ekspeditory*). Fortunately, these are comparatively minor items. More serious are the following points:

(*a*) The much larger relative number of British draughtsmen, as against the Soviet 'draughtsmen and designers', seems probably due to the fact that the Soviet professional qualification is higher.

(*b*) The British 'foreman' is often considerably less well qualified than his Soviet opposite number. Many a Soviet 'foreman' (*master*) is a graduate engineer in his first job.

(*c*) On the other hand, Soviet 'librarians' are clearly at a much lower level of professional competence than those so described in the British statistics.

(*d*) As already suggested, the British 'farmer' has no Soviet *vis-à-vis*, and the comparison with various Soviet farm officials is largely devoid of meaning. The many British working farmers are particularly difficult to 'place'.

(*e*) The same is true of the managerial groups on both sides. Thus some British working shopkeepers (self-employed, or with a handful of employees) are obviously not to be compared with directors in Soviet retail distribution. Consequently, the most sensible comparison is between owners, managers *and* shop assistants, etc., added together.

(*f*) The same kind of difficulties arise in other spheres, though perhaps not to the same extent. The small man who owns two or three lorries does not exist in the USSR. The directors of *large* British companies—for instance, ICI or Shell—would be *state* administrators in the USSR, since at that level they would correspond with ministers or senior officials in government offices charged with administering the economy. Obviously we cannot hope for more than the roughest degree of comparability. Fortunately, here and elsewhere, certain crosschecks are possible with other forms of labour statistics, and these will be presented in Table 3.

(*g*) Census figures on British civil servants cover higher clerical officers and above. The Soviet total of 'administrators of state and social organizations' is both larger and smaller in definition. Smaller because, according to information kindly provided by a Soviet colleague, a 'head of sub-section' appears to be of higher status than a British HCO; larger because, firstly, it covers both local government and 'social' organizations (the latter include trade union officials, the Union of Soviet Writers, probably also the Dynamo sports club, the Soviet chess federation, the equivalent in Leningrad of the Manchester Statistical Society, if there be such, etc., etc.); larger also because both the central and local government undertake functions which are carried out by private enterprise in the West.[1]

(*h*) Some activities, ranging from funeral arrangements and pawnbrokers to hotel-keeping, are grouped in Soviet statistics under the heading 'communal services'; though often under the local Soviets, the officials in charge do not figure as 'state administrators'. In the above table, an (inadequate) attempt has been made to find some British equivalent categories for purposes of comparison.

(*j*) The sizeable Soviet category 'economists, statisticians, planners' may cause much misunderstanding. A few of them may indeed correspond to their professional equivalent in Great Britain. Mostly, however, they work in enterprises on jobs which resemble cost-accounting or involve the preparation of statistical returns. The British figures give 3,500 persons under the heading of 'mathematicians, statisticians, actuaries and economists', but these much higher-level individuals belong more logically under 'science'.

(*k*) Half of the British 'science' category consists of 'chemists, not pharmaceutical', and much of the rest is described as 'other scientists'. It is possible that the qualifications of these may on average be lower than those of Soviet 'scientific personnel'. Otherwise, given the vast scientific effort of the USSR, it would be hard to account for these constituting a relatively smaller number of the total occupied population, the more so as the Russian word 'science' (*nauka*) is wider than the English, and would include archaeologists, philologists and anthropologists, for instance.

(*l*) The British figures for arts, etc., include many persons concerned with the commercial side of entertainment, which distort the comparison with the USSR; it is not really likely that the

[1] See addendum for further comment.

British figures are relatively higher on a comparable basis.

(*m*) Whereas the British figures are exhaustive, the Soviet data leave out 1.8 million 'brain workers'. These could include communist party officials—who are certainly omitted from the state and social organizations figures in the table—and also police officers, priests, possibly banking and insurance officers (they seem to fit nowhere else), and some others unknown. Obviously, so large a 'remainder' is unsatisfactory, and may upset the validity of some comparisons.[1]

Now let me turn to some significant comparisons.

The USSR has far more *medical doctors*, though this may in part be due to the necessities of caring for a population scattered in isolated villages. Also Soviet doctors are known to carry out duties (for instance in hospitals) which fall in this country to nursing staffs.

As might be expected, the USSR is far ahead in the number of *engineers*. Her relative superiority in *laboratory staffs* may be due partly or wholly to differences of definition.

The Soviet Union is known to have a much lower pupil-teacher ratio than Great Britain's, and this is reflected by the much larger number of *teachers*.

A very interesting problem arises in respect of the *Civil Service*. How, it may be asked, can the Soviets have a relatively lower figure when the role of the state is so much greater? The facts, as will be shown, become even more surprising if Civil Service clerks are included, as will emerge from Table 3. Despite all doubts as to coverage of the figures, there is here a significant difference based on different ways of conducting affairs. This will be discussed later on.

Communal services are notoriously poorly developed in the USSR. The 'comparable' British figures, in fact, omit a number of persons who are in this Soviet heading, because the statistics do not permit them to be identified. It may seem that house agents are a species unknown in the USSR, but managers of apartment-houses, belonging both to local authorities and economic enterprises, are in the Soviet figure, and this would seem a fair equivalent.

[1] It has been possible to identify and reduce some of this 'remainder'. See addendum.

The number of *enterprise managers and their deputies* in Soviet industry, transport and communication seems very small, even absolutely smaller than their nearest British equivalent, as the table shows. One reason could be the much smaller number of small businesses. Another is that the heads of many sub-units and departments of Soviet enterprises would be treated as managerial in British statistics but are not so treated in the USSR because they would not hold the formal appointment of either director or deputy-director of an enterprise. For example, the head of a machine-shop in the famous Kirov (formerly Putilov) works in Leningrad might be in charge of thousands of workers and of complex technological processes, but he may well appear in the figures as an engineer (if he is one), or possibly among the 'unknown' remainder of 1.8 million. His British equivalent would certainly be included as a manager.[1]

More real is the vast difference in those engaged in *trade*. Over 9.1 per cent of the entire British labour force seem to be concerned with wholesale and retail trade, even excluding the purely manual grades such as storekeepers and warehousemen. The Soviet equivalent adds up to barely 3.2 per cent. Table 3 will serve to confirm that there is indeed a big difference. No attempt will be made here to draw a moral.

Most striking of all is the colossal disproportion in the numbers of clerical workers. It is not altogether impossible that the picture is affected by differences of definition. There could be some miscellaneous clerks among the Soviet residual. Yet the term used in Russian—*deloproizvodstvennyi personal*, or personnel concerned with papers and files—should include office clerks and typists, who appear to 'belong' under no other head. It will later be shown that there are remarkably few clerks in the Soviet Civil Service, and this, one suspects, is generally true of their way of doing business. Far fewer letters, far smaller offices. Visitors to large Soviet enterprises have often noticed the smallness of the offices. Much more seems to be decided by more senior staff, and by word of mouth, by personal dealings or at meetings. The disproportion between the two countries is so great that even if a million or more of the residual of non-manual workers were

[1] This is a misinterpretation of the Soviet figure, which has been more clearly defined in the census volume and certainly includes heads of shops and of other enterprise departments.

added to the Soviet total of clerks, it would still be a little over 2 per cent of the total occupied labour force, or little more than a quarter of the British percentage. One suspects that some of the residual could be low-level clerks, because a table given by the same source (*VS*12, p. 21) shows that a very high proportion of those listed as *deloproizvodstvennyi personal* have had a secondary education.[1]

Soviet figures for clerks, and possibly also Government employees, may have been affected by repeated and deliberate efforts on the part of the authorities to limit or reduce the numbers in these categories. This may well have led Soviet administrators and directors in the localities to reclassify persons carrying out such duties under other heads in order to escape the wrath of Government establishment inspectors. Whereas in Great Britain a white collar is a status symbol, and in the presence of countervailing pressures there may be a contrary tendency to describe as clerks persons of marginal clerical status. These considerations may well affect the statistics and therefore the comparisons we are making.

Workers by Hand

Table 2 represents an attempt at a comparison. It is less enlightening and probably less reliable than are the figures in Table 1. It would be useful to compare particular skills, but although the Soviet figures do include some of the necessary information for some sectors, the attempt was abandoned because definitions were too vague and the figures incomplete. One hopes that problems of definition have not unduly distorted the table as it stands. In one or two instances non-comparabilities seem clear from the designations used. Thus the British figure for 'laundry workers and dry cleaners' is wider in coverage than the Russian, which excludes dry cleaners; the latter are presumably to be found with 'other commercial services'. Similarly, it may well be that bookbinders are not in the Soviet figure for printing workers, in which case they must appear in the residual.[2] The extraordinarily low Soviet total for paper workers may also be explained by omission of stationery and paper-bag making, which are in the 'comparable' British figures. It is also, unfortunately, very doubtful if the

[1] For further evidence on this point, see addendum.

[2] Not so. The figure includes bookbinders (51).

Soviet's 'power plant and material moving' heading has its British equivalent opposite it.[1]

However, certain conclusions can still be usefully drawn. Dominating the table is the USSR's immense almost ten-fold preponderance in the proportion of *agricultural workers*. There are some interesting detailed points arising in respect of the agricultural data. One is the much greater degree of specialization of Soviet tractormen. Their number is relatively much higher than might be expected from a comparison of the machinery available; British tractors and other machines are less extensively used and are often operated by the farmer himself or some 'other agricultural worker' as and when needed. Another point concerns the vastly greater number of 'shepherds and cowherds' in the USSR explicable by lack of fencing and of well-trained dogs (and also partly by the omission of cowherds from the British figure).

The figures for particular industries largely speak for themselves. It would be interesting to try to derive some rough labour productivity comparisons from them, but this would take us beyond the scope of the present paper.

In *transport*, the USSR naturally possesses a larger number of railwaymen, but it is more surprising to find that so many are engaged in road transport in a country with a relatively modest number of lorries and few good roads (though we must allow for some owner-drivers who appear with the non-manual group in the British figures). The Soviet lorries are certainly used much more intensively, and the state of the roads doubtless calls for much more maintenance and repair. A high Soviet figure for *loaders* is scarcely unexpected since this is a notoriously under-mechanized sphere of activity. The relatively small number in *public catering* in the USSR is probably explainable by the small number of bars and cafés. (But it should be noted that hotels are not in this Soviet figure.)

Why do the Russians have so many *cleaners*? The category within which they appear in the census return seems to exclude the possibility that domestic servants are part of the very high figure under this head. There just must be many charwomen and cleaners in Soviet offices and other premises wielding unmechanized brooms, mops and buckets. (Street cleaners are not in this total; they must appear under 'communal services'.) But the

[1] It has! See addendum.

most striking contrast of all is under the heading of '*guards and watchmen*', where the Soviet total of two million is relatively nine times the greater. It is certainly an observable fact that Soviet factories and offices have a more developed system of guards and passes than do the British, though it is possible that the British figure is not strictly comparable in that some of the work done by Soviet guards is done over here by receptionists of various kinds.

All the comparisons are somewhat distorted by the fact that over three million rank and file members of the Soviet Armed Forces appear under the heading appropriate to their civilian occupations. Presumably this serves to inflate most of all the total of agricultural workers.

A Cross-check: Employment Classification—1959

Both British and Soviet figures exist for a variety of years giving the sector breakdown of the labour force by broad groups of activity. This differs in conception and source of publication from the census returns of the two countries. But it can serve to cross-check some points where differences of definition in the census data might well lead to confusion. The figures appear in Table 3.

The British figures relate to June 1959, and are adapted from the Annual Abstract of Statistics, 1960. One is compelled to use the tables which relate to the United Kingdom as a whole. The general table in the Abstract gives data both for the United Kingdom and for Great Britain, excludes the unemployed and includes the employers and self-employed. Unfortunately it is necessary to use more detailed figures, which the Abstract gives for the United Kingdom only and which include a part of the unemployed while excluding the employers. In the table, an attempt has been made to present the figures consistently, inclusive of employers and excluding the unemployed, but this has meant some rather rough adjustments on occasion.[1]

The Soviet figures are taken from current labour statistics, but these, in the form in which they are published, are confined to state-employed persons. This has necessitated a whole series of

[1] For example the Abstract gives 711,000 under the heading of 'catering including hotels,' but this includes 29,000 unemployed and excludes an unknown number of employers.

upward adjustments whose accuracy should not be exaggerated. The most important of these is the adoption of a figure of thirty-three million for agriculture, for reasons already explained.[1] Several other headings require upward amendment in respect of collective, co-operative and individual employment. The total cannot be made to add up to 99.1 million, since it more or less represents man years. It must be admitted that it does so imperfectly, since the adjustments are rough and the underlying Soviet figures are not consistently in terms of man years. None the less, the major part of the figures are reasonably firm and the discrepancies are likely to be too slight to matter.[2]

The total checks fairly well against the implied evidence of various official tables. Thus, according to *NK*59, health and education account for 10.4 per cent of the civilian labour force. These two headings, with which 'Science' is certainly included, total 9.26 million workers and employees. Since it is very unlikely that anyone other than state workers or employees are engaged in these branches of activity, it follows that the total, which is not given as such by the source, must be around eighty-nine million. Adding 3.6 million military personnel would bring it to only a little above the total shown in Table 3.

The main non-comparabilities in this table concern, firstly, *education*, where the Soviet figure includes library and club staffs and excludes higher educational institutions (which are with Science), whereas most British librarians are under local government, and university staffs are listed under education. There is also, again, the problem posed by the large Soviet heading '*housing and communal services*', which includes so varied a group as pawnbrokers, waterworks men, funeral attendants, dry cleaners, hotel staffs, inquiry bureaux, laundries, street cleaners, etc., etc. Most of the persons concerned are employed by local Soviets, some by various economic enterprises (for instance, janitors of apartment blocks belonging to a factory). Clearly this formidable

[1] On page 263, above.

[2] Alas, some discrepancies are certain. Thus in *NK*59, p. 585, we find 'agriculture and forestry' credited with 41 per cent of the total civilian labour force, which figure is quite inconsistent with Table 3 and with the census. This discrepancy may be due to the fact that the agricultural figures are not strictly on a man year basis. The Soviet source adds a note to the effect that 'the figures may be amended in the light of the census of 1959'. They no longer appear in the following year's statistical handbook.

list cannot be matched by any group in current British statistics. The analogous British individuals are included partly under local government, partly under catering (with hotels) and partly under miscellaneous services. A *very* rough equivalent has been given in the table. Finally, there are the unemployed. There are no unemployed in the USSR according to innumerable official statements. Some are in fact under-occupied in collective farms, others —such as young people who have not found a job after leaving school—are simply not listed as either employed or unemployed.

Allowing for these and some other difficulties, some conclusions may still be drawn. One is the expected very large relative 'superiority' of the United Kingdom in the numbers engaged in *trade*, and also in *insurance*, *banking* and *finance*. The USSR is well ahead in *agriculture*, in *military personnel* and, even after allowing for differences in coverage, in *education*. An important question is raised by the apparent British preponderance in the relative number of *civil servants*. This is not as great as it looks. Many Soviet equivalents to British local government employees appear in the housing and communal services heading. The powerful communist party machine is not included in this Soviet figure,[1] and nor is the police, uniformed or secret.[2] But the Soviet figures include not only state officials but also officers of trade unions and a variety of other social organizations, as well as the economic and planning bureaucracy. If one bears all this in mind, it is not merely remarkable but truly startling to see that the British percentage for *central* government employees is higher than the Soviet total for central and local government.

It is true that there is some danger of overstating the British figures on a comparable basis. 'State administration, central', which appears as 541,000 in the *Annual Digest of Statistics*, should in principle exclude all industrial civil servants, who ought to appear under the appropriate industrial heading, and all postmen, who are included under 'communications'. Unfortunately, figures given in different tables in the *Digest* show inconsistencies, and it appears possible that some miscellaneous semi-industrial staffs have been included in the 541,000 and ought not to be so included. On the other hand, this figure excludes the employees of a number of bodies whose opposite numbers in the Soviet

[1] But it *is* included in Table 1 (see addendum).
[2] For more about the police, see addendum.

Union would certainly be regarded as engaged in administration: for instance, the National Coal Board, the Central Electricity Generating Board, the Cotton Board, the Iron and Steel Board. This to some extent offsets any error there may be. It is also significant that a sizeable proportion of the British total consists of persons employed by the Service departments. These would not, of course, include industrial personnel. However, they may well cover individuals carrying out tasks which would be classified elsewhere in the USSR (for example, they may be undertaken by military personnel and therefore included in the Armed Forces). When all this is allowed for, and when the quite large number of communist party officials (thought by many to be around 250,000) are added to the Soviet total, it seems virtually certain that the genuinely comparable figures, if ever they can be obtained, would reduce the British lead in civil servants. Yet on the evidence there still is a significant, if unwelcome, superiority in this respect. This extends also to local government (British figures do not include police and fire brigades).

Why this disproportion? A clue may be found in the contrast between the number of administrators of the ranks of 'heads of sub-units and above' (392,000 given in the census) and the total number employed in administration (1,268,000). These figures must be interpreted in the light of the small number of clerical staffs in the USSR shown in Table 1. It seems clear that subordinate staffs are much smaller in the Soviet Civil Service. Much more business is done by personal contact at fairly high levels. Far fewer personal cases are handled by correspondence in Government offices. The administrative pyramid is much narrower. This explains why so much time is wasted by officials and others in the waiting rooms of various institutions, waiting to see some senior official (this is a traditional feature of Russian administration). The smaller number of persons employed is easily observable by anyone who compares the size of the offices of the London County Council with those of the Moscow city soviet. Indeed the municipal offices of my own London borough (Wandsworth) are about as large and fully staffed as those of a major Soviet city. A Russian economist with whom I discussed this question drew my attention to the widespread use of unpaid voluntary social workers in local government and to the efforts that are made to make do with the absolute minimum of paid staff. It would be instructive to attempt a detailed comparative analysis of administrative procedures and organization in the two countries. It is hardly possible to take the matter further in the present context, except perhaps to remark that 'Parkinson's law' is well known in Moscow, the book having been published in a Russian translation. Whether for this reason or not, the numbers employed in the state administration have shown a downward tendency; in 1940 they amounted to 1.82 million, against less than 1.27 million in 1959. It would be worth inquiring closely about how this was done.

At the beginning of my talk I expressed the hope that it would be possible to derive some general conclusions concerning the effects of the two social systems on manpower utilization. It is hard to say much that is new in this respect. The contrast to which differences in system is most relevant obviously relates to the numbers engaged in trade. The disproportionately large number in Soviet agriculture is clearly not to be explained by the nature of the Soviet system but by the Russia which the communists inherited; Soviet policies have endeavoured to industrialize and urbanize as quickly as possible. The much smaller number of Soviet clerks may also have a traditional-Russian rather than any ideological explanation, unless a romantic preference for physical labour played its role. The excessive preoccupation with security doubtless helps to explain their vastly greater numbers of guards and watchmen, while a more creditable preoccupation with education and health also leaves its mark on the relative figures. Most people probably expected that the USSR would have a particularly gigantic bureaucracy arising out of the nature of its political and economic system, but, however conscious one may be of the imperfections of our statistics, our conclusions rather surprisingly lead the other way. The last words of this paper must again draw attention to the regrettably large margin of error in many of the calculations made here. It is also necessary to point out that much more could be done on the basis of the Soviet census data: for instance, an analysis of female employment, educational qualifications in various occupations, the numbers qualified in certain trades, and much else besides. But this will have to be left to some other occasion.

* * *

Since the above was written, several Soviet census volumes have appeared, providing much new information. Several articles could be based on the figures which have been published. In the present context, however, all that will be done is to incorporate such additional information as bears on the preceding text and tables. The text and tables have been left unchanged, save for repairing an inadvertent omission in Table 3, two brief footnotes correcting statements now shown to be wrong, and references to this addendum.

Firstly, there is more information about *clerical labour*. The total is made up as follows:

	(*thousands*)
Office supervisors	17
Shorthand writers and typists	130
Secretaries, filing clerks, other clerks ..	388
	536

(*Source: Itogi vsesoyuznoi perepisi naseleniya 1959 goda* (hereafter *Itogi*) M., 1962, p. 166.)

The total can be split between main branches of activity from a table which divides in this way all the principal professional and trade groupings, as follows:

Clerical labour	(*thousands*)
Industry*	88
Construction	30
Agriculture	17
Transport	19
Trade and supplies	25
Housing and communal services ..	20
Education, science, art	74
Govt., admin., credit, etc.	192
Other unspecified	71
	536

(*Source: Itogi* . . . , pp. 146–58.)
Note: *Manufacturing, public utilities, mining, fishing.

This is all very small-scale. In particular, 130,000 shorthand writers and typists in all the Soviet Union is incredibly low. In Great Britain in 1951 there were 559,000 shorthand-typists and typists! It could mean that many Soviet officials type their own letters, or, more probably, that there are few typewriters. Perhaps this is one reason why punctual replies to correspondence with Soviet addresses are so rare.

Secondly, additional information is provided on the interesting total (in Table 1) of those engaged in *Administration of state and social organizations*. It is made up as follows (in thousands):

Heads of state organs and their sub-units		247
of which: (All-union, republics, provinces, big cities	51)	
(Districts, other cities	91)	
(Rural soviets, chairmen and secretaries	104)	
Heads of Party, Komsomol,* trade union, co-operative and other social organizations and their sub-units ..		146
of which: (All-union, republican, provincial, area, big city	26)	
(District, other cities	62)	
(Heads of primary organizations ..	58)	

(*Source: Itogi*..., pp. 157, 158.)

Note: *Young Communist League.

This makes it abundantly clear that the communist party bureaucracy is 'in' Table 1. Of course, the figures are not a full reflection of the *total* party or state bureaucracy, since only officials in charge of something are included. However, this goes down pretty low in the hierarchy; thus 'secretaries of rural soviets' are most humble chaps with an income about equal to that of an unskilled labourer. Yet a man with much higher pay and higher rank would not be in the above figures if he were, for instance, a junior member in a sub-unit or sub-department in Moscow. It is an odd way of drawing a statistical line; it is as if military statistics included as 'commanders' sergeants in charge of detachments but not lieutenants holding junior staff appointments.

As already seen in Table 3, the total inclusive of junior personnel and clerks is still very small. It should be noted, however, that party employees may not be included in Table 3, the figures for which come from a different statistical source.

It may also be of interest to cite the detailed breakdown of the item given in Table 1 as '*Inspectors, checkers, auditors*', since this is an item relevant to the procedures of a planned economy. The census gives the following details:

	(*thousands*)
Heads of planning, financial, economic-reporting and statistical depts. of enterprises	48
Inspectors, auditors	347
Operators of accounting machinery	22
Checkweighmen, tallymen, etc.	440

(*Source: Itogi . . .*, p. 166.)

The doubt about 'power plant, materials moving' and similar workers proved to be baseless. The figures are broadly comparable. The Soviet figure for power plants *only* exceeds a million, the high number being due to the many small and inefficient generating stations. It is roughly ten times the analogous British figure in absolute terms.

Finally, *police*. The census gives a figure of 261,954 under 'protection of socialist property and social order' (*Itogi . . .*, p. 158). This must cover all 'normal' police forces, but may or may not cover what is commonly known as the 'secret police'. It is likely that the home security forces and frontier guards are considered to be military, and those serving in them are treated as if they were in the army for statistical purposes. Assuming that officers and 'other ranks' are in the same proportion as in the British police (1 : 13), the residual in Table 2 includes some 240,000 policemen. (Presumably, 20 or 21,000 police *officers* are part of the residual of 'workers by brain' in Table 1, though this is conjectural, since we do not know the rank at which the Soviets consider police to be using brain rather than brawn.) The Soviet Union would then have, proportionately to its population, slightly fewer police than Great Britain. One explanation may be the importance in the USSR of part-time unpaid volunteers (*druzhinniki*), who try to keep order and fight 'hooliganism'.

Note: The preparation of the tables was very largely the work of Mr D. Matko, of the Research division of the London School of Economics, to whom the author wishes to express his thanks. (He is now at the University of Glasgow, and helped also with the addendum.)

TABLE 1

'WORKERS BY BRAIN' (NON-MANUAL)—GREAT BRITAIN AND USSR

(Percentages are of *total* occupied population)

Great Britain (1951)

	Thousands	*Per cent*	*Group %*
Law	26	0·12	—
Medical doctors	43	0·19	
Dentists	14	0·06	
Veterinary surgeons	5	0·02	1·34
Medical auxiliaries	242	1·07	
Engineers	85	0·38	
Draughtsmen and designers	135	0·59	
Laboratory assistants and technicians n.e.s.	72	0·32	3·70
Foremen and supervisors (*a*)	480	2·13	
Clerks of works (building)	10	0·04	
Surveyors (38) and other prof. and technical	62	0·28	
Teachers	357	1·58	1·69
Matrons and stewards in schools, etc.	25	0·11	
Librarians	15	0·06	—
Authors, journalists, editors, etc.	29	0·13	—
Arts, acting, music, cinema, etc.	80	0·35	—

USSR (1959)

	Thousands	*Per cent*	*Group %*
Law	79	0·08	—
Medical doctors	382	0·39	
Dentists	32	0·03	
Veterinary surgeons (45) and assistants (110)	155	0·16	1·87
Medical auxiliaries	1,289	1·29	
Engineers	834	0·84	
Draughtsmen and designers	297	0·30	
Laboratory staffs (436), Technicians (513)	949	0·95	4·21
Foremen (*master*)	753	0·75	
Other technical personnel	1,373	1·37	
Schoolteachers (2,245), University teachers (138)	2,383(*b*)	2·41	2·69
Kindergarten and other educational staff	275	0·28	
Librarians	239	0·24	—
Literary, press	104	0·11	—
Arts	191	0·19	—
Other cultural activities	223	0·23	—

Great Britain occupation	No.	%	Group %	USSR occupation	No.	%	Group %
Scientists (incl. chemists)	49	0·22	—	Scientific personnel	178(*b*)	0·18	—
Farmers and farm managers	317	1·40	1·48	Collective-farm chairmen and deputy chairmen	103	0·10	1·20
Farm bailiffs and foremen	18	0·08		State-farm directors and deputy directors	15(*c*)	0·02	
				Forestry staffs	44	0·05	
				Brigade-leaders in farms (740), and agronomists, etc. (278)	1,018	1·03	
Civil servants (HCO and above)	81	0·36	0·69	Administration of state and social organs (heads of sub-units and above)	392	0·40	0·40
Local government officers	29	0·13					
Social welfare workers	23	0·10					
Other civil service and local officers (not clerks)	16	0·07					
Officials of political, industrial and trade associations	6	0·03					
Misc. services	130†	0·58	—	Communal services staffs	277	0·28	—
Commercial and industrial office managers	61	0·27	1·98	Enterprise managers and deputies in industry, transport, communications	837(*d*)	0·84	0·84
Managers in industrial undertakings	297	1·32					
Managers and proprietors in transport and communications, railway officials	85	0·38					
Company directors	3	0·01					
Proprietors and managers, wholesale businesses	136	0·59	9·12	Directors of shops and trading organizations	335	0·34	2·43
Proprietors and managers, retail businesses and other commercial occupations	692	3·06		Salesmen, shop assistants, dept. heads in shops and restaurants	1,166	1·17	
Proprietors and managers, restaurants	87	0·39		Other staff in distribution, supplies, procurements	767	0·77	
Salesmen, shop assistants, roundsmen, etc.	1,006	4·46					
Commercial travellers and canvassers	140	0·62					

TABLE 1 (continued)

	Thousands	Per cent	Group %
Postal, telephone, telegraph staffs	126	0·56	—
Secretaries of companies, accountants	68	0·30	2·86
Costing, estimating, accounting clerks, book-keepers	490	2·22	
Other office machine operators	77	0·34	
Shorthand-typists and typists	567	2·51	7·82
Other clerical	1,198	5·31	
All other non-manual	275‡	1·23	—
Total Non-Manual	7,657	33·9	
Total Occupied Population	22,578	100·00	

	Thousands	Per cent	Group %
Agents and dispatchers	146	0·15	—
Postal, telephone, telegraph, radio operators	476	0·48	—
Economists, statisticians, planners	308	0·31	3·50
Inspectors, checkers, auditors	963	0·97	
Book-keepers and accountants	1,817	1·82	
Cashiers	413	0·42	
Clerks	536	0·54	0·54
All other non-manual	1,886(*e*)	1·90	
Total 'by Brain'	21,235	21·4	
Total Occupied Population	99,130	100·00	

† (Baths 7; Water and Electricity distribution 15; Estate agents 24; Hotel managers and proprietors 28; Funerals 5; Moneylenders 2; Lodging house keepers 49).

‡ (Military officers 46; Police officers 6; Religion 49; Architects 19; Bankers 19; Insurance managers 28; Stockbrokers, etc., 4; Insurance brokers 5; Insurance agents and canvassers 67; Other brokers, agents, factors 28; Other finance 4.)

(*a*) Class 9 of the Census less warehousemen.

(*b*) The Soviet census grouped university staffs with scientists; the former were subtracted on the basis of data in *NK59*, p. 754.

(*c*) Deduced from the number of state-farms (the census grouped them under other state-enterprise managers).

(*d*) The total as given in census, less collective-farm and state-farm managerial personnel.

(*e*) The residual does *not* include military officers, who are said to be classed in their civilian occupations. It may include banking, insurance, police officers, communist party officials and other groups unknown.

TABLE 2

'WORKERS BY HAND' (MANUAL WORKERS)

Great Britain (1951)	*Thousands*	*Per cent*	*Group %*	*USSR (1959)*	*Thousands*	*Per cent*	*Group %*
Agriculture:							
Agric. machinery and tractor operators	82	0·36	3·71	Tractormen and 'combiners' (*b*)	2,576	2·60	33·44
Shepherds	11	0·05		Shepherds and cowherds	754	0·76	
Veg., mkt. gdners., seeds	58	0·26		Veg. and orchard workers	191	0·19	
Gardeners, other	145	0·64		Livestock workers (excluding shepherds)	4,133	4·17	
Other agric. workers (*a*)	542	2·40		Other farm labour (*c*)	25,501	25·72	
Forestry and woodmen	31	0·14	—	Forestry	231	0·23	—
Mining and quarrying	638	2·83	—	Lumbermen	751	0·76	—
				Extractive industries	1,187	1·20	—
Treatment and processing of mining products	206	0·91	—	Processing of minerals	538	0·54	—
Chemicals (incl. rubber and plastics)	266	1·18	—	Chemicals	395	0·40	—
Metals and engineering	3,393	15·03	—	Metals and engineering	9,304	9·39	—
Textile workers (including upholsterers)	821	3·64	—	Textile workers	1,130	1·14	—
Tanners, fellmongers, fur dressers, leather workers	51	0·26	—	Hides and leather	145	0·15	—
Footwear	133	0·59	—	Footwear	372	0·38	—
Garment workers (incl. hat and cap)	486	2·15	—	Clothing	1,302	1·31	—
Food, drink and tobacco	252	1·12	—	Food (incl. drink and tobacco)	815	0·82	—
Wood, cane, cork workers	486	2·15	—	Wood processing	1,407	1·42	—
Paper (incl. stationery and bags)	80	0·35	—	Paper	36	0·04	—
Printers, bookbinders	189	0·84	—	Printers	212	0·21	—
Stationary engines, cranes, power stations, etc.	265	1·17	—	Power plants, material moving	1,721	1·74	—
Building and contracting	844	3·74	5·25				
Painters and decorators	340	1·51		Building labour	5,094	5·14	—
Fishing	29	0·13	—	Fishing	128	0·13	—

TABLE 2 (continued)

	Thousands	Per cent	Group %
Railwaymen	303	1·34	
Road transport (except horse)	753	3·34	5·27
Water transport (on boats)	113	0·50	
Horse-drivers, grooms, etc.	22	0·09	
Dockers, stevedores	93	0·41	1·67
Porters, packers, etc.	284	1·26	
Warehousemen, storekeepers	336	1·49	
Postmen, P.O. sorters	103	0·46	—
Assistant nurses, ward orderlies, etc.	142	0·63	—
Public catering (*d*)	193	0·85	—
Laundry workers, dry cleaners	141	0·62	—
Caretakers and officer keepers	70	0·31	—
Charwomen and office cleaners	247	1·09	—
Watchmen	49	0·22	—
Firemen	28	0·12	—
Other personal service (*e*)	197	0·87	—
Domestic service, indoors (*f*)	845	3·74	—
Miscellaneous unskilled labour	583	2·58	—
Civil defence	21	0·09	
Police	78	0·34	4·72
Armed forces	530	2·34	
All others (*g*)	442	1·95	
Total Manual	14,921	66·09	
Total Occupied Population	22,578	100·00	

	Thousands	Per cent	Group %
Railwaymen	1,664	1·68	
Mechanized road transport	3,395	3·42	6·24
Water transport	244	0·25	
Road transport, animal	784	0·79	
Loaders	1,632	1·65	1·87
Porters	216	0·22	
Warehousemen, weighters, etc.	905	0·91	—
Post office workers	243	0·25	—
Medical orderlies, etc.	895	0·90	—
Public catering (excl. cooks)	262	0·26	—
Launderers	193	0·19	—
Janitors	202	0·20	—
Cleaners (indoor)	1,733	1·75	—
Watchmen and guards	2,030	2·04	—
Firemen	137	0·14	—
Other communal services	730	0·74	—
Cooks (*h*)	522	0·53	—
Miscellaneous unskilled labour	2,462	2·48	—
Others	1,723	1·74(*j*)	—
Total workers by hand	77,895	78·58	
Total Occupied Population	99,130	100·00	

(*a*) Including estate labourers and other occupations ancillary to agriculture.
(*b*) Including other farm machinery operators.
(*c*) Including work-gang leaders. (*Zvenyevye*), 157.
(*e*) Hall and hotel porters 23; photographers 25; window cleaners 34; chimney sweepers 5; gamekeepers 6; others 105.
(*f*) Includes cooks and kitchen-hands
(*g*) Including costermongers, coal hawkers, newspaper sellers, cinema operators, footballers, jockeys, makers of musical instruments, etc.
(*h*) Other domestic servants are presumably in the residual.
(*j*) Does *not* include military, which are in the other headings in accordance with civilian occupation.

TABLE 3

SECTOR CLASSIFICATION

(all personnel engaged)

	UK 1959	*UK* Per cent		*USSR* 1959	*USSR* Per cent
Manufacturing	9,366	37·9	42·7	22,000 (*a*)	23·9
Mining	827	3·3			
Fishing	27	0·1			
Gas, electricity	344	1·4			
Building	1,550	6·3		6,000 (*a*)	6·5
Agriculture	1,026	4·2		33,000 (*b*)	35·9
Forestry	25	0·1		370 (*a*)	0·4
Transport and communication	1,704	6·9		7,000 (*a*)	7·6
Wholesale and retail trade	3,061	12·4		3,500 (*a*)	3·8
Banking and insurance	509	2·1		258	0·3
Education	790	3·2		4,549 (*i*)	4·9
Health	770	3·1		3,248	3·5
Science and scientific services	165	0·7		1,462 (*i*)	1·6
Catering	750 (*f*)	3·0		1,000 (*a*) (*g*)	1·1
Housing and communal services	350 (*e*)	1·4		1,710	1·9
State administration, central	541 (*j*)	2·2		1,268 (*d*)	1·4
State administration, local	600(*c*)	2·4			
Military	565	2·3		3,623	3·9
Firemen	199	0·8		3,012	3·3
Others (*h*)	1,083	4·4			
* Wholly unemployed ..	414	1·7		—	—
Total	24,714	100·0		92,000	100·0

(temporarily unemployed: 25)

* Temporarily unemployed are included in the number of civil employment, while wholly unemployed are given separately.

(*a*) Source (*NK*59, pp. 588–9) gives lower figures, but upward allowance (rough) has been made for non-state employees.

(*b*) *VS*12, p. 5.

(*c*) Excluding police and firemen.

(*d*) Including administrative staffs of 'social organizations' and co-operatives.

(*e*) Laundries, cleaning and dyeing, hairdressers, water supply, etc. The real equivalent of the Soviet figure under this head is probably higher.

(*f*) Including hotels.

(*g*) Excluding hotels.

(*h*) Professional and miscellaneous services, plus police.

(*i*) Higher education is included with Science, and libraries and 'cultural clubs' included with Education.

(*j*) This may be rather too high (see text).

16. *Economic irrationality and irrational statistics*

The subject-matter of the present article was suggested by the apparent paradox of the coexistence of misallocation of resources and high rates of growth. This is particularly noticeable in communist countries, but the evidence and the conclusions are by no means confined to them. One suspects they are of more general application, and are certainly relevant to policy choices in developing countries. Or rather, more precisely, they are relevant to our *ex post factum* assessment of the *results* of policy choices, in so far as these aim at growth as a primary objective, or where the achievement of growth is a vital criterion of the success of the policy adopted.

First of all, we must be clear what we mean by irrationality. It is of little use in this context to make any assumptions about consumer sovereignty or the maximization of welfare in its conventional sense. By 'irrational' I mean such behaviour as is not in practice consistent with the attainment of given objectives at least cost. These objectives could theoretically be indicated by a free market, by a dictator, by the central committee of the communist party, by wise men sitting in Brussels, or any combination of these. I am well aware, of course, that in the real world the distinction between means and ends, objectives and methods, is very difficult to draw. This is particularly so if one tries to define the nature of so-called 'planners' preferences' in a command economy of the Soviet type. In one sense, any command issued by the planners expresses 'planners' preferences', for otherwise it would not be issued. None the less, there is a significant conceptual difference between the general policy objectives of the planners and the executive commands which they issue in pursuit of these objectives. This distinction holds even though it is not possible to identify clearly in each individual case what is a basic objective and what is a mere means to an end. Quite clearly, planners, and others, are capable of making wrong decisions, can allocate resources irrationally in terms of their own objectives. Were it otherwise, we would be forced to the ridiculous conclusion that any order actually issued by planners is rational because it is issued by planners and therefore by definition in accord with 'planners' preferences'. This would be as circular as assuming that in the real Western world every investment decision must be rational because it is taken by reference to market forces.

One complication is that where growth itself is a primary objective, the attainment of impressive statistics might become an end in itself, but it seems reasonable to assume that not even the most growth-conscious government desires statistics for their own sake. They would like these statistics to reflect the increased volume of actual useful goods and services which is envisaged in the plans.

In the analysis that follows I abstract from social, political and strategic considerations. Needless to say, these are very important in the real world. Governments often make decisions with these considerations in mind, and these decisions can affect both the ends and the means of economic activity. There is no reason why social, political or strategic rationality should not take precedence over economic rationality. But one point which might emerge from this analysis is that the economic cost of such decisions may be concealed, that in particular their effect on statistics of growth is often quite indeterminate. I shall argue that the same is true of certain kinds of accidental or incidental misallocation of resources, such as might be due to confusion in planning offices, or artificially fixed prices, or import restrictions, or other possible causes.

Let us begin by identifying certain types of resource misallocation which undoubtedly do have an adverse effect on growth, in any type of economy. The following categories may be distinguished:

i. Materials are destroyed, lost or stolen (though in the latter case they may be used for productive purposes, as when a peasant steals potatoes to feed his pigs).

ii. Materials are wasted unnecessarily, as when too much metal goes into metal shavings, or excessive quantities of coal are burnt in inefficient furnaces.

iii. Materials do not arrive, thus bringing a factory to a halt.

iv. Existing capital equipment remains unused, or partly used, owing to lack of business.

v. Construction projects remain unfinished for many years, freezing capital recources to no purpose.

All the above examples have in common the characteristics that they are concerned either with the non-use of existing resources, or with the wasteful use of inputs of a kind that leads to no measurable output. Thus the statistical effect of excessive use of coal is to diminish the net-product of the coal-using factories by the value of the coal they waste, without any compensating item. It is true, of course, that waste can stimulate production of the wasted commodity. Similarly, the destruction of a factory by fire no doubt provides employment for human and capital resources, which might otherwise not have been employed. In certain circumstances, i.e. when there is a recession or unemployment, we all know that this could have desirable effects on the growth of the economy. However, while keeping such considerations in mind, it would be reasonable to leave them out of account in the subsequent analysis because it is economic growth rather than the trade cycle which is the subject with which we will be primarily concerned.

Let us begin with a category of waste different in its statistical effects from those listed above. Let us suppose that men are paid to dig a useless hole in the road, and then to fill it up again. (Anyone working in the University of London may recall the prolonged existence of just such a hole, a stone's throw from the administrative buildings of the university.) While this activity is as wasteful as all the others, it differs from them by being in itself a contribution to the national income. It forms part of GNP, but is useless. This pointless activity has an opportunity cost; resources could have been used for some more sensible purpose. In terms of human welfare, or the purposes of the state, there is clearly a loss. There is also a loss in terms of consumable end-products. Is there a statistical loss? Not necessarily. Suppose the men who dug the hole were paid £x, and that this represents the conventionally-measured net product of their activity. Suppose that they would have otherwise produced potatoes, choral music, office furniture, or lectures on economics, which would have also been 'worth' £x. Then statistics may not recognize the difference.

Statistics are blind. A man travels to Edinburgh to meet his beloved, but she is not there, so he returns sadly to London, but statistically he has contributed the same sum to the net product of transportation as if he had married her. This is an imperfect measure of human welfare, as we must recognize.

Some may say—but who digs useless holes? Alas, it is not as uncommon as it sounds. In the USSR geological prospectors have drilled holes for the sole purpose of fulfilling a quarterly plan expressed in metres of drilling.[1] Nearer home, roads dug up for electricity and, soon after, again for gas or telephone, will do as a parallel.

Now let us move one step forward and consider processes which do make actual goods, useful goods, but the goods are not as durable as they should and could be. American and (especially) Soviet examples abound. In the American case, some 'durables' are given a short life, either physically or by a planned speedy obsolescence. In the USSR, poor materials and workmanship, plus an incentive system based on quantity and/or costs per unit of output, lead to similar practical consequences. This is more familiar ground. In the American context, it can be argued that a short life for 'durables' stimulates output and therefore growth, and that resources released by a switch towards more durables would remain unemployed. In the USSR, with many unsatisfied demands for resources, this last argument would not hold. However, since the Soviet price system does not even pretend to express opportunity cost or relative scarcities, it follows that statistics based on Soviet prices will not express them either. Suppose that Soviet television tubes last half as long as British ones and that, consequently, twice as many have to be produced for a given number of sets. If by adopting a new process the life of Soviet tubes can be doubled, resulting in the halving of output and the release of half the labour force, it does not follow that the prices of the alternative goods and services will yield any more GNP than the now unnecessary tubes. Of course, if the released resources would generate some more useful output, people would be better off. But GNP may be unchanged, or grow, or fall; and we cannot know which. There is, however, the possibility that the adoption of the new process would enable the production of tubes to be concentrated in efficient factories, thus

[1] *Pravda*, August 3, 1955.

reducing costs per unit and releasing a disproportionately large volume of resources, in which case statistics will after all show a net benefit.

Still another point concerns quality, and range of choice, which are notoriously tricky to express statistically, a fact which greatly complicates international and inter-temporal comparisons and which may substantially distort growth measurement. This is, or ought to be, well known, so that it will be considered extremely briefly here. Peter Wiles rightly devotes some vigorous pages to this aspect of the subject.[1] In the present context, the only point which must be made is that range of choice and measurable growth are often contradictory objectives, and, conversely, improved quality and wider choice are often not reflected in growth statistics. Anyone who has not adventured into this field should try, for a start, to compare living costs between a country with rationing and one without (e.g. Britain in 1949 with the United States at the same date) (or with Britain in 1959), or the Soviet Union now (no rationing, but shortages, or uncertain supply at state-established prices) with any Western country.

The subject of production consciously orientated to growth statistics, of a product mix 'adapted' to the task of reporting plan fulfilment in quantitative terms, has also been fairly extensively discussed by critics of the Soviet planning system. It is certainly true that, despite their many deficiencies, Western statistics of output do not suffer from this particular kind of distortion (true, misallocation is possible, but its effect on growth is quite uncertain; it may increase it or reduce it). Firms tend to pursue profit and to show marked lack of interest in the statistical effects of their decisions on gross or net output, while government statisticians usually have no political or personal interest in demonstrating that the curve slopes steeply upwards. In the Soviet Union, decision-makers can affect indices consciously: since aggregations of changing product mixes are always somewhat imperfect approximations, there is scope for choice, and this can create quite a difference between the growth of useful output and of output as measured by official statistics. In fact, many commonly-cited statistical measures derive such validity as they possess from *not* being consciously sought after at operational

[1] See his 'Growth versus Choice', *Economic Journal*, June, 1956, and also his *Political Economy of Communism* (Blackwell, Oxford, 1962).

levels. Imagine, for instance, what would happen to the meaningfulness of labour productivity statistics if firms deployed their labour force and chose their processes with one eye on the effect of their decisions on the statistics! This whole question of the misleading statistical effects of the pursuit of growth in the USSR was vigorously explored by Michael Polanyi: in his article 'Towards a Theory of Conspicuous Production'. He rightly wrote that 'economic productivity must be judged by the creation of economic value. Products are not goods merely by virtue of their bodily existence.'[1] Unfortunately, his very sound arguments on the adverse effect in terms of usefulness of the pursuit of output targets were accompanied by a misleading picture of the nature of the Soviet system. Further, his criticism was confined to Soviet-type economies, whereas some of the arguments he raised, and are raised here, seem to have much wider application.

But we ought to pass on to a less explored area, that of the consequences of irrational investment decisions. Let us assume that the irrationality consists of adopting a variant which achieves the desired results at unnecessarily high cost. At first sight the answer to this problem is so obvious that there is no problem. If there were a saving in costs, the net product would be higher, resources would be freed for other uses, and the growth of the economy would be more rapid. It is certainly true that in a model of a classical competitive free-enterprise economy the answer *would* be obvious, for by definition any alternative to the optimum solution would yield less net product, which would be the true measure of welfare. However, let us forget pure models for a moment, and consider the following question: What are costs? Let us suppose that the investment decision is irrational because a steelworks is sited too far from sources of fuel and/or materials. (Plenty of examples of such errors may be found in the Soviet bloc, and we may also see instances in some developing countries obsessed with steel as a status symbol.) Suppose that the unnecessary costs consist of rail transport, i.e. of the labour of railway workers, of extra locomotives, wagons, rails, etc., etc. These are all a contribution to GNP. They are not final output, of course, but GNP is not confined to final output. The production of the extra rolling stock, or the running of the heavily-used railway line, may in itself be extremely efficient, and labour pro-

[1] *Soviet Survey*, October-December, 1960.

ductivity statistics may be very impressive. Opportunity cost? Yes, but what grounds have we to suppose that the net product of the resources deployed on freight transportation (and in industries serving it) will be higher if used elsewhere? Even in the real (as opposed to the textbook) Western world, it need not be so. *A fortiori* it need not be so in the Soviet Union.

These considerations may help to explain the coincidence of inefficient resource allocation and high growth rates. The following example may clarify matters further. Suppose that agricultural mechanization takes the form of providing economically inefficient equipment, its inefficiency being measured by the fact that the same output is obtained from the same land at 5 per cent higher cost per ton. Suppose further that the supply of this equipment made possible the release of 10 per cent of the agricultural labour force, and that precisely this number is now required to make, distribute and service the new equipment and to provide the fuel necessary to operate it. Their wages are higher than they were in agriculture. Now consider the statistical consequences. Agricultural productivity goes up. Industrial output goes up. The net output of agriculture is reduced by the additional inputs of fuel, the annual amount of depreciation of the equipment, etc. Against this, the net output of industry increases significantly. The net product of the men released from agriculture is almost certain to be higher in their new occupations. In actual statistical practice, their move from the villages would lead to additional generation of national income arising from urbanization, but even if we neglect this we are surely bound to get a misleadingly favourable picture. In the end, on our assumptions, all we really have is the same amount of farm produce at slightly higher cost. We also have a marked rise in the relative importance of the output of intermediate products, of 'means of production' as Marx would call them. Greater round-aboutness will have been achieved, and this will show as higher output in general, as higher output of producers' goods (as distinct from consumers' goods) in particular: yet not only could this be consistent with irrational resource allocation, it could have such misallocation as its cause. I do not suggest that the above picture fits the history of Soviet agriculture. However, the institutional arrangements were such that mechanization could have had such a result. Machinery was allocated administratively, its use prescribed administratively, and no effort was made to assess costs in agriculture. (Things are changing now.)[1]

Another Soviet example is worth exploring. Speaking at a recent conference in Moscow, a representative of the Bashkir economic region remarked on the fact that his region had doubled labour productivity in the oil industry in five years, yet costs rose by 5 per cent. Apparently wages changed insignificantly, and the speaker did not affix any of the 'blame' on diminishing returns. He drew instead the moral that the planners, pursuing high physical output per man directly engaged, may have overlooked the 'labour embodied' in the capital goods and other inputs used by the oil industry. We cannot tell if he is right, but let us imagine that this was indeed the correct explanation. Consider its statistical reflection.

So far as the official Soviet industrial output index is concerned, there is no doubt at all about the answer: the effect will be to increase growth rates. This is because this index is arrived at by adding together the outputs of every enterprise and converting the result into constant prices. The value of the oil, of pipes, of drilling equipment, etc., etc., will all be counted, so long as they are made by different enterprises (inputs made by one enterprise and used within that same enterprise are not counted twice). If in each separate sector, as in the oil industry, higher labour productivity is recorded (though perhaps achieved with equal lack of economic logic), then industrial labour productivity as a whole rises impressively, since this is calculated by dividing the increase in the gross value of output of all enterprises by the increase in the labour force. Yet, as the above-cited Soviet economist is aware, this is hardly a very meaningful 'victory' on the economic front. Be it noted that this is not quite the same point as the one rather more commonly made by critics of Soviet statistics, concerning the effect of vertical disintegration on growth. It is certainly true that if an existing process of production is divided between two different enterprises, instead of being carried out in one, the effect is to exaggerate growth of 'gross industrial output' in its Soviet computation (or to understate it if vertical integration takes place). But the point made here is valid even if no new enterprises are created; I am only exploring the consequence of

[1] In *Voprosy ekonomiki* No. 1/1964, A. Efimov pointed out that the relative rate of increase of consumers' goods output, at a given total rate of growth, is a guide to efficiency in resource utilization.

a situation in which inputs purchased by one from another have the effect of raising costs, i.e. (*ceteris paribus*) are irrationally chosen. A further example may illustrate this. Another Soviet participant in the wide-ranging discussion now raging over the principles of Soviet economics has pointed out that all the usual efficiency indicators for freight transportation—ton-kilometres carried, cost per ton-kilometre carried, ton-kilometres per employee—'benefit' from long hauls, even though the economy as a whole loses.[1] In the same way, indicators designed to measure successful operations of other sectors taken in isolation can cause serious resource misallocation, when, as in the USSR, these indicators are either quantitative or are expressed in inflexible prices of a 'cost-plus' type. Academician Nemchinov has declared himself convinced that much waste is occasioned in the USSR by planning growth targets for intermediate goods. The state, he asserts, should plan *final* output.[2]

That Soviet 'gross industrial output' statistics benefit from this kind of irrationality is beyond doubt. What about *net* output, i.e. industry's contribution to the national income? In this case one cannot say that growth will be statistically stimulated. But neither can we assert that it will be adversely affected. The answer is indeterminate, particularly with Soviet prices. Our measure of GNP or national income does, in fact, take into account any legitimate economic activity, rational or no. It is true that they are much superior to the Soviet 'gross industrial production', since double-counting is eliminated. However, increased output of such plainly 'non-final' items as machine tools, to give one of many examples, is bound to 'count' in GNP, whether these kinds of tools are economic or no. We have already established at perhaps excessive length that irrational activities count, and that a loss can only come to light if the opportunity forgone would have yielded a higher net income. This would happen by definition in a textbook model of a perfect free-market economy, or in a mathematically programmed command economy (provided the latter can define what it is that is to be maximized or optimized). It need not happen in the Soviet economy as it is. And not only in the Soviet economy. For, plainly, it is easy to think of circumstances which favour this species of misallocation in the West

[1] A. Birman, *Ekonomicheskaya gazeta*, January 5, 1963, p. 5.
[2] *Pravda*, January 21, 1962.

also. Thus the earlier agricultural example could be a consequence of subsidies and other 'market imperfections'. Suppose that most farming, and the use of most of the tractors or combine-harvesters, would be unprofitable in Lancashire but for subsidies. Who is the loser and how can the loss be measured? There is certainly an income redistribution between town and country. It could be said that the citizens would be better off if farm subsidies did not stimulate unnecessary demand for unnecessary tractors; i.e. we could say that living standards would have been higher with a different resource utilization pattern, with more food imports and possibly fewer tractors, and resources freed to make other things. No one disputes that, if the opportunity cost consists of consumers' goods forgone, this affects living standards. If tractors and freight transport could, at the margin, be replaced by shoes and socks, no doubt welfare would increase. But would the net product of the shoes and socks be larger in money terms?

Some of these considerations apply also to discussions of the effect on growth of tariff barriers. Let us assume that a country, let us call it Belgium, would be able to acquire soap at least cost by selling brussels sprouts to Britain and buying the soap from Port Sunlight. Let us further imagine that the Belgians put a duty of 40 per cent *ad valorem* on imported soap, and set up a factory of their own in Belgium, which produces initially at 35 per cent, later at 25 per cent, higher cost and continues to do so indefinitely (no 'infant industry' argument applies). Suppose further that the factory is staffed by workers released from the brussels sprouts fields by the fall in exports to Britain, and that the investments needed to start up the factory might have been devoted to increasing the production of some less high-cost commodity. It does not require demonstrating that the Belgians would then be less prosperous than they might have been. For one thing, soap consumption would go down. But what about growth statistics?

At this point a complication needs to be introduced, which in fact is relevant to most of the preceding argument. Growth is measured in index numbers, and index numbers have some strange properties. If one seeks to measure the growth of an economy over some ten- or twenty-year period, it is notorious that results are liable to differ substantially according as one uses early-year or end-year prices as weights. There have been wise words spoken on this subject, notably by Gerschenkron,[1] Bergson,[2] Moorsteen,[3] Wiles.[4] It remains to apply these ideas to the subject-matter of the present paper.

Let us remember that, other things being equal, the less efficient an industry is, the larger its weight in an output index—provided its inefficiency is within its own value-adding activities, and does not take the form of wasting inputs. Reverting to the (imaginary) Belgian example, the high-cost soap might be high-cost because, owing to the restricted market, it was not possible to benefit from certain economies of scale. *Because* it is dear, soap then acquires a sizeable weight in the output index, and so a rapid increase in output affects the aggregate index considerably. If in the course of the first few years costs and prices of soap fall, the preservation of the base-year price would be very good for the health of a growth index. One can envisage a situation in which the initial inefficiency of the import-saving industry and its positive effect on growth are in a real sense correlated. This was certainly true of the engineering industry in Russia in the period 1928–37, provided one used 1928 price weights. The following results were obtained by Moorsteen, using a sample of machinery output which, though not all-inclusive, was the same (only the price-weights varied; the official index, however, had a wider coverage).

SOVIET OUTPUT OF MACHINERY, 1937
1927–28=100

Soviet official index, '1926-27 prices'	1,509†
Rouble price weights of 1927-28, Moorsteen ..	1,792*
Rouble price weights of 1937, Moorsteen ..	889*
Rouble price weights of 1955, Moorsteen ..	550*

* Exclusive of arms output.
† Inclusive of arms output.
Source: Moorsteen, *op. cit.*, p. 115.

Needless to say, since there is a tendency for *relative* prices of newly-established machinery industries to fall as they become more firmly established, the above pattern may be regarded as a genuine economic 'regularity'. It is widely known as the 'Gerschenkron effect', since it is Gerschenkron's study of Soviet and

[1] *Review of Economics and Statistics*, May 1955.
[2] *The Real National Income of Soviet Russia since 1928* (Harvard, 1961).
[3] *Prices and Production of Machinery in the Soviet Union, 1928–1958* (Harvard, 1961).
[4] *Political Economy of Communism*, especially pp. 222–52.

American dollar prices and growth rates for machinery which brought it to general notice. It is one instance of the contribution which the study of the 'abnormal' Soviet economy and its statistics can bring to our general understanding of economics.

All this seems at first sight to have some rather startling implications. An underdeveloped country with a far-sighted chief statistician would be well advised to develop its most high-cost industries, provided costs can be somewhat reduced in due course and the chief statistician is a believer in Laspeyre. (This amounts to an advocacy of a 'law of comparative disadvantage'.) It also follows that the index of growth must in no circumstances be recalculated with later base-year weights, a point well understood by the Soviet Central Statistical Offices, whose output-indices for the period 1928–50 were and are in so-called 1926–27 prices. (Typically, Paasche is found to be more convenient for calculating cost-of-living and real wage indices, for here the use of early-year weights leads to unfavourable results. This is a good illustration of 'party statistics', i.e. a politically-influenced choice between several possible 'correct' answers.) Wiles put the general point well when he spoke of the advantage, in terms of growth statistics, of operating in the area of increasing returns. But it is arguable that, even if there is no appreciable reduction in costs over the years, the effect on the index of the choice of a high-cost variant may well be positive, if this is measured in terms of the given country's prices. True, the opportunity-cost is high because the costs are high. But this very fact imparts a heavy 'weight' to that commodity in the output index. Investment in the area of 'comparative disadvantage' may well be consistent with quite high *per capita* output (again in terms of local currency) of the workers engaged. Rewards in the 'modern' sector usually compare favourably with the very poor pay and low productivity of labourers in overpopulated underdeveloped countries. Once again, real costs and final consumable products are seldom measured effectively.

What conclusions can be drawn from all this? Let us begin by making it clear that this is not an essay in denigration of Soviet or anyone else's economic performance. Still less is it an attack on 'growthmanship'. It may be perfectly justified to plan a sharp rise in output, and to do so by allocating resources in ways other than those indicated by a market. This may be a legitimate political decision even if a more or less effective market exists, and in many developing countries the market is highly imperfect anyway. Progress through planning should not be shunned merely because it contributes to imprecision in statistics. It is not my purpose to 'prove' that these policies are wrong, or to argue that the output of the countries which practise planning is largely useless. The essential point, surely, is to underline the weakness of our statistics, or rather of the concepts of statistics, when used to measure aggregates of dissimilar goods and services in a changing society, particularly if prices are no longer market prices. It is obvious, surely, that conventional measures in money terms presuppose that, however roughly, the figures measure cost, or usefulness. In a planned economy, 'cost' in this sense must mean opportunity cost in terms of planners' preferences, and usefulness (or utility) must relate to the relative importance of the effort made in terms of achieving the planners' objectives. In no possible sense can 'cost-plus' prices express such magnitudes. These prices (e.g. in the USSR at present) reflect wage payments, prices of inputs, depreciation, plus a percentage profit mark-up.[1] They will do so whether or not the decision to undertake the activity in question is rational in terms of the objectives of the planners. To repeat an earlier point: anything 'economic' that we do 'counts', and the higher its cost the more it counts. 'Cost plus' will always have this effect, it must be neutral as between different degrees of usefulness of output. In the competitive model these misleading effects are prevented by competition itself, and by the reasonable assurance that capitalists will not knowingly invest in an unprofitable activity. We are far from being in this situation in Great Britain. Planned economies are further still.

Therefore, the conventional indices which express growth have only limited validity, as a measure of the growth of real, usable and desired output, and as a criterion by which growth-inducing policies may be judged to have succeeded or failed. The bias need not be all one way (save in the special case of the 'Gerschenkron effect'). Thus the consequences of a decrease in irrationality, or an increase in the range of choice, will tend to be understated statistically. True, with all their imperfections, the orders of

[1] In fact they depart from this standard fairly widely in both directions for a variety of reasons, but for no systematic economic purpose or cause.

magnitude suggested by some indices do obviously have some meaning. Thus the USSR grows faster than the USA, France faster than Great Britain. But we must be acutely conscious of the limitations of our statistical tools of measurement.

VI. IDEOLOGY

Communism *

Communist parties rule over a quarter of the earth's surface, over a third of the earth's peoples. They claim to be acting in the name and in the spirit of Marxism, and to be leading the people over whom they rule towards a communist society, in which each will give freely of his abilities and receive freely in accordance with his needs, in which abundance exists and money does not, and the state has withered away. Needless to say, this is not any actually-existing society; reality has been very different.

Marxism as a philosophy can be, and has been, used as a foundation for two very different political attitudes. One of these stresses the evolutionary aspect of the doctrine. Since socialism and communism are products of changes in the economic and social structures, it is unnecessary and indeed un-Marxist to speed up the process by violent revolutionary action before the necessary changes in the basis of society have matured, especially as Marxism predicted the inevitability of final victory. This interpretation inspired moderate social-democratic movements on the European Continent, and on this basis the Mensheviks in Russia opposed the 'premature' seizure of power by socialist parties in general, and the bolsheviks in particular, in 1917. Lenin, on the other hand, found inspiration in the revolutionary aspects of Marxism. Philosophers, said Marx, had hitherto interpreted the world; the point, however, is to change it. In Lenin's view, a seizure of power by a highly-disciplined party, even in so backward a country as Russia, could be used to change society, to change the economic basis, by deliberate political action. To those brought up on Marxist economic determinism, this seemed to be standing Marx on his head. True, Lenin was acutely aware of Russia's backwardness, of the difficulties which this caused.

* From the *Financial Times*, February 11, 1963.

However, he envisaged Russia's revolution as merely the beginning of the world revolution, which might be speeded up by a communist seizure of power at a weak point of the capitalist-imperialist front. The developed countries of Europe would come to Russia's aid when, as he thought, they too would overthrow capitalism in the very near future.

But there was no world revolution. After victory in a bitterly contested civil war, Lenin and his successors maintained a tight dictatorship, in the name of the working class, in a predominantly peasant country. The struggle over Lenin's succession was mixed up with the argument about how to set about transforming Russia. Stalin won and, in 1929, launched the ruthless 'revolution from above': vast programmes of industrialization, forced collectivization, with rigid centralization to enforce the state's priorities. Millions were deported, many died of hunger (millions? the numbers are still a state secret). Coercion on a vast scale gave greater arbitrary powers to the police, at first on behalf of and then over the Party. At the so-called 'congress of victors' in 1934, the Party was told by Stalin that the enemies of socialism had been shattered.

But it was a very different Party. Already in 1920, Lenin himself placed severe limits on free discussion in its ranks. The task of ruling over a recalcitrant or indifferent majority, and subsequently forcing through such bitterly unpopular measures as collectivization, called for toughness and discipline, not fine speeches and rebellious idealism. Many of the old communists had perished in the civil war. Others had been soured by harsh realities. Still others had been thrust aside by Stalin, and were later to perish at his hands. The new generation of hard-headed party secretaries were of a different mould. They served Stalin, but they also made him.

The transformation of the Party into a disciplined caste of rulers, within which the mere suspicion of dissent became a crime, was completed by the shattering Great Purge of 1936–38, in which the large majority even of the leadership elected in 1934 disappeared, along with the most military officers, captains of (state) industry and many, many others.

This drastic blood-letting could hardly have failed to affect the real nature of the party or its ideology. Yet on the surface the ideology was unaltered. It has frozen into a series of unquestioned dogmas, an oversimplified catechism, with a compulsory interpretation of every philosophical, economic or sociological question. Intellectual life was subjected to a great frost. Stalin became the demi-god dictator.

It is this stage of Soviet life which became known in the West from the novels of Koestler and the stories of displaced persons who made their way west during and after the war. This apogee of terror, of total control over arts and sciences, of false accusations and abject confessions, became fixed in people's minds as Soviet 'normalcy'. It is hard to persuade some otherwise well-informed persons, especially in America, that times have changed.

But they took a long time to change. There remained the terrible experience of the war. Stalin, amid the appalling disasters of 1941, appealed to patriotism, and in the name of patriotism, rather than communism or the party, the people responded. To give Stalin his due, he foresaw this necessity several years earlier, when, on his orders, history books changed their flavour and began to extol the past of Russia, even Tsarist Russia. Never far beneath the surface at any time, despite the nominally internationalist character of the revolution and of communism, Russian nationalism was vastly strengthened by the dearly-bought victories of war. The final triumph in Berlin gave a forceful impetus to the identification of the Soviet régime with the national interests of Eternal Russia. There was hope that the end of the war would bring relaxation, the end of the terror.

Yet, the terror system returned, and new and exceedingly severe restrictions were imposed on intellectual life. There seemed every likelihood of a new mass purge when, in March 1953, Stalin died.

Meanwhile, the international position of communism had changed radically. After the original failure of the world revolution to materialize, and especially after Stalin's accession to the 'throne', Soviet foreign policy adopted a basically defensive posture. Conscious of isolation in a hostile world, fearful of some deadly combination of imperialist 'interventionists', Stalin and his henchmen used all available means to strengthen their position. Among these means was the Comintern. Conceived originally as the general staff of the world revolution, it became a branch of the Soviet foreign office, and the process of 'bolshevizing' the various communist parties in *partibus infidelium* turned them into obedient instruments of Moscow, purged of any sign of independence.

When Moscow imagined that the hostile coalition was based on Paris and London, with Chamberlain and Poincaré cast for the role of villains, then the world's communists attacked them by preference, neglecting until too late the much greater menace of Nazi-fascism. When Hitler threatened the Soviet state, and this led to the discovery that Paris and London could perhaps be allies in an effort to stop the Nazis, the world communist movement embraced the 'Popular Front'. This tactic did, in fact, win a good deal of support for the communists, especially in Western Europe, because of the genuine attractiveness of the slogan of 'unity against fascism'. Yet when Stalin found it expedient to sign his pact with Hitler in 1939, the world's communists had to perform a humiliating somersault, demonstrating to all who cared to see their essentially puppet status. Of course, the German attack in 1941 quickly made them turn about yet again. In 1943, perhaps because he was hopeful of an agreement with his Western allies, or to lull their fears, Stalin formally abolished the Comintern.

But after the war the situation was transformed. The Chinese communists won control of their enormous country. Communist régimes established themselves, or were established by Russia, in most countries of Eastern Europe. The USSR had ceased to be an island in a 'capitalist' sea. As the wounds of war were healed, she emerged as a great industrial and military power. Nuclear weapons changed the nature of war.

Yet Stalin's methods did not change. His efforts to control the 'ruling' communist parties in Eastern Europe led to a clash with Yugoslavia. Deep suspicion and hostility towards the West led to a series of actions which brought about the cold war.

While he lived, he treated the communist movement almost as his personal power-instrument. Towards the end of his life, he seems to have become alarmed at the 'nuclear' reaction which he had provoked in the West. But he was incapable of changing. He preferred to have either enemies or puppets, nothing in between. Thus in his last years he was quite unable to adjust to the anti-colonialist revolution. To him Nehru, as a non-communist, was simply another imperialist stooge.

His death released tremendous pent-up forces for change within the communist world. It is hard for us, with a still inadequate historical perspective, to assess what has occurred, still less forecast future developments. But at least we can discern the following, sometimes, divergent trends.

Within the USSR, there followed the relaxation of the terror, amnesties, efforts to improve living standards. Regardless of personal differences, Stalin's successors sought to win the allegiance of the masses by a visible concern for their material good. Intellectual life revived, as greater freedom was granted to science and the arts. True, this was and is accompanied by a reassertion of the Party's right to decide the limits of the permissible. So long as the Party has a monopoly of power, and appoints all editors, censors and the top members of the scientific hierarchy, and controls contacts with the West, it is indeed premature to talk of real freedom. Yet one must be deaf, dumb and blind not to see that there have been big changes for the better, that there is real life stirring, which the Party's professional bureaucrats are striving to hold or push back, with varying success.

Despite the great power concentrated in Khrushchev's hands, a return to Stalinism seems extremely improbable. Khrushchev knows well that times have changed, and indeed has sought to gather personal-political credit for the changes in his repeated attacks on Stalin. The USSR is not a beleaguered fortress, in which everything must be sacrificed for the rapid build-up of an industrial base. Such a base already exists. Stalin's economic system, by ruthlessly enforcing priorities, by neglecting agriculture and exploiting the peasants, did succeed in making of Russia a mighty industrial and military power. But the economic techniques—and political methods—of that period have become obsolete.

The Party itself is caught in a dilemma. By long-ingrained habit it tends to enforce administrative solutions on the economy, by issuing orders. But the Party also wishes the fulfilment of an extremely ambitious programme of economic growth ('overtaking America'), for which purpose greater efficiency in the use of resources is essential. Consequently we see repeated organizational experiments, contradictory edicts on centralized Party control and decentralized enterprise initiative in industry.

Impatience with the continued backwardness in agriculture is also leading to a series of reforms, though here the tradition of political interference is more firmly established. The trend may be towards a greater merging of the Party and state (especially state-economic) apparatus, which, in the name of Party control, may continue the process of transforming the Party into a nationalist ruling *élite*, with ideology kept for appropriate formal occasions.

In the rest of the communist world, meanwhile, complex changes were afoot. De-Stalinization demoralized some satellite communist parties, and led directly to the Hungarian revolt and the transfer of power in Poland to Gomulka, who had been imprisoned as a 'national' deviationist. While elsewhere in Europe the façade of communist monolithism was more or less maintained, there were visible strains. The leadership had been placed in command by Russian power, not by their own actions, let alone by the desires of their fellow-citizens. Many had acted as Stalin's personal agents, had killed and imprisoned fellow-communists at his behest. It was hard for them to stand on their own feet. The solutions adopted in different countries varied widely, underlining the break-up of the monolithism of the Soviet world; we can no longer assume that any communist party acts because Moscow tells it to. This applies not only to communists in government but also, though in varying degrees, to communist parties in the capitalist West. Thus, no student of the Italian Communist Party can fail to observe a new note of independence, unthinkable a few short years ago.

But, of course, it is the split with China which looms largest in the internal life of the communist world.

The Chinese revolution owed little or nothing to Soviet support. Mao Tse-tung apparently showed deep respect for the Russian revolution and for Stalin. However, he and his colleagues were understandably proud of achieving command of the world's largest people and most ancient state, and were in no mood to take orders. It was to be only a matter of time before they asserted their independence. The Chinese communist revolution implied the ultimate end of Russian control over the world's communist movement. But apart from the question of who controls whom, there was another factor in operation. The Chinese revolution was young, its leaders filled with passionate will to change China and to undertake the most radical social experiments. The present Soviet leaders were youths or small children in 1917, they rule over a country which has much to lose from social and international convulsions. The Chinese leadership became increasingly convinced that the USSR, for all its nominal adherence to the revolutionary doctrines of Marxism-Leninism, is becoming a settled, national, 'have' state, genuinely anxious to reach an accommodation with the West. They cried treason, and sought to take over from the 'corrupted' hands of Khrushchev the leadership of true revolutionary communism. We cannot yet fully apprehend the drastic consequences of all this for the world's communist movement, or indeed for the world.

Yet these Chinese accusations do not fit into the customary Western interpretation of Soviet foreign policy. The Chinese are accusing the Russians of believing in co-existence, while the West is apt to regard Russian professions of a desire for accommodation as a fraudulent tactical manoeuvre. What, then, is the truth? The following is a possible interpretation.

Khrushchev inherited the cold war, and, as he sees it, both the USSR and the West are busily manœuvring, trying to change the balance of power in their own favour. To lower one's guard is to invite a punch on the nose. Yet, in an age of nuclear weapons, it is vitally necessary to avoid an open conflict which would wipe out everything. Khrushchev claims that the forces of history are on the side of communism, that the Western world will founder amid its own contradictions. The older belief that these will manifest themselves as ever-deepening crises within the major capitalist states has largely given way to the more soundly-based expectation of collapse in underdeveloped countries. Here there is indeed some prospect of violent social convulsions, and the likelihood is that moderate or traditionalist methods, of the type backed by the West, will fail to achieve results. Then power could slip into the hands of pro-communist elements, *à la* Castro.

An economically powerful USSR can then come to the rescue. A militarily powerful USSR can use its possession of H-bombs not only to deter attack upon its own positions but also to avert 'the export of counter revolution', that is American attempts to turn back the forces of history by military intervention. Far from proving the falsity of the above interpretation, Cuban events fit it like a glove, including the withdrawal when nuclear war threatened.

The Soviet policy seems to be a combination of cautious

manœuvring in the cold war with a high priority for avoiding an open clash with the West ('peaceful co-existence'), and a species of 'historicist' optimism which seeks to reconcile caution with the will to win in the end. The Chinese evidently believe that the optimism is but a rationalization of the caution, that the USSR really has no wish for conflict. Not that the Chinese communists 'want war'. We must not accept Moscow's caricature of Chinese motives and policies. Mao is also aware of the destructive power of H-bombs. But he is in a much more dynamic mood, he is willing to take greater risks, and he believes that the West's implacable hostility dooms all efforts at negotiation to failure, and that therefore it is psychologically erroneous to appear to wish to negotiate at all. Certain intransigent Westerners should be able to see their own mirror-image.

At this point sceptical Western critics are apt to demand some proof of a 'change of aim' or a 'change of heart' on the part of the USSR. In the absence of evidence of this, they would deny the validity of the preceding analysis and of the Chinese accusations. (The latter would then become primarily ideological missiles in a power struggle.) However, the sceptics pose the question in a misleading way. The party exercises its dictatorship in the name of the principles held by the founding fathers. It must declare that its aims are unchanged. Indeed, they *are* in a sense unchanged, but the will to make sacrifices and take risks in pursuit of them may have decisively diminished. ('Aims' are, in any case, a vague term. Both a burglar and myself might have the common aim of acquiring £1,000, but men's reactions to our activities differ, for good and sound reasons.)

Meanwhile the pressures and counter-pressures of the cold war maintain mutual hostility and give rise to actions which reinforce traditional attitudes on both sides. For example, given a powerful American presence in the Middle East, which his military advisers doubtless regard with some alarm, Khrushchev uses his best endeavours to weaken the West in this area, using for this purpose, *inter alia*, anti-imperialist propaganda and local pro-communist movements. Such actions are by no means inconsistent with the 'Chinese' interpretation, but also fit into Lord Home's.

Communism is evolving, is changing rapidly and unevenly in an unstable world. It is odd that Marxism, originally concerned with the triumph of the working class in the most advanced capitalist states, has become the industrializing ideology of backward countries. Marx would have been amazed. His ideas are losing ground in the West, but in Asia or Latin-America a crudely over-simplified version may inspire ambitious revolutionaries to join together in a tightly-knit party to drag predominantly peasant fellow-citizens into the twentieth century. In a real sense, Stalinism was just such a crude form of Marxism. It has been outgrown in the USSR itself, where economic and social development has passed beyond it, and we see an active search for new ways of interpreting old theories. The USSR is challenged by China, which is still in the earlier stage, and, in denouncing the trends towards relaxation in the USSR as 'revisionism', is bidding for leadership of the present and future rebellions in the underdeveloped world. Faced with this challenge and reacting to it, will the USSR and the West be able to find a basis for genuine co-existence, and will the many ugly features of Soviet social and political organization gradually give way to something more tolerable and tolerant? It is foolish to try to 'answer' such a question, but a certain cautious optimism is not out of place.

GLOSSARY

The following Russian words and abbreviations occur in the text without always being accompanied by a translation or explanation:

Gosstroi: State committee on construction.

Kolkhoz: Collective farm.

MTS: Machine tractor stations (abolished in 1958).

Obkom: Oblast (i.e. provincial) Committee of the Communist Party.

Raikom: Raion (district, usual rural) Committee of the Communist Party, abolished under that name in 1962.

RSFSR: Russian Soviet federative socialist republic, or Russia proper.

Sovkhoz: State farm.

Sovnarkhoz: Abbreviated form of *Sovet narodnovo khozyaistva*, Council of national economy (Regional economic council, unless otherwise specified in the text).

Trudoden: (plural *Trudodni*) 'Workday-unit', measuring quantity and quality of work on collective farms.

VSNKh: Higher (or Supreme) Economic Council. Abbreviation used in 1960-62 for the RSFSR Sovnarkhoz, but since 1963 it relates to the *all union* supreme co-ordinating body (see page 117).

NOTE ON THE ROUBLE

In 1961 the internal value of the rouble was multiplied by ten; i.e. all prices and wages were divided by ten. (The external value, i.e. the official exchange rate, was increased by much less than this, thereby effecting a disguised and long overdue devaluation.) Throughout this volume, unless otherwise stated, all rouble figures are in *old* roubles.

INDEX

NAMES INDEX

For Product Safety Concerns and Information please contact our EU
representative GPSR@taylorandfrancis.com
Taylor & Francis Verlag GmbH, Kaufingerstraße 24, 80331 München, Germany

www.ingramcontent.com/pod-product-compliance
Ingram Content Group UK Ltd.
Pitfield, Milton Keynes, MK11 3LW, UK
UKHW022011180926
475701UK00003B/314

* 9 7 8 0 4 1 5 6 8 4 9 6 5 *